JOHN WESLEY (1703-1791)

John Wesley, the founder of Methodism, is noted for his evangelistic campaigns throughout the British Isles and America. Wesley committed his life to Christ in 1738 and promptly began a great revival campaign that spread rapidly, making him one of the world's most effective and popular evangelists of all time.

Reading Wesley's fascinating life story will provide a model of inspiration and encouragement for readers of all ages. Today, as in 18th century England, the proclamation of the Good News continues to be our challenge from God. John Wesley's story gives us a real-life account of how one man can have the impact God intends each of us to have on our world.

HEROES OF THE FAITH has been designed and produced for the discerning book lover. These classics of the Christian faith have been printed and bound with beauty, readability and longevity in mind.

Greatest care has gone into the selection of these volumes, with the hope that you will not only find books that are a joy to read, but books that will stir your faith and enlighten your daily walk with the Lord.

Titles available include:

Fanny Crosby, Bernard Ruffin

Dwight L. Moody, W.R. Moody

George Müller, William Henry Harding

John Wesley, C.E. Vulliamy

John Wesley

C.E. Vulliamy

P48 purpose of Movement to improve
p. 49 wesley Hamahr + do good to others
p. 49 A Methodist is one who lives according
to the Method set down in the Bible

Barbour and Company, Inc.
164 Mill Street
Westwood, New Jersey

ISBN 0-916441-14-8
(Canadian ISBN 0-920413-91-9)

Published by: **Barbour and Company, Inc.**
164 Mill Street
Westwood, New Jersey 07675

(In Canada, HEROES OF THE FAITH,
960 The Gateway, Burlington, Ontario L7L 5K7)

EVANGELICAL CHRISTIAN PUBLISHERS ASSOCIATION MEMBER

Printed in the United States of America

John Wesley

PREFACE

It is now realized that Wesley's importance is not confined to his work as the founder of Methodism. His influence upon the social, industrial and religious life of the eighteenth century was undoubtedly one of the prime historical factors of that period. The materials for a biography of Wesley are therefore extremely varied, and distributed over a very wide field. Those materials are found not only in biographies, but in a wide variety of historical and sociological records.

The influences of Methodism spread far beyond the limits of the Methodist organization, not merely sparking a new sense of religious life in other bodies, but producing reactions throughout the entire social structure. It cannot be doubted that Wesley, during his lifetime, was the dominant personality of the age, and that he was more widely known than any other Englishman of the time.

His life began in the first decade and finished in the last decade of the eighteenth century. For at least fifty years, his personal influence was felt.

Such a life may be looked at from more than one point of view. A merely departmental study of Wesley would obscure the vigor and brilliance of his life, and would not give a true picture of his character. Wesley cannot be understood without reference to the progress or nature of the Wesleyan revival, and the revival cannot be understood without reference to its own special phenomena and to the circumstances that produced it.

In this book, an attempt has been made to show Wesley not only as the remarkable person he was, but also as the leader of a great religious movement without parallel in the history of the Christian Church.

CONTENTS

CONTENTS

CHAPTER I

EPWORTH

THE people of the Lincolnshire fens in 1700 were equally incapable of knowing God or of acquiring even a moderate degree of respectability. They were drunken, surly and violent. If they disliked a man, they maimed his cattle, burnt his roof, or tried to drown him. They lived upon soggy land, lately redeemed from the marshes and liable to winter floods. Inhabited and surrounded by such people, and standing in the midst of a green, flat, soft and watery landscape, the village of Epworth was not a happy place for one of learning and of gentle manners.

Samuel Wesley, the rector of Epworth in 1700, certainly had the inclinations of a quiet, studious man, though he may have been a little rough and hasty in speech, a little impetuous in action. He was a man of solid, almost pugnacious piety. He loved poetry and dissertation. As a youth of twenty-two he had published a book of poems under the singularly unattractive title of *Maggots*. Ten years later he produced a heroic poem on the life of Christ. In 1704 he dedicated to Queen Anne a rhyming history of the Bible in three duodecimo volumes. But his most prodigious work, *Dissertationes in Librum Jobi*, was not completed until shortly before his death in 1735. Besides his more ponderous labours, he wrote pieces for Dunton's *Athenian Gazette or Casuistical Mercury*, he published elegies and sermons, polemics and works of practical religion.

The rector of Epworth was the descendant of notable dissenting theologians, but he was himself a stiff Tory Churchman. After a curacy in London and nearly a year's service as the chaplain of a man-of-war, he had been appointed to the hamlet of South Ormsby in Lincolnshire. He was then a married man, and he gave up the living of Ormsby when the mistress of the Marquis of Normanby, his patron, took to calling upon his young wife. Such assertions of principle were in keeping with his manly character, but effectively barred the way to favours and preferment. In 1697 he had received the living of Epworth. Well might he exclaim in his poem on Marlborough:

"Far from the sun and regions bless'd and mild,
Almost to utmost *Thulë* here exil'd,
Forgetting and forgotten long I lay,
Nor once wak'd up, nor had one thought of day."

Susannah, the wife of Samuel Wesley, was the daughter and the twenty-fifth child of Dr. Samuel Annesley, the famous Nonconformist. Religion had been the serious affair of her life from infancy, and when she was thirteen she had decided formally, without emotion and upon purely theological grounds, to join the Church of England. Her decision, made at so tender an age, marked the firmness and resolution of her character.

She was a beautiful woman, with many accomplishments. In clearness of thinking, and in quiet insistence on what she considered right, she was obviously superior to her husband. She was never loud or fussy. Her will, gently but deliberately enforced, ruled the affairs of Epworth Rectory; her influence, religiously impartial and consistent, operated in no uncertain way upon the growing minds of her children. Austere yet cheerful, dutiful, serene, with noble integrity of purpose, it may be that she relied too much upon exact regulation and the iron principles of unvarying discipline.

The first child of Susannah and Samuel Wesley, named after his father, was born during the curacy period in London. He was followed, between 1690 and 1709, by eighteen other children, of whom only nine survived infancy.

John Benjamin Wesley, born at Epworth on the 28th of June 1703, was the fifteenth child of his parents, and at the time of his birth he had only five sisters and one brother living. The brother was Samuel, the first-born, and the sisters were Emilia (or Emily), Susannah, Mary, Mehetabel (Hetty) and Anne. The three surviving children who came after him were Martha, born in 1706, Charles, born in 1707, and Kezia, the "fire child," born in 1709.

Life at Epworth Rectory was diversified by curious and

painful occurrences. There were sharp collisions of will and principle between the rector and his wife; for although Mrs. Wesley dutifully obeyed her husband in matters of conduct, it was different with matters of conscience. Susannah could not support the House of Orange, and when, in 1701, her husband prayed for King William, she refused to say Amen. "Very well, Sukey," said the rector, "if we are to have two kings, we must have two beds," and he saddled his horse and rode off to London. The extravagance of this action is fortunately mitigated by the fact that he was "a convocation man," and had business in London at that time. But the rector was really a most affectionate husband, and his more serious troubles were caused by a rash fervour in politics and a total incapacity for the management of his own affairs.

The Epworth revenues amounted to about two hundred pounds a year, yet the rector was three hundred in debt at the beginning of the century. He had a run of bad luck. Like many other country parsons, he was partly dependent upon his profits as a farmer and cultivator. His flax was burnt, his barn fell, and his crops failed. He had also, through some local intrigue, been deprived of the chaplaincy to a foot regiment. At the end of June 1705 he was confined in the prison of Lincoln Castle for a debt of less than thirty pounds.

This imprisonment coincided with a vigorous and brutal persecution of the Epworth family by the parishioners. Samuel Wesley was hated, partly because he was so aggressively Christian, and partly because he was a fierce Tory partisan, with a stern, High Church attitude towards Dissenters. A riotous mob with drums and guns paraded outside the rectory. The rector's cows were stabbed. The Axholme people swore that if they got the parson in the Castle Yard at Lincoln they would squeeze his guts out. One of these brutes, seeing the Wesley children at play, cried out, "Oh ye devils! we will come and turn ye all out of doors a-begging." Somehow or other the debt was paid, and Samuel Wesley was released from jail before the end of the year.

But the fury and malice of the Lincolnshire men could go far beyond mere mobbing and the maiming of cattle. In 1702, they had made an attempt to burn down Epworth Rectory by throwing fire upon the thatched roof. In February 1709, when John Wesley was five and a half years old, a second fire took place, and the rectory was totally destroyed.

The rescue of John Wesley from the burning house is the best-known episode of his childhood. The rectory, a dry mass of thatch and timber, blazed furiously. In the horrid confusion of the rush for safety, John was left asleep in the attic. When the child woke the fire was roaring along the rafters above his head. The staircase was already in flames. But John, even at the age of five and a half, sh wed extraordinary presence of mind. He dragged a chest up to the window, climbed on it and thus showed himself to the people below. At that very moment his father, in agonies of despair, was commending the infant soul to God. Two brave fellows, who were certainly not of the heathenish kind, saw the boy at the window, and saved him just before the collapse of the roof. It was in memory of this escape that Wesley so often referred to himself as "a brand plucked out of the burning."

Epworth Rectory was rebuilt before the end of the year, and the family, dispersed for a time in friendly houses, came back to the wise control of Susannah. The intermission of that control, she said, had been disastrous. Her children, formerly so gentle and well-mannered, had become loud and clownish; they had learned songs which were not fit for good children, and were careless in the observance of Sunday. Mrs. Wesley countered these ill effects by the more strict enforcement of her system.

The system on which Mrs. Wesley reared and taught her children may well seem a little harsh to a soft, indulgent age. She believed in the steady application of principles and the exact performance of duties. The vagueness of a mere theory would have been intensely repugnant to her precise nature. Yet her discipline, though rigidly maintained, was never the cruel discipline of a tyrant.

Susannah Wesley had a store of godly cheerfulness, a heart overflowing with affection. To her, there was nothing morally questionable in training infants of a year old "to fear the rod and cry softly." The rod was a piece of moral apparatus, enforcing the appropriate lesson of punishment, and approved by the Scriptures. "The first thing to be done with children," said Mrs. Wesley, "is to conquer their will." And observe the happy result: "That most odious noise of the crying of children was rarely heard in the house: but the family usually lived in as much quietness as if there had not been a child among them."

To this native air of discipline John Wesley owed the ruling principles of his own mind. He was a Methodist from the cradle. If he showed any precocity at all, it was a precocity of logic and hard reasoning. "Our Jacky," said his father, "would do nothing—*non etiam crepitare*—unless he could give a reason for it." Probably there was less to be learnt from his father's example, but from him he certainly received a love of letters and of classic erudition.

Between John Wesley and his elder brother Samuel there was an interval of thirteen years. John cannot have known Samuel very intimately in his childhood, for Samuel was a Westminster scholar in 1704, and was rarely at home. The playfellows of John were his young sisters and his brother Charles. Emily, the eldest of the sisters, was eleven years older than John, and Kezia, the last child of the Wesleys, was six years his junior.

All the Wesley daughters were intelligent, vivacious and pious girls. All of them had a greater or lesser degree of literary aptitude. Mehetabel, or Hetty, helped her father in his laborious compilations, and wrote some passably good verses for the *Gentleman's Magazine*. Martha, in her later life (as Mrs. Hall), became one of the friends of Johnson. With the exception of Kezia, who never married, these young women were unhappy in their choice of husbands, and their marriages were almost equally tragic. We cannot help suspecting that Mrs. Wesley's parental discipline, applied with a rigid conscience but little perception, may have been partly responsible for these disasters.

And it is clear that the Wesley girls were sacrificed, as girls were then commonly and dutifully sacrificed, to the advancement of their brothers. The first concern of the rector and his wife was to provide for the education of their sons: the others—and indeed, the parents themselves—had to endure privation cheerfully.

When her children were five years old, Mrs. Wesley began their systematic education. The hours of teaching were from nine to twelve and from two to five. Only one day was allowed for learning the letters of the alphabet. Each lesson was firmly impressed upon the child's mind by a method of patient repetition. "It is almost incredible," said Mrs. Wesley, "what a child may be taught in a quarter of a year by a vigorous application if it have but a tolerable capacity and good health."

At dinner-time, the children ate their food and drank their small beer at a little table close to their parents. If they wanted anything, they had to whisper softly to the maid, who, in her turn, conveyed the message to Mrs. Wesley. "Mornings they always had spoonmeat; sometimes at nights. But whatever they had, they were never permitted at those meals to eat of more than one thing, and of that sparingly enough." Strict manners and exact propriety were insisted upon, and one of the most serious misdemeanours was to speak rudely or imperiously to a servant.

It will be noticed that the rector himself makes no appearance in the scheme of domestic administration. We know practically nothing of his relations with his children, and it would seem as if he took no part, even in the education of his sons. No doubt he was chiefly occupied, either in sturdy efforts to win the heathen men of Axholme, or in the quiet pursuit of learning.

John's miraculous escape from the fire appeared to his mother as a proof of the clear intention of Providence, and John became the particular object of her solicitude. The child was habituated to pious exercise; he was docile, calm and reasonable.

The few anecdotes of Wesley's early years all show him to have been singularly free from petulance or caprice, and

6

singularly endowed with self-control and patience. It is certainly remarkable that the horrors of the fire left no harmful impression upon his nerves or mind. When he was ill with the smallpox in his ninth year, he suffered without complaint. His habits of deliberation and love of argument became so strongly marked as to cause his father occasional annoyance. When he was offered fruit or sweets between meals, he would say gravely, "Thank you; I will think of it." He must have been a solemn little boy, though not entirely without a normal capacity for merriment.

Unfortunately, we lack the materials for a close, familiar study of Wesley's childhood. Only the exuberance of a sentimental imagination could provide us with such a study; it has been more than once attempted, with results rather ingenious than convincing. But there can be no doubt that the Epworth family was exceptional in more ways than one. It was a family in which the governing principles were invariably religious, and that in itself was remarkable enough at a time when piety was out of fashion. Samuel Wesley not only had the regular services every Sunday, but every Wednesday and Friday as well. He observed every fast and every festival of the Church. His children were brought up on the catechism of Beveridge, and were taught long passages of the Bible; some of them knew practically the whole of the New Testament by heart. Even before they could walk and talk, the little Wesleys were trained in the observance of Sunday, they behaved with reverence and composure during the family prayers, and were taught how to ask by signs for a blessing.

It is important to remember that the Wesleys were both geographically and socially isolated. There were no cheerful acquaintances, no friendly relations with the outer world, no visiting boys and girls to play with the children. The family led its own life within its own boundaries. The influences and associations of Wesley's childhood were therefore essentially domestic, and they were essentially feminine: he was taught and formed by his mother, he played and talked with his sisters. The isolation of the family was doubtless unwholesome, but it would have been infinitely more unwholesome if it had not been for the vigour and cheerfulness of the central personality—that of Susannah. We know that Mrs. Wesley encouraged play as well as piety, and that she would even take her part in a game of cards with the little girls. Until his departure for school, the ruling influence in Wesley's life was certainly that of his mother, and it was to her, rather than to his father's example of truculent piety, that he owed the solid foundation of his own religious character.

In January 1714 John Wesley entered the Charterhouse on a nomination from the Duke of Buckingham. He was then ten and a half years old.

Sufficient ridicule has been poured upon Tyerman's grotesque assertion that Wesley "entered the Charterhouse a saint and left it a sinner." Wesley, who always judged his own character with extraordinary harshness, states that he was "guilty of outward sins, which he knew to be such, though they were not scandalous in the eyes of the world." He still read the Scriptures, and said his prayers at morning and evening. He still hoped to be saved, because he was not so bad as other people, had "a kindness for religion," read his Bible, and went to church. Only from the elevation of a full spiritual experience could this be looked upon as a state of sin; it amounts to little more than the loosening of home traditions which is the usual consequence of life in a public school. Indeed, that Wesley preserved inviolate so much of the home tradition after six years of life as a gown-boy at the Charterhouse, is a very striking proof of the depth and value of his early impressions. There is not much in school routine which conduces either to religious habits or to serious thought. Nor is it customary for little boys to pay attention to their personal holiness. Young John was a boy with an exceptional sense of religion, and to say that he "lost his religion" at school is mere nonsense.

Soon after John's admission to the Charterhouse, his brother Samuel became an usher at Westminster. Charles came to Westminster in 1716, and from this year until 1720 the three Wesley brothers were together in London.

Samuel, the usher, was a churchman of the dry, uncompromising type, with firm and formal notions upon the importance of doctrine. He had a clear mind and a terse way of expressing his thoughts. He gave many proofs of merely scholastic ability. As a poet, he was ingenious, though never inspired. Above all things, he was a practical man. He did everything in accordance with rules and principles. He was upright, exact, reliable, severely controlled, and superior to every emotional weakness. He seems to have endured the life of an usher cheerfully for nearly twenty years, and in 1732 his dogged merit was rewarded by the headmastership of Blundell's at Tiverton. He died in 1739, at the age of fifty, leaving behind him a wife and a daughter. His *Poems on Several Occasions*, a medley of hymns and of humorous pieces, was published in 1736.

Brother Samuel kept a watch over young John at the Charterhouse. "Jack," he wrote to their father, "is a brave boy, learning Hebrew as fast as he can."

We may suppose that John and Samuel met frequently, but it seems as if the relations between them were never of the most cordial or intimate kind. The attitude of the elder brother towards his junior was always rather stiff, critical and patronising, and we shall see later how widely the two brothers were separated by their essentially different ideas of a valid religious faith.

Little is known of John Wesley's life at the Charterhouse. He was there for six years, and was a frequent visitor at his brother Samuel's house in Dean's Yard, Westminster, where he probably spent his holidays. The story of Wesley preaching to the little boys does not seem to be authentic, and the only anecdote which he himself relates of this period is that of his meeting with the notorious Dr. Sacheverell. This meeting took place shortly before John left the Charterhouse, and it was not a happy one. The Doctor looked at him sternly, and observed: "You are too young to go to the University; you cannot know Greek and Latin yet; go back to school."

The Charterhouse was probably no worse than the other public schools. Little boys were beaten and bullied into appropriate forms of English manliness; their food was taken by the older boys; and they were encouraged, by methods harshly practical, to learn hard, lie hard, and fight hard. Yet there must have been compensations, for Wesley could look back to his Charterhouse days, not only without bitterness, but with actual pleasure. On Founder's Day in 1727 he was one of the stewards for the annual dinner of old Carthusians, when, at the moderate cost of about thirty pounds, the old Carthusians ate roasted pike, fried whitings, venison pasties, pigeons, sirloins of beef, spitched eels, asparagus, roasted lobsters, almond tarts, custards, florentines, jellies, and a great variety of other dainty or substantial dishes, to the musical accompaniment of two French horns. And on several other occasions he paid friendly visits to his old school. To the Charterhouse he owed, at least, his admission to Christ Church as an exhibitioner.

The natural force and purity of his character, and the deep influences of a religious training, preserved Wesley at the Charterhouse from the ordinary vices of a great school. Judging from the impressions of those who first saw him at Oxford in 1720, he was a brisk, sensible youth, with a fine classical taste, a manly view of life and extremely acute powers of reasoning when he came up to the University.

In the winter of 1716-1717 the letters from Epworth conveyed to Samuel (not to John) an account of strange disturbances at the rectory. These letters were read to John and produced an immediate and lasting impression on his mind. The story of the "Epworth noises" must be reckoned among the decisive influences of Wesley's childhood, for it certainly determined his attitude towards what we now call psychic phenomena, an attitude which, in later life, exposed him so often to the charge of credulity, and made him so eager to record or investigate any occurrence which might appear supernatural. It is extremely important to recognise this element in Wesley's mind and to follow its consequences.

The Epworth noises began on the 1st of December 1716. Groans and knockings were heard in every part of the house, and by every member of the family except the rector. A maid-servant noticed "a most terrible and astonishing noise, as at the dining-room door, which caused the up-starting of her hair, and made her ears prick forth at an unusual rate." The sounds quickly became more varied and more alarming. There was a noise of breaking glass among the bottles under the staircase, and the man-servant, Robert, heard "someone come *slaring* through the garret to his chamber," and gobbling like a turkey cock. Robert also declared that he saw a hand-mill at the head of the garret stairway turning of itself with incredible speed. Then the iron casements, the lids of metal pans and the latches of the doors began to ring and rattle. A rumbling, drumming and stamping seemed to move from room to room, shaking the walls and windows. Sounds were heard like those of lumps of coal being flung and splintered on the floor, pewter dishes being thrown about or glasses broken. At other times it seemed as if sheets of clanging metal were dropped heavily on the boards. Occasionally they could hear something like the rubbing of a beast along the walls. But there were never any visible signs of damage or disturbance.

Presently it was observed that the sounds were accompanied by certain definite signals or regulations. Before the knockings began, there was a preliminary noise like that of the rusty gear of a windmill creaking and veering in the wind, or like the winding-up of a jack, or the shearing of a carpenter's plane.

All this had been going on for about a fortnight before it was brought to the notice of the rector. He smiled incredulously and suspected the girls; but before long he was convinced by personal experience. Knockings were heard on the side of his bed, and one night these were so violent, accompanied by "great noises below," that he got up and went round the house with Mrs. Wesley. As they went down the stairs, there was a sudden crash among the stored bottles, and immediately after this, a sound as if a pot of money had been poured out over Mrs. Wesley's bosom: it seemed, she said afterwards, as though hundreds of silver coins had flowed tinkling along her nightgown to her feet. In the hall, they were met by the house dog, cringing and crying in a state of terror.

It is typical of the sturdy Wesley character, that none of the family was frightened, or at least not for long, by these occurrences. Kezia was only seven years old, and Martha was ten. Emily, the eldest of the girls, was twenty-four; and Hetty, who is often supposed to have been associated in some way with these manifestations, was nineteen. The young children would tremble in their sleep, but without waking, when the sounds were heard; yet, in a little time, they all listened to the noises with amusement or even indifference. Charles Wesley, at that time nine years old, was at Westminster, and probably heard nothing about the events at Epworth.

Emily seems to have been the first who had the idea of connecting the sounds with a personality and of giving that personality a name. She called him "Old Jeffery." The idea was a happy one. By giving the supposed visitor a name so ordinary and familiar, with a suggestion of the ludicrous, she helped them to regard him as a mere harmless nuisance. "Ah!" they would say when they heard the knocking, "there is Old Jeffery at his tricks again." And the little girls told each other it was time to go to sleep when Jeffery began to rap on the walls.

Mrs. Wesley was at first inclined to believe that the sounds, varied and peculiar as they were, might be due to rats. She therefore caused a horn to be loudly blown in every room in the house. After this, the knockings were much more frequent, and were heard by day as well as by night.

Actual movements or direct sensations of contact were very rarely observed. Latches were seen lifting and doors opening, and the rector was once or twice roughly pushed as he was going into his study. Anne's account of the bed on which she was sitting being lifted into the air is not well authenticated, and is not repeated in the summary which Wesley himself gave in the *Arminian Magazine*. Emily felt a door strongly pushed against her, but by pressing it back with her shoulder and knee she was able to close it.

On three occasions, a small supernatural creature appeared. First, when Mrs. Wesley looked under a bed in the nursery, "something ran out pretty much like a badger, and seemed to run directly under Emily's petticoats, who sat opposite to me on the other side." One evening, Robert saw the same creature sitting by the dining-room fire: it ran past him, went through the hall, and disappeared. On the third occasion, it was seen to scuttle out from behind the oven-stop in the back kitchen, in the form of a white rabbit.

Jeffery would repeat the raps given by members of the family, and he learnt the rector's peculiar rhythmic knock on the front door. But the answering sounds were often so thunderous and heavy, they seemed as if they would shiver the very beams, and the entire house trembled with their violence. At the reading of morning prayers, Jeffery made a great noise when they came to the prayers for the king, and the children called him a Jacobite. It was often observed by the girls that the raps were immediately under their feet, a circumstance which is recorded in many reports of similar happenings.

By the end of January 1717, the noises had entirely ceased, and we have no particular account of the final episodes. According to Emily, the knocks were last heard on the outer walls of the house.

The evidence relating to the Epworth noises is exceptionally reliable. Apart from the testimony of the rector and his wife, of whose veracity there can be no doubt whatever, we have that of Mr. Hoole, the vicar of Haxey. In addition, we have separate accounts, written or dictated at various times, by Anne, Mary, Emily and Susannah. Whatever may be the explanation of these disturbances, their occurrence is beyond question.

Two or three points in connection with these mysterious noises may be profitably considered. First, there is the close resemblance between the Epworth events and the ordinary manifestations of the *poltergeist*. Such manifestations are supposed to occur most frequently in new houses, and the rectory, rebuilt after the fire in 1709, was practically a new house. Secondly, our attention is often drawn to the fact of the noises appearing to follow or accompany Hetty Wesley rather than any other person; and we are asked to remember that she alone, of all his elder sisters, was the only one who failed to give her brother an account of the Jeffery episodes. From this, it has been inferred that she was consciously responsible for the noises. But she was often asleep when the noises occurred, and at other times she was absent from the room in which they were palpably located. Apart from the obvious mechanical difficulty of producing the noises, we must remember a circumstance given by Wesley in his careful analysis of the main features: "The sound very often seemed in the air in the middle of a room, nor could they ever make any such themselves by any contrivance." Thirdly, we have an important note, apparently made by Wesley in 1726: "The first time my mother ever heard any unusual noise at Epworth was long before the disturbance of Old Jeffery. My brother, lately come from London, had one evening a sharp quarrel with my sister Sukey, at which time, my mother happening to be above in her own chamber, the doors and windows rung and jarred very loud, and presently several distinct strokes, three by three, were struck. From that night it never failed to give notice in much the same manner against any signal misfortune, or illness of any belonging to the family." Now, in considering only the evidence of reliable witnesses and the carefully prepared account by John Wesley, and ruling out the stories told by Robert and the maids, we are bound to admit that the Epworth noises are not to be explained as the result of ordinary crude methods of trickery or malice. To Emily, it was all due to witchcraft, and the grey badger and the white rabbit were appearances of the witch herself ; to John, it was the work of supernatural beings or a persecuting devil; and to the sturdy rector, it was just the thing to make "a glorious penny book for Jack Dunton." All the phenomena come into line with other accounts of similar experiences (of which, as far as we know, none of the Epworth family knew anything at all), and, like them, present us with an unsolved problem.

One of the first concerns of John Wesley when he came

home from Oxford in 1726 was to collect from every available witness an exact account of the noises. He took them seriously, and they formed, indeed, the basis of a firm and consistent belief in what we now call spiritualism. To hold such a belief, at a time when the English forms of righteous complacency on the one hand and of arrogant cynicism on the other were never more fully and more precisely developed, was a striking proof of original character, especially in one whose clear mind repelled with contempt any sort of vagueness or mystery, and to whom the methods of keen logic and close argument were always congenial.

In the interval between school and college, Wesley did not return to Epworth. Probably he lived in the house of his brother Samuel at Westminster, but we have practically no information in regard to him at this period. He does not seem to have made any definite plans, nor is there anything to suggest that he contemplated ordination.

Undoubtely his father hoped that John would enter the Church. The rector of Epworth was growing old. He found it no light matter to carry out his duties. In addition to his work at Epworth, he had to walk or ride over the streams and marshes to the wretched hamlet of Wroote. His eldest son had taken up the profession of a teacher. Charles, in 1720, was only thirteen years old. It was reasonable to hope that John might be induced to think of a curacy at Epworth. But we have no direct evidence of the home influences at this period. Neither have we any material which gives us an account of Wesley's own state of mind at the beginning of his University life.

CHAPTER II

OXFORD

ENGLISH life in the eighteenth century was marked by the awkwardness and horrors of transition, with a tendency to seek refuge in mere formulas. On the one hand there was a cumbrous deadness, and on the other a heartless vivacity. Below a smooth shell of tawdry elegance, the age was coarse, dark and brutal. Philosophic doubt, brightly scintillating with a new brilliance and freedom of thought, forced orthodoxy to assume the most rigid, and also the most extravagant, forms. Churchmen were deeply discouraged, and the ministry of the Church was not far removed from a state of demoralisation. Here and there, a dim kind of religion struggled feebly under a mantle of gloom, and put forth a little despondent poetry about graveyards.

Speaking of the Church of England in the eighteenth century, Abbey and Overton do not hesitate to describe it as "a dark scene of melancholy failure." This failure was not entirely due to the social atmosphere in which the Church was breathing so painfully, but was largely caused by the weakness of her own administration. The great evils of pluralities and non-residence are sufficiently clear. By the corrupt disposal of preferment and the flagrant abuse of patronage, clergymen were receiving emoluments from parishes which they seldom, if ever, visited; and we are told that a certain Welsh bishop had only once seen his diocese, because he preferred to live among the lakes of Westmorland.

The Church, at all times presenting curious varieties of practice or discipline, was never less uniform in constitution. In 1689 the Nonjuring clergy, refusing the oath of allegiance to William and Mary, had been ejected from the Establishment. Men who set principle before interest are not likely to be men of inferior character. The loss of the Nonjuring clergy was morally disastrous. The total number of the dissentients in 1689 was about four hundred, including

the Archbishop of Canterbury and the Bishops of Bath and
Wells, Chichester, Peterborough, Ely, Gloucester, Worcester and Norwich. William Sancroft, the Nonjuring
Archbishop, claimed to be the legitimate head of the Church
of England, and requested the exiled king, James II, to
nominate two new bishops to assist him: George Hickes
was therefore appointed Bishop of Thetford and Thomas
Wagstaffe, Bishop of Ipswich. Nor did the death of James
in 1701 allow the Nonjurors to change their attitude, for
they had promised allegiance to his lawful successors. And
although the accession of George I in 1714 made it difficult
for men to believe that all kings were divinely appointed,
the separatist elements could not be reconciled to the State
Church. There were thus two Communions, each claiming
to be the lawful and original Church of England. The Nonjuring bishops had been ejected by the State without synodal
action and for reasons that were definitely political, and they
were still bishops in fact as well as in name. Among their
following were churchmen of great eminence and ability,
such as Law, Jeremy Collier, Spinckes, Brett, Fitzwilliam
and Kettlewell. Oxford, the home of every lost cause except
that of pure religion, became a Nonjuring centre, with a
marked concentration at Balliol and Edmund Hall.

It is hardly correct to speak of the Nonjuring movement
as a schism. The question at issue was not doctrinal but
dynastic, and no subsequent divergence in ritual was in
itself an original part of the Nonjuring policy. Nor would it
be correct to associate the movement too closely with the
Jacobite cause, although it is true that many Nonjurors were
Jacobites. Whether the expelled clergy were right or wrong,
they command respect as men who possessed the fine courage
of minorities, and who had given up all hope of reward or
preferment on a matter of conscience. Probably they
represented the best, the most learned and most religious
elements in the Church. But the effect of their action was
certainly disastrous. Not only was the official Church
deprived of the service and influence of a number of brilliant
and courageous men, but the fear of disturbance had a
fatal effect upon the ecclesiastical policy of Walpole. Apathy

in the Church became a test or standard of political virtue, and the qualities most encouraged were those of docility and obedience.

If the weakness of the Nonjurors lay in a too formal insistence upon orthodoxy, the State Church contained weaknesses of another kind. The influence of Tillotson, congenial enough to the new lazy ideals of the Establishment, gave rise to a Church so broad that it had no definable boundaries. Where Tillotson had been merely speculative or tolerant, the Broad Churchmen were easy-going to a most reprehensible degree. And here again there is an obvious connection between the latitudinarianism of the early eighteenth century and the political system of Walpole.

Philosophic deism was another menace to the integrity of the Church. Tillotson himself, by asking men to make reason the test of faith, had prepared the minds of religious people for a new sort of dizzy speculation. He was too ready to soften the idea of future punishment or to allay the fears of those who accepted the literal meaning of the Bible.

These various circumstances had naturally produced in the Church of England, during the first decades of the eighteenth century, a state of affairs which was truly deplorable. The spiritual purpose of the Church was almost entirely obscured by faction, apathy, or the meanest of complaisances. People behaved in church with an irreverence which would even now shock the least religious. They lolled and talked in the pews, they put their hats on the Communion Table and even sat on it, they stood on chairs and hassocks in order to bow and smile to their acquaintances. Very few attended church at any time. The appearance of a lively interest in religion was carefully avoided by clergy and laity alike, and nothing was more dreaded than the reproach of being mystical or zealous. The concept of clerical duty, in so far as it existed at all, was rigidly parochial. And yet there was so little contact between the pastor and his people that such irregularities as private baptism were prevalent in every part of the kingdom, and the celebration of the Eucharist was not only infrequent but was perfčrmed in a manner so careless as to be a grave scandal.

At no time was the clerical character so low in the public estimation. Hogarth, with a fierce vehemence of satire, has shown the worst view of the English clergyman in two of his most admirable engravings: the final scene in the *Harlot's Progress*, published in 1732; and the *Midnight Modern Conversation*, published in 1733. Even at a later period, the popular idea of a clergyman was that of a sleek, lazy creature whose least offensive aim was to be quiet and comfortable. When Johnson met his old college friend Edwards in 1778, the following conversation took place: "*Edwards.* 'I wish I had continued at College.' *Johnson.* 'Why do you wish that, sir?' *Edwards.* 'Because I think I should have had a much easier life than mine has been. I should have been a parson, and had a good living, like Bloxham and several others, and lived comfortably.'" The muddy figure of the boisterous fox-hunting parson, or some "honest Harry" drinking his pints of beer in the servants' hall, may be taken as representing those qualities which were most likely to find favour with patrons. A saintly man, particularly one with a keen sense of duty, was looked on as a pedant or a fanatic. There can be no doubt that moral laxity among clergymen, even if it was not condoned, was looked upon with a leering or cynical indulgence. Sheer ignorance, amounting to illiteracy, was no bar to ordination. According to Bishop Burnet, "The much greater part of those who come to be ordained are ignorant to a degree not to be apprehended by those who are not obliged to know it." Pious men, like Secker and Watts, were in despair.

Examples of honesty and virtue were rarely found among people of high rank. A hollow elegance and measured affectation concealed an almost universal depravity of manners. Foul speaking and hard drinking, with a free indulgence of brutal sensuality, were signs of genteel behaviour. The systematic torture of animals provided the most popular forms of amusement. The public shows and fairs were scenes of crude beastliness and debauchery, attended surreptitiously by women of fashion. Drunken bands of young gentlemen, calling themselves Mohocks, ran about in the streets of London, knocking people down, slitting their noses and squeezing their eyes out. Highwaymen, though much less deadly than automobiles, took travellers' money on every night of the year. The law treated men, women and children with fierce impartiality, and strung them up on hundreds of gibbets in every part of the kingdom. At the same time, crimes of savagery and violence were never so frequent.

In the whole life of the nation there seemed to be a fatal decay of moral fibre. Parliamentary interest was openly bought and sold. It may be doubted, even in the face of modern procedure, whether fraud and perjury have ever been more cynically employed in the ordinary transactions of commerce. Satire, professing to lash the follies of the age, was a mere excuse for written or pictured indecencies of the most nauseating and elaborate kind.

The Universities, like the Church, had sunk to the common level of rottenness. Speaking of Oxford in 1726, Hearne wrote: "There are such differences now in the University of Oxford . . . that good letters decay every day, insomuch that this ordination on Trinity Sunday . . . there were no fewer than fifteen denied orders for insufficiency, which is the more to be noted because our bishops are themselves illiterate men." In practice, the only qualifications for a degree were money and residence. The candidates were allowed to choose the masters who should examine them, and these were naturally "their old cronies and toping companions." "In the University of Oxford," said Adam Smith, "the greater part of the public professors have, for these many years, given up altogether even the pretence of teaching . . . the public schools are much less corrupted than the universities." Butler, at Oriel, had to endure "frivolous lectures and unintelligible disputations." Religion was treated as mere flabbiness and eccentricity. The Fellows, with no incentive to work, lived lazily upon their emoluments, feebly tolerating the idleness and impudence of their scholars. "Easy men," said Gibbon, "who supinely enjoyed the gifts of the founder . . . Their conversation stagnated in a round of college business, Tory politics, personal anecdotes of scandal; their dull and deep potations excused the brisk intemperance of youth."

Oxford life presented the general picture of a succession of men waiting for other men to marry or die. The scholars, who were not under the slightest obligations even to appear learned or pious, amused themselves by drinking, smoking, playing bowls or billiards, or dallying with the toasts of the town in Merton garden or Magdalen walks. Those of a more vigorous or wealthy sort pulled boats on the Isis, took their fowling-pieces to the woods, or raced their tidy nags on Port Meadow. Coffee-houses were opened; and amiable young men clinked their pint pots over the board at the Mitre. It was "a country flowing with syllogisms and ale, where Horace and Virgil were equally unknown." Gibbon regarded the fourteen months he spent at Magdalen as "the most idle and unprofitable of his whole life."

John Wesley came up to Christ Church as a Commoner on the 13th of July 1720, not long after his seventeenth birthday. He had an allowance of forty pounds a year from the Charterhouse, with small occasional gifts from the pinched family at Epworth.

His letters during the first four years of his residence show a light-hearted, manly spirit. He does not seem to have thought seriously about religion. But here, as at the Charterhouse, he gave proof of an exceptional character. Neither the intellectual paralysis nor the moral decay of Oxford had the least effect upon his cheerful, busy and lucid nature. Unlike the greater number of his companions, he worked industriously, had a fondness for learned controversy, and took pains to acquire a neat classic style in writing. He was poor, and troubled with small debts. Of anything worse than debts we have no evidence.

Wesley always reviewed his own life with extreme candour, and often with a degree of harshness which he would never have exercised in his judgment of any other person. He was only reticent when he was afraid of injuring someone else; never reticent in the exposure of what he believed to be his inward faults.

In looking back at the early Oxford years he was far from satisfied. "I still said my prayers, both in public and private, and read with the Scriptures several other books of religion. . . . Yet I had not all this while so much as a notion of inward holiness; nay, went on habitually, and for the most part very contentedly, in some one or other known sins, though with some intermissions and short struggles, especially before and after the holy Communion, which I was obliged to receive thrice a year." This points to no grievous failings, beyond those of slackness or indifference—"known sins," perhaps, but sins quickly outgrown. At no period of his life, not even during his youthful independence at Oxford, could Wesley have been described as a sinner in the ordinary sense of the term, or in any sense comprehensible to the ordinary mind. But he himself admits (in 1785) than when he came up to the University he had no idea beyond *inter sylvas Academi quaerere verum.*

There is no mention in his early Oxford letters of religious aims or views. Nor does it appear that the rector of Epworth had urged his son John to prepare for Holy Orders. It is true that his mother "wished with all her heart" that he would be ordained, and would assist his father at Epworth. In 1724, neither of his parents had seen John for a very considerable time, and they must have thought of his future with some anxiety. But John did not show the evidence of his great vocation until the spring of 1725.

And yet, while judging himself with unrelaxing severity, he was not averse to some of the milder amusements of youth. From the short notes of his cipher diary we find that he sat in the coffee-house, or at the King's Head, read the *Spectator*, and read (without comments) the story of *Jane Shore*. In one of the terse entries he wrote: "Boasting, greedy of praise, intemperate sleep, detraction . . . heat in arguing." He "disputed warmly on a trifle . . . talked of marriage with Griffiths, walked round the meadow . . . drank tea with Mr. Rigby, talked of predestination." On one occasion he was "treated by

Ditcher at the Coffee-House and Tennis Court." He notes
that he "played two hours at tennis." These few diversions
are simple enough; and the candid avowal of warmth in dispute, of boastfulness and the habit of detraction (charges
which are doubtless exaggerated) marks the beginning of
a spiritual advance.

It was presumably in the summer of 1725 that he made
his first experiment in conversion. Writing to his mother
in January 1727, he says:

> "About a year and a half ago I stole out of company
> at eight in the evening, with a young Gentleman with
> whom I was intimate. As we took a turn in an aisle of
> St. Mary's Church, in expectation of a young Lady's
> funeral, with whom we were both acquainted, I asked him
> if he really thought himself my friend; and if he did,
> why he did not do me all the good he could. He began
> to protest; in which I cut him short by desiring him to
> oblige me in an instance, which he could not deny to
> be in his own power; to let me have the pleasure of
> making him a whole Christian, to which I knew he was
> at least half persuaded already; that he could not do me
> a greater kindness, as both of us would be fully convinced
> when we came to follow that young woman.—He turned
> exceedingly serious, and kept something of that dis-
> position ever since. Yesterday was a fortnight, he died
> of a consumption."

The deep religious character of Wesley was therefore
clearly marked, though far from maturity in 1725, when he
was twenty-two years old. That solemn conversation in
the aisle of St. Mary's, that keen sense of pious opportunity,
showed the grace, the fervour and kindliness of the growing
spirit.

Young Wesley "altered his conversation, and set in earnest
upon a new life" in 1725. He saw that a true religion must
penetrate every aspect of the personality, and have its deep
centre in the heart. He sought, logically enough, the comforts and assurance of ritual. He communicated every
week, and set apart an hour or two every day for serious

reflection. At this period he was deeply influenced by "a religious friend" (whose identity is not clear) and by his first reading of Thomas à Kempis and Jeremy Taylor.

On Sunday, the 19th of September 1725, he was ordained a deacon by Dr. Potter, the Bishop of Oxford. Soon afterwards he preached his first sermon, at South Leigh near Witney.

Early in 1726, John visited the family at Epworth. He had not seen his home for many years. Little is recorded of the visit, but we know that he collected eagerly some further evidence concerning the "noises," and that he preached a funeral sermon on the death of a young parishioner. He wrote sermons for his father, noted in his diary that "levity slays," paid calls and drank tea, cut stakes and made rustic benches for the arbour, helped his father in transcribing the great work on Job, read *The Half-pay Officers*, *The Royal Convert*, and *The Orphan*. He must have discussed with his father the prospects of obtaining a Fellowship at Lincoln, a matter in which the old man was greatly interested.

Lincoln, almost alone of the Oxford colleges, had a solid reputation for piety and learning. Wesley was young for a Fellowship, but he too had a reputation for piety and learning, and in March 1726 he was elected.

The rector of Epworth had only five pounds to carry him and his family over the six months preceding the harvest, "*Sed passi graviora!*" he cried bravely. "Wherever I am, my Jack is Fellow of Lincoln." John got leave of absence, and came home for a little while to help his father.

The new Fellow entered seriously upon his duties at the beginning of the October term. In November he was appointed Greek lecturer and Moderator of the classes. As Moderator, presiding over the daily disputations, he delighted in the keen exercise of logic, of all exercises the one most congenial to his mind. He received the happiest impressions of the other Fellows. "As far as I have ever observed," he wrote to his brother Samuel, "I never knew a College besides ours, whereof the members were so perfectly satisfied with one another, and so inoffensive to the other parts of the University. All I have yet seen of the

Fellows are both well-natured and well-bred; men admirably disposed as well to preserve peace and good neighbourhood among themselves, as to promote it wherever else they may have acquaintance."

But no mere amenities could distract him from his fixed intention to work hard, nor would he allow the slightest deviation from the rules which he prepared for himself in matters of conduct, learning and piety. He became austere, chilly to the idle or importunate, firmly settled in the ways of self-discipline. Writing in 1774, he said: "When I formerly removed from one College to another, I fixed my resolution, not to be hastily acquainted with any one; indeed, not to return any visit, unless I had a reasonable hope of receiving or doing good therein." His courteous affability never prevented an occasional dryness in retort. In 1726, his brother Charles, a gay though not ungodly youth of eighteen, had come up to Christ Church from Westminster, declaring that he "would not be made a saint all at once," and we can imagine the Moderator looking at young Charles with a touch of brotherly disapproval.

John Wesley was a neat little man, not more than five feet six inches in height. His constant weight was about eight stone ten pounds. He was trim and muscular, thin but never emaciated, with a suggestion of paleness and fragility in early manhood. He wore his dark hair long; it flowed smoothly from a central parting and rolled over in two plain curls upon the shoulders. He could not afford a wig or the attentions of a barber. From his youth until the end of his life he wore his hair in the same fashion. His calm facial beauty must have reminded many who saw it of the pictures of Milton. Yet a slight protrusion of the lower lip, a squareness of jaw, and the quick lift of the eyelids, gave his face a marked character of energy. He was never hurried or excitable in speech; in every gesture he was carefully restrained. If there are spiritual qualities peculiar to good breeding, he certainly possessed them. No man ever had a more perfect nervous balance or a more absolute control of temper.

On the 14th of February 1727, Wesley took the degree

of Master of Arts. He chose three varied themes for his disputations: one was on The Soul of Brutus, one on Julius Cæsar, and one on the Love of God. Although his attainments were not prodigious, he can be fittingly described as a learned man. In addition to the ordinary classic studies, he read Hebrew and Arabic, metaphysics, natural philosophy, poetry and divinity. He was acquainted with the work of S'Gravesande and Newton, and had made a few optical experiments.

He now designed for himself an even stricter method of living, and a more severe application to study. He had written to his mother at the beginning of the year (1727):

"I am shortly to take my Master's degree. As I shall from that time be less interrupted by business not of my own choosing, I have drawn up for myself a scheme of studies, from which I do not intend, for some years at least, to vary. I am perfectly come over to your opinion, that there are many truths which it is not worth while to know. Curiosity, indeed, might be a sufficient plea for our laying out some time upon them, if we had half a dozen centuries of life to come; but methinks it is great ill-husbandry to spend a considerable part of the small pittance now allowed us, in what makes us neither a quick nor a sure return."

In response to what may very well have been the somewhat desperate appeals of the family, John Wesley left Oxford in the summer of 1727 and went to help his father, who, at sixty-five, was already infirm and broken.

Wesley, in view of a later refusal, has been taxed with indifference to his father's troubles. But he was now renouncing the joys of a studious and most congenial life, and all the pleasing responsibilities of his Fellowship, in cheerful answer to the call of duty. All his dear designs and careful preparations were abandoned at once. And the actual performance of his duty must have been exceedingly trying.

The dogged ministry of old Samuel had raised his

parishioners from a level of ignorance and brutality to a level of depressing dullness, but no higher. Wroote, where John was principally occupied, was dirty, damp and muddy, even in summer-time. It was known as Wroote-out-of-England. Everything was neglected, untidy and dismal. Pigs, hens, puppies, ducks and geese ran everywhere freely, and the litter of careless husbandry made the place nauseous and unwholesome. Hetty Wesley described the people of Wroote, in her vivacious way, as "asses dull on dunghills born." Here indeed was a change from the learned industry, the peace and comfort of a Fellow's life at Lincoln.

Yet it would be not only unjust, but contrary to all that we know of him, to suppose that John Wesley was unhappy or resentful during the period of his curacy at Wroote and Epworth. He was always glad to be among his own people, and his family affections were certainly profound. What is more, he often felt at this time the need of retirement.

He must have got into close and baffling touch, for the first time, with the deadness and sullen ignorance of the English peasant. All his life he regarded the salvation of the peasant as an extremely difficult matter, and he spoke of him sometimes with a despair in which there was a note of petulance. And if the boor was unredeemable, the farmer was almost equally hopeless. In a letter written many years later to John Trembath, he speaks of "the men whose talk is of bullocks; who have little enough to do either with religion or reason; and have but just wit enough to smoke, drink, and flatter you." Elsewhere, he describes the ordinary condition of the farmer: "Our eyes and ears may convince us there is not a less happy body of men in all England than the country farmers. In general their life is supremely dull; and it is usually unhappy too; for, of all people in the kingdom, they are the most discontented, seldom satisfied either with God or man."

He paid occasional visits to Oxford. He was there in October 1727; and in the following July he went up to be ordained priest by Bishop Potter at Christ Church. When, in the summer of 1729, he was again at Oxford, he met a little group of serious young men, who, at the suggestion of his brother Charles, met together for reading and quiet study.

In October 1729, John Wesley received a letter from Dr. Morley, the Rector of Lincoln, telling him that the junior Fellows who were also Moderators were required to attend personally to their duties unless they could find a substitute. One of the other Fellows, Mr. Fenton, had worked his way into a safe perpetual curacy; and another, Mr. Robinson, had to serve "two cures about fourteen miles from Oxford." It was therefore desirable that Wesley should return to his post. "Your father," said Dr. Morley, with a placid disregard of circumstance, "may certainly have another curate, though not so much to his satisfaction." John Wesley did not hesitate. He returned to Oxford in November, and remained there, almost continuously, for nearly six years.

Old Samuel Wesley, though we may be sure that he was too brave and too proud to complain, must have seen John go with a sinking heart. It is true that he found other curates—first Romley and then miserable Whitelamb— but it was hard to lose so dear and congenial a helper a John. But then, "my Jack is Fellow of Lincoln." My Jack, bless him! has the duties of a responsible man at the University, and he must attend to them.

When John Wesley left the Epworth family at the end of 1729, one, at least, of the unfortunate marriages had taken place. Poor, vivacious Hetty had become Mrs. Wright. She had been engaged to a young gentleman who was a lawyer, but her father, believing that the lawyer was unprincipled, forbade the marriage. Mr. Wright had then come forward, with the cordial approval of the rector.

And who was Mr. Wright? He was a plumber and glazier, uncouth, unlettered, coarse, faithless and drunken. No matter; he was in good circumstances. Better a homely plumber, with all his little faults, than a flashy rogue practising the devil's own trade of the law.

It is shocking to find the rector of Epworth urging his daughter to marry such a man, and not only urging her, but using the most direct methods of his grim authority.

Old Samuel Wesley was in some ways a most admirable man, but he had the dull obstinacy of a rigid formalist. Here, indeed, he seems to have acted without intelligence or kindness or the least atom of common sense; we have to suppose that Mr. Wright put on his best clothes when he came to the rectory and looked honest and plausible. We have to suppose something of the kind, because we know that the rector was not really a wicked old fool, resolving to bring about the total destruction of his daughter's happiness.

Mrs. Wesley, it would seem, gave her assent to this marriage. The Wesley parents managed to do as badly for their daughters as they had done well for their sons. But Hetty saw clearly enough, and her sister Mary saw clearly enough, what would be the results of this wretched alliance. Mr. Wright took his wife to his miserable establishment in Frith Street, Soho, where they were both nearly poisoned by the fumes of lead, and where all their sickly children died in infancy.

The shadow of this tragedy was already seen at Epworth in 1729. The family was terribly pinched, and was to be pinched yet more in finding the means to clothe and educate graceless Whitelamb, who was afterwards to bring tragedy into the life of Mary Wesley.

It cannot have been a happy household that John left when he returned to Oxford. He did not think it necessary to resign his Fellowship in order that he might stay at Epworth, nor is it likely that anyone suggested he ought to do so, yet it would be interesting to know whether his parents and his sisters watched him depart with any sensations a little more positive than mere regret.

Three years afterwards, the old rector appealed to Samuel for assistance, and in 1734 he appealed again to John. But neither Samuel nor John would go to Epworth. It is easy to say that John Wesley was always conscious of the great work to which he was called (though he himself denied this), that he was moving by ordered stages towards the fulfilment of a tremendous purpose, that he was controlled by the promptings of divine guidance; but still there lingers in our mind a doubt whether he need have left his father with such little concern in the miseries and infirmities of what were clearly the last years of his life. Such a doubt, even if it is not well founded, is not entirely without excuse. *Sed passi graviora!*

The life of John Wesley, after his return to Lincoln in 1729, entered upon a new phase, and one of extraordinary importance. The rise of Oxford Methodism must naturally be considered in a separate chapter. But here it is proper to notice a new influence in Wesley's religious development.

In 1726, William Law, the son of a grocer, had published a book called *Christian Perfection*, and this was followed in 1728 by the *Serious Call*.

Law was born in 1686 and ordained in 1711. His two books were probably the most influential religious writings of his period. He was the exponent of a new German theosophy in which the elements of medieval mysticism were harmonised with habits of modern thought.

We do not know at what time Wesley first met the *Serious Call*: Professor Winchester thinks it was probably in 1728. The influence of Law upon young Wesley, though not lasting, was unmistakable. Until the Moravian example gave to Wesley's religious life an essentially practical tendency, he inclined strongly towards mysticism. He was attracted by the glowing fervour of Law, and by the peculiar force and exaltation of his manner. Law frowned upon the vanities of social life; and young Wesley refused idle visitors. Law taught, or implied, the isolation of the holy man; and such a view, though it might have deprived Wesley of wholesome social recreation, helped to intensify the more speculative or emotional side of his religious nature.

The *Serious Call* played its part in confirming the habits of personal discipline and of pious exclusion which marked the life of Wesley at Oxford from 1729 to 1735. At the same time, it did more. It brightened the fire of spiritual ambition. It brought a rosier glow to the rather pallid gleam of aspiring faith, and gave a more intense conviction of religious reality.

Even in the use of his alarum clock, Wesley showed the ascetic influence. First, it was put to wake him at seven, then at six, then at five; and finally he was called at the cold hour of four every morning. In this habit of early rising he continued, except for short interruptions of sickness or emergency, for the whole of his life. So he conquered the sin of "intemperate sleep." And he attributed to this measure of discipline, not only the freshness and vigour which he felt when he woke, but the excellence of his general health.

CHAPTER III

CYRUS AND ASPASIA

IN 1725, or perhaps earlier, John Wesley had become acquainted with Robert Kirkham of Merton. Mr. Kirkham was a cheerful young man, the son of the rector of Stanton in Gloucestershire. His cheerfulness did not lead him away from serious things, he had an honest piety, and became one of the first of the Oxford Methodists. He has left a jovial picture of himself in a letter to Wesley, dated February 1727:

"With familiarity I write, dear Jack.—On Friday night last I received your kind accusation. You generously passed by, or pardoned, all insipid expressions; but I am condemned for brevity before I could put forth my defence. . . . I am just going down to a dinner of calve's head and bacon, with some of the best green cabbages in the town. I wish I could send you a plate of our entertainment while it is hot. We have just tapped a barrel of admirable cider. . . . Your most deserving character, your worthy personal accomplishments, your noble endowments of mind, your little and handsome person, and your obliging and desirable conversation, have been the pleasing subject of our discourse for some pleasant hours. You have often been in the thoughts of M. B., which I have curiously observed, when with her alone, by inward smiles and sighs and abrupt expressions concerning you. . . . Keep your counsel, and burn this when perused. . . . I must conclude, and subscribe myself, your most affectionate friend, and *brother* I wish I might write."

Instead of being burnt, the letter has been preserved, to shock Dr. Rigg, and to give us the first romantic view of Wesley. The girl who smiled and sighed when she thought of that "little and handsome person" was Robert's younger sister, Betty Kirkham.

Young Wesley appears to have paid many visits to the Cotswold villages of Stanton, Buckland and Broadway, where he found an intelligent and well-bred society very much to his liking. At Stanton he was made welcome by the Kirkhams, and at Buckland, little over a mile away, by Colonel Granville's family. At Broadway, he stayed with the rector, Mr. Griffiths, or in the friendly house of the Allens. And here, among the glorious bluff slopes of the Cotswold hills, he used to walk with Betty Kirkham, and her sister, gentle Damaris.

It is about forty miles from Oxford to these delectable places: a day's ride for Wesley. As he came near the final stages of his journey, with a few books and clean clothes in his saddle-bags, or in a wallet slung over his shoulders, he must have seen with delight the tower of the church at Stow-on-the-Wold rising over the long line of the hills. He must have looked forward with gladness of heart to the welcome at Stanton, the brisk hilarity of Robert, the kind smiles and happy glances of Betty and Sarah. After 1726, young Charles became a friend of the Kirkhams, and he too rode over the hills from Oxford. Both these young men found a rare and wholesome pleasure in the society of their Cotswold friends.

The earliest references to Betty Kirkham in the writings of Wesley are in the brief notes of the first Diary, under the date of September 1725. Betty had already assumed the fancy name of *Varanese*, a practice in conformity with the social and literary affectations of the period. The entries (there are two of them) are the same: "Writ to Varanese."

That Wesley, even at twenty-two, was deeply in love with Betty Kirkham, or that he was ever deeply in love with any woman, is highly improbable. He seems to have looked on women with an habitual delicate idealisation which saved him from all extravagance in thought or conduct, if it made him curiously blind to things which a coarser nature would have quickly apprehended. He could be sentimental, even excessively sentimental, but never dashing. From the cruder sort of passion he turned with abhorrence. He was exquisitely courteous, gentle and forbearing; and every

33

phase of his life was treated as a phase of spiritual experience
by his deeply religious nature. He had the natural defences
and inhibitions which are a part of such a character, as well
as the finer qualities of good breeding. Yet he was fond
of the society of women; and we know that at one time he
feared he might become too fond of it. A pretty woman, if
she was also serious, always attracted him. He was never
tempted by the "gay, fluttering things" of high life, by
those who were trivial, slight or vain.

Wesley himself was unquestionably attractive to women.
He was manly, vivacious, a good talker, with a rare beauty
of countenance and the quiet ascendancy of genius or power.
There could be no greater mistake than to imagine him
sour, disdainful or petulant, or to suppose that, because he
was religious in the most exalted degree, he was lacking
in sociability or the desire to please. Every account of him
shows that he was extremely good company. He was a
friendly man, with no liking for solitude. He was not
averse to dancing, or the simple amusement of parlour games.
Even as a youth, his wide reading and deep thinking must
have provided him with an unusual variety of ideas. He
read not only theology, metaphysics and classical authors,
but plays and novels. In the privacy of his Oxford room she
had spent an hour or two "acting." This he might severely
condemn as mere levity or waste of time; it showed, at least,
a normal susceptibility to enjoyment of a rational kind.
In dress he was neat, clean and proper; without a trace of
affectation, but with a rigid insistence upon order and
comeliness.

Young Wesley was therefore *persona gratissima* to the
Kirkham ladies, as he was, later, to Mrs. Granville and her
daughters.

Betty Kirkham was thoughtful and religious. It has
been suggested, indeed, that she was the first "religious
friend" of Wesley, and that she introduced him to Thomas
à Kempis. If that is so, her influence in 1725 would have
to be reckoned among the vitally important influences of
that critical year. Be that as it may, she was one of the
central figures in Wesley's personal experience from 1725

to 1731. It is clear enough, not only from Robert's letter, but also from letters by Martha and Emily Wesley, that John's affection for Betty was well known.

We are left in doubt as to any proposal of marriage that may have taken place. Probably there were some reasons against an engagement, and no proposal was ever made. Nor must we forget that marriage would have involved the loss of the Lincoln Fellowship. Betty married a Mr. Wilson in 1731; but Tyerman and Winchester are clearly mistaken in saying that she died in 1732, for John Wesley still wrote to her in 1735, and Charles Wesley appears to have met her in 1737.

A more remarkable lady came into Wesley's life towards or during the summer of 1730, after he had entered zealously upon the work of Oxford Methodism. This lady was Mrs. Pendarves, afterwards Mrs. Delany, a woman of very exceptional charm and character.

Before her marriage, Mrs. Pendarves was Miss Mary Granville, the daughter of Bernard Granville, who was the brother of Lord Lansdowne. She was born in 1700 at Coulsdon in Wiltshire. In her youth, she had spent some time in the house of her aunt, Lady Stanley, at Whitehall. She was married in 1718 to Alexander Pendarves of Roscrow near Falmouth, an ill-tempered, rough and gouty man of about sixty, who had a fine estate, and is said to have married to spite his nephew. His wife called him Gromio. He had told her of "all his good qualities and vast merit," and pointed out "how despicable she would be if she could refuse him because he was not young and handsome." This unpleasing person died in 1724.

Mrs. Pendarves, a beautiful and rich widow, moved virtuously serene among a shoal of importunate suitors. Neither Alcander, Bassanio nor Carlo could win her affection. She lightly gave her friends such playful names as Chatter-chops and Ha Ha, and refused "the American Prince," Lord Baltimore. She loved music. "Yesterday," she wrote to her sister in 1728, "I dined at the Percivals and tweedled away upon a lovely harpsichord, and I was not bid to *mind my time.*" Her virtue was almost phenomenal.

35

She lived in gay innocence among lively and fashionable people, never losing either head or heart or common sense. Hogarth "promised to give her some instructions about drawing." She admired the *Brutus* of Voltaire. When she could find time for them, she attended carefully to the duties of religion. In 1743 she married Dr. Patrick Delany, who was then fifty-eight; a popular Irish preacher; according to Swift, "the most popular preacher we have."

In later life, Mrs. Delany won the friendship and the admiration of nearly all the distinguished men of the age. She was "a truly great woman of fashion," said Burke; "the highest-bred woman in the world." Great men could freely admire her, for she never rivalled them in performances of the intellect; it was her gift to be universally charming and to excel in the pretty devices of paper mosaics and "flower work." She became the godmother of the Duke of Wellington. Her last years were spent in the intimacy of the royal family at Windsor, where the king gave her a house near the castle. It was here that Fanny Burney was introduced to George III. and the "dear queen." She died in 1788, three years before Wesley, and at precisely the same age.

Wesley owed to the Kirkhams his introduction to Mrs. Granville and her two daughters, Ann Granville and Mrs. Pendarves. It is reasonable to suppose that he met them at Buckland, some time before they moved, as they afterwards did, to Gloucester.

A pleasant little society of young people, writing to each other and reading and talking together, was formed by the two Granville girls, the Kirkhams, and John and Charles Wesley. In a letter from John to Mrs. Granville he speaks warmly of his gratitude and of his desire to be of spiritual service, and finishes by saying: "My brother joins with me in his best respects both to yourself and those good ladies whom we love to call your family."

Mrs. Pendarves, in 1730, was in her thirty-first year—three years older than John Wesley. She had taken to calling herself Aspasia. John became Cyrus; his brother Charles, Araspes; Ann Granville was known as Selina, and Sarah

Kirkham, Sappho. Whether John was called Cyrus at an
earlier date, or when he first met Aspasia, are not matters of
great importance; but it may be noted that Mrs. Pendarves,
in a letter to her sister Ann written in March 1727, says:
"You shall have Cyrus as soon as I can get him." It was
certainly not before 1730 that Cyrus felt for Aspasia something less temperate than a mere ordinary friendship.

Perhaps the affection of Wesley for his "dear Varanese"
was now of a more tranquil kind; or perhaps Betty had
already perceived the approach of Mr. Wilson. But there is
nothing to suggest that Wesley transferred his affection
from Varanese to Aspasia before Miss Betty had shown a
certain change in her own. In the first letter of Cyrus to
Aspasia he says: "While I was transcribing the letters,
these last monuments of the goodness of my dear Varanese, I
could not hinder some sighs which, between grief and shame,
would have their way." This letter is dated August 1730.
Nearly a year afterwards, in the summer of 1731, he wrote
to Mrs. Pendarves: "You will easily judge whether the
remembrance of *Aspasia* made that entertainment in particular less enjoyable which I enjoyed last week, in the almost
uninterrupted conversation of dear *Varanese*. 'On this spot
she sat,' 'along this path she walked,' 'here she showed that
lovely instance of condescension,' were reflections which,
though extremely obvious, could not but be equally pleasing,
and give a new degree of beauty to the charming arbour,
the fields, the meadows, and Horrel itself."

Telford (one of Wesley's later biographers) misses the
point of this when he supposes that the loving reflections of
Cyrus apply to Varanese. Clearly they do not. They are a
part of "the remembrance of Aspasia." Wesley, walking
with his Varanese, calls to mind a walk with Aspasia among
the same scenes, and is melted by the thought of her
"lovely condescension." Mrs. Pendarves, in her reply,
said: "How I please myself with the thought that I was not
quite forgot at that interview; perhaps I was wished for."
Betty is not less dear, but she has become the subject rather
of melancholy tenderness and of sighing respect than of
lively aspiration.

Mary Pendarves, a gracious visitor from the world of fashion, must have beamed among the homely Cotswold people with a mild though superior charm. She must have brought to the heart and mind of Wesley new images and new emotions. Betty Kirkham, with all her sweetness and piety, may well have lacked the attractions of this beautiful, virtuous, amusing and yet religious young widow.

In the singularly interesting correspondence of Cyrus and Aspasia we are struck by the peculiar formality, discretion and obscurity of the letters. They are so far from being love letters of the usual kind that several biographers have been left in doubt as to the real nature of Wesley's attitude towards Mrs. Pendarves, or the real meaning of his allusions to Betty Kirkham.

We have to bear in mind that Cyrus and Aspasia very seldom met each other. The Granvilles probably moved from Buckland to Gloucester before the end of 1730. Mrs. Pendarves did not often visit the country. She visited her friends in London, or lived with her aunt Stanley at Whitehall. Her life was that of a society woman, and it was obviously the life which she chose for herself, and preferred to any other. By a strange coincidence, a great deal of her time was spent in the town house of the Wesleys or Westleys or Wellesleys of Meath. Richard Colley, in whose cheerful family Mrs. Pendarves was on a footing of intimate friendship, had inherited the name and estates of Garrett Wesley of Dangan and Mornington; he was raised to the peerage with the title of Mornington in 1746. Colley Wellesley was the grandfather of the Duke of Wellington.

How often, and in what circumstances, Wesley actually met Aspasia, we do not know. Her "lovely condescension" permitted her to walk with him among the woods and meadows of Stanton, and even to linger in the arbour. Wesley records, with overflowing sentiment, at least one of these walks. If we are to take him literally, Mrs. Pendarves represented an almost heavenly degree of perfection. He felt himself far behind her in the matter of holiness. "The penitent," he said, "cannot avoid being left behind by the innocent." The sheer glory of her spirit "brightened the dear hill, the fields, the arbour." She seemed to him a superior creature, joining the radiance of earthly beauty to a most angelic profusion of divine grace. And she, for her part, was clearly attracted by this grave and handsome young man, who was so unlike her gay Alcanders, her importunate Bassanios. In all probability her religion, as far as it went, was true enough: that a woman of fashion had any religion at all was certainly remarkable. For rather more than a year she kept up a correspondence with Wesley, and she preserved his letters.

In every godly nature there is a trace of sentiment. A man without sentiment is a man without religion, for sentiment is the natural idealisation of gentleness and goodness. Cyrus is no trivial assumed personality. He is young John Wesley, very deeply fascinated by the charm and piety of his Aspasia. His letters are not those of an ordinary lover; perhaps they are not those of a lover in any obvious sense of the word; they are full of reverence, discretion, restraint, the softest of admonitions; but they are also sentimental.

When he wrote these letters, Wesley was twenty-seven. The value of his correspondence with Aspasia is that it shows us, more clearly than his meditated work, those tender sensibilities which were a permanent part of his nature; possibly an occasional source of credulity and weakness, but always among the most lovable of his qualities and the most human.

Soon after their exchange of letters had begun, in the late summer of 1730, Cyrus wrote to Aspasia the most romantic of all his passages:

"I spent some very agreeable moments last night . . . thinking to how little disadvantage *Aspasia* or *Selina* would have appeared even in that faint light which the moon, glimmering through the trees, poured on that part of the garden in which I was walking. How little would the eye of the mind that surveyed them have missed the absent sun! What darkness could have obscured gentleness, courtesy, humility—could have shaded the image of God! Sure none but that which shall never dare to approach them; none but vice, which shall ever be far away!"

Selina is decorously included in the moonlight vision; for even in mental imagery Cyrus cannot admit a situation which is not strictly proper.

Varanese is frequently mentioned in these letters. Both to Cyrus and to Aspasia she is the object of affectionate regard: Aspasia calls her "our dear inimitable Varanese," and complains that she has not even had time to write to her. Wesley refers often to "dear Varanese"; he would "shelter himself under the protection of Varanese and Aspasia and Selina." The most suggestive of these references is in a letter from Cyrus written in the winter of 1730:

"But whether I could do what I ought, I have great reason to question. I much doubt whether self-love would not be found too strong for a friendship which I even now find to be less disinterested than I hitherto imagined. . . . While I am reflecting on this, I can't but often observe with pleasure the great resemblance between the emotion I then feel and that with which my heart frequently over-flowed in the beginning of my intercourse with our dear V. Yet there is a sort of soft melancholy mixed with it, when I perceive that I am making another avenue for grief, that I am laying open another part of my soul, at which the arrows of fortune may enter."

He is passing from one avenue of grief to another. In a later letter, he laments that he is "denied the happiness of conversing with such a friend (Varanese)."

We are bound to infer that some barrier had arisen between him and Betty Kirkham. It may have been that Betty's father, or Betty herself, considered that Wesley, by this time, should have made his intentions clear, and hon-ourably advanced or retired. It is conceivable that Betty was piqued by the palpable admiration of Cyrus for Aspasia. Or perhaps, as we have suggested before, Mr. Wilson had already shown his topsails in the offing. What is clear from

Wesley's letter is that he feared, in becoming the friend of Mrs. Pendarves, to expose himself to another sorrow. On the 25th of November 1730, he sent Aspasia a letter in which occurs the following passage:

"O that our friendship (since you give me leave to use that dear word) might be built on a firm foundation! Were it possible for you to find me any way of repaying part of the good I experience from you, then I would not dare to doubt I should still have some place in your thoughts. And why should I doubt? since He who has hitherto sustained me is the same yesterday and for ever; and since, so long as I own and depend upon them, His wisdom and strength are mine. . . . Would that, when humility, which sitteth by His throne, is sent down to rest upon you, one ray of it might glance upon my heart, to remove the stony from it, to make it duly sensible both of its own many infirmities, and of your generous desire to lessen their number! For want of this, I cannot follow you as I would. I must be left behind in the race of virtue. I am sick of pride: it quite weighs my spirits down. O pray for me, that I may be healed. I have the greater dependence on your intercession, because you know what you ask. Every line of your last shows the heart of the writer, where with Friendship dwells Humility. Ours, *dear Aspasia*, it is to make acknowledgements; upon us lie the obligations of gratitude."

Whatever now happened to Wesley was primarily a matter of religious experience, nor is it difficult to see in this idealisation of Aspasia something more than a mere courtliness of phrase. He saw in this lady, whose gravity was so becoming, and whose religious confidences were probably quite sincere, all the noble fascinations of a saintly mistress. A sense of deep humility certainly accompanies the finer sorts of love; and although it would be going too far to assume that Wesley ever admitted, even to himself, that he was in love with Mrs. Pendarves, she represented, for him, an experience that was new, delightful, and yet disturbing. At the end of 1730, he wrote:

"Should one who was as my own soul be torn from me, it would be best for me, it would be the stroke of mercy. . . . But is it a fault to desire to recommend myself to those who so strongly recommend virtue to me?—ardently to desire *their* esteem, who are so able and willing to make me in some degree worthy of it? Tell me, *Aspasia*—tell me, *Selina*—if it be a fault that my heart burns within me, when I reflect on the many marks of regard you have already shown."

No one could find, in this reverence and decorum and rather timid formality, the materials for an exciting romance; and yet the unmistakable suggestion of romance is always present in these letters. The attitude of Mrs. Pendarves herself is not quite clear. It has been said that she could never have thought of marrying Wesley; but she ultimately married a man greatly inferior to Wesley in birth, charm and distinction. Dr. Delany, however worthy and pious he may have been, was the son of a judge's domestic, and his manners were rough and homely: he was fifteen years older than Mrs. Pendarves, and there seems to be no reason for describing the marriage as eminently suitable.

The general tenour of the Cyrus and Aspasia correspondence is definitely religious, marked, on the side of Wesley, by the evidence of a warmly sentimental attachment. There is nothing in the correspondence which goes beyond the limits of the sentimental. Yet the episode was unique in the life of Wesley, and it shows, not only how the intensely religious nature meets the ordinary experience of youth, but Wesley's own particular capacity for idealised or sanctified emotion.

In 1731, Mrs. Pendarves was in the whirl of fashionable life. We do not know if she ever met Wesley after the autumn of 1730. But for some time, at any rate until she went to Ireland with the Wesleys of Dangan, the exchange of letters continued. And we cannot help seeing a shade of jealousy in Wesley's religious warnings. "That *London* is the worst place under heaven for preserving a Christian temper," he tells her, "any one will imagine, who observes that there can be none where its professed, irreconcilable enemies, 'the lust of the eye' and 'the pride of life,' are more artfully and forcibly recommended."

But Aspasia turns to him for guidance:

"Every Sunday evening," she wrote to him, "there is a gentleman in this town has a concert of music. I am invited there to-night, and design to go. I charge you, on the friendship you have professed for me, tell me your sincere opinion about it, and all your objections. For, if I am in an error by going, you ought to prevent my doing so again."

Cyrus gravely answers: "Far be it from me to think that any circumstances of life shall ever give the enemy an advantage over Aspasia. He who has overcome the world and its princes shall give His angels charge over her, to keep her in all her ways. . . . To judge whether any action be lawful on the Sabbath or no, we are to consider whether it advances the end for which the Sabbath was ordained. Now, the end for which the Sabbath was ordained is the attainment of holiness. Whatever, therefore, tends to advance this end, is lawful on this day." But he avoids an express ruling on the question of the concerts.

Mrs. Pendarves was now enjoying herself prodigiously, but with perfect innocence, in London. Most of her time was spent, so it would appear, with the Wesleys of Dangan. She played with Mr. Wesley's new orrery, and watched Hogarth painting the family group. She went to plays, routs and operas. Perhaps she enjoyed most of all the little "jaunts" to Richmond or the river, which Mr. Wesley was so expert in devising. She laughed at the amusing talk of "Mr. Coot and Harry Usher." She went to church and she went to Court; she went everywhere. But still she was the "dear Aspasia" of Cyrus; and Cyrus, with a shade of melancholy and apprehension, reminds her of the vanity of the world:

"If Providence has used me as an instrument of doing

43

any good to Aspasia, I had almost said, 'I have my reward.' Some part of it I have, undoubtedly. The thought of having added anything to your ease will make many of my hours the happier. Yet, perhaps, I ought not to desire that you should be easy at the common conversation of the world; which, if once it come to be indifferent to us, will scarce be long before it be agreeable. We are, indeed, as to this, in a great strait. Either it displeases; and who would be in pain, could it be avoided?—or it pleases; which surely causes, if it does not spring from, an entire depravation of our affections."

Aspasia herself recognises the perils of a society whose one concern is amusement. God has no place in the heart of a fool, and Aspasia sees that she is surrounded by every possible variation of ungodliness and folly. And yet those water-parties were so delightful, the opera so exciting, and the Wesleys could provide her with such elegant, friendly and cheerful entertainment! After all, she is not less religious than she was formerly. Providence calls her to play her part among these gay multitudes, and she may even be the means of doing good. In July, she answers a letter from Cyrus. She has just received a letter from him, in which he tells her that he has been accused of "carrying things too far in religion."

"The imputation thrown upon you is a most extraordinary one. But such is the temper of the world; when you have no vice to feed their spleen with, they will condemn the highest virtue. O *Cyrus*, how noble a defence you make! and how are you adorned with the beauty of holiness! . . . How ardently do I wish to be as resigned and humble as *Cyrus*! . . . As you say, my lot is fallen among those who cannot be accused of too much strictness in religion. So far from that, they generally make an open profession of having no religion at all. I cannot observe my fellow creatures in such manifest danger, without feeling an inexpressible concern. But God in His good time may make them sensible of their blindness. . . . *Company is come and will not allow me a long*

44

conversation. I cannot always submit to this sort of life. It encroaches too much. *Adieu.*"

The alarms and warnings of Cyrus became more emphatic. As he thinks of the hardened hearts and the empty heads of her friends, he himself is aware of "an inexpressible concern." He cannot believe that such friends can honestly justify themselves by saying they do no hurt. "It is no hurt to rob you of your time . . . to turn your very sweetness of temper against you? . . . Must Aspasia ever submit to this insufferable misfortune? Every time a gay wretch wants to trifle away part of that invaluable treasure which Thou hast lent him, shall he force away a part of hers too?— tear another star from her crown of glory? O 'tis too much indeed! Surely there is a way of escape."

Aspasia feels the force of the argument: "While I read your letters," she says, "I find myself carried above the world; I view the vanities I left behind with the disdain that is due to them, and wish never to return to them. But, as it is my lot to dwell among them as yet, I will at least endeavour to defend myself from their assaults; and, with your assistance, I hope to baffle and turn aside their sting."

After Mrs. Pendarves had gone to Ireland with the Wesleys of Dangan, her correspondence with Cyrus became more fitful, and finally ceased altogether. There was so much to do, and so much to think of. Aspasia met Swift, and Laetitia Pilkington, and the amusing society of the Castle at Dublin. Her dear Miss Wesley "performs miracles at the Castle, and is by much the best dancer there." Perhaps her desire to emulate Cyrus in godliness was not as consistent as it had been. In March 1732, she wrote to her sister with a touch of remorse: "Cyrus by this time has blotted me out of his memory, or if he does remember me, it can only be to reproach me; what can I say for myself?" She could only make the feeble excuse of "want of time." A year later, she was still watching the progress of Wesley with sympathetic interest: "As for the ridicule Cyrus has been exposed to, I do not at all wonder at it; religion in its plainest dress suffers daily from the insolence

45

and ignorance of the world." But it was not until 1734, after a silence of nearly three years, that she wrote again to Wesley. Her letter began with a humble statement of confusion. Cyrus had now become the leader of a new religious movement in Oxford—indeed, the only religious movement in Oxford, or in England, for that matter—and his answer, severely polite and gravely conclusive, proved that the old sentiment had become a matter of pious memory:

"Alas, Aspasia! Are you indeed convinced that I can be of any service to you? I fear you have not sufficient ground for such a conviction. . . . You declined the trouble of writing, not because it was a trouble, but because it was a needless one. And if so, what injury have you done yourself? As for me, you do me no injury by your silence. It did, indeed, deprive me of much pleasure, and of a pleasure from which I received much improvement. But still, as it was one I had no title to but your goodness, to withdraw it was no injustice. I sincerely thank you for what is past; and may the God of my salvation return it sevenfold into your bosom! And if ever you should please to add to those thousand obligations any new ones, I trust they shall neither be unrewarded by Him nor unworthily received by Aspasia's faithful friend and servant, Cyrus. *Araspes*, too, hopes you will never have reason to tax him with ingratitude. *Adieu!*"

So the correspondence, and the friendship, came to an end. Charles Wesley (Araspes) met Mrs. Pendarves in 1737; but it seems as though she never saw John again.

The last echo of the Cyrus and Aspasia episode came out of the faded remembrance of Mrs. Delany, when she was an old woman of eighty-three. "Ah, yes!" she told her friend Miss Hamilton at Bulstrode; "she had known the Mr. Wesleys—the Methodist preachers; she knew them when they were young men. . . . They were of a serious turn, and associated with such as were so. . . . That was a happy beginning, but the vanity of being singular and growing *enthusiasts* made them endeavour to gain proselytes and adopt that system of religious doctrine which many reasonable folk thought *pernicious*. Well, well! Perhaps they did some good to the common people. . . ." And so we can imagine the old lady rambling on to other reminiscences of a livelier kind, or to other reflections of a sterner nature.

CHAPTER IV

THE HOLY CLUB

THE ultimate form of Methodism was not the result of any original prepared scheme or planned organisation taking the full measure of possibility and foreseeing every line of development. It grew stage by stage, governed in policy, at least until 1744, by the shifting play of circumstance. Wesley himself admitted, in 1785, that he had been "insensibly led, without any previous plan or design."

The "first rise of Methodism" was the work, not of John, but of Charles Wesley at Oxford. Great religious revivals commonly start in places where religion has most completely decayed. The first Methodist society consisted of three young men—Charles Wesley, Robert Kirkham and William Morgan. In November 1729, John Wesley became their leader.

Now, the purpose of these young men was not to found a religious movement, but simply to improve themselves and to do good to their fellows. We have seen Robert Kirkham; a cheerful and honest, though not a remarkable character. William Morgan was a fervent, consumptive lad from Dublin; he combined philanthropy with shrewdness and an anxious regard for detail; he was the missionary of the group, and visited the prisoners in the Castle and the jail of Bocardo.

The term Methodist seems to have been first applied to the original group of three by a "young gentleman" of Christ Church in 1729. Although an extremely appropriate and very honourable term, it was applied in derision. To the young gentlemen of Christ Church, and probably to all the other young gentlemen of Oxford, there was something inconceivably funny about these grave lads who made a regular practice of piety, met each night for serious reading, and proposed to visit the poor and to lead people into the way of salvation.

Methodist was not by any means a new term, and it may

even, as Workman suggests, have been borrowed from current slang to fit the occasion. It had been applied to schools of botany and medicine, and had been used in 1647 in a purely theological sense. By the end of the seventeenth century it had certainly acquired a sectarian meaning, although no sect bearing the name was in existence, as far as we know, at the time of the Oxford meetings. The term occurs in a dictionary of 1706, and is there merely defined as "One that treats of method or affects to be methodical." This would imply that the use of the word had become slightly ironical, or had a derogatory implication. The term was forced upon the movement by popular usage; it was adopted by Wesley under protest, for to him the idea of religious differentiation was always abhorrent. Wesley's own definition has a magnificent simplicity: "A Methodist is one who lives according to the method laid down in the Bible."

In the course of time, a few other young men and a few tutors joined the little group or society. They met regularly, and usually in Wesley's rooms at Lincoln. Although the motives which drew them together were religious, they used, at first, to devote some of their time to the study of the classics. To study anything, and above all to study religion, was entirely at variance with the usual practices of young men at Oxford. It was considered more correct to be idle, infidel and irresponsible. The Wesley group had therefore an appearance of singularity.

"Almost as soon as we had made our first attempts this way," wrote Wesley, "some of the men of wit in Christ Church entered the lists against us, and between mirth and anger made a pretty many reflections upon the *Sacramentarians*, as they were pleased to call us. Soon after, their allies at Merton altered the title, and did us the honour of styling us *The Holy Club*."

They were also called the Enthusiasts, the Bible Moths, the Reforming Club, and Supererogation Men. But of all their nicknames, that of the Holy Club was the most popular, and it was probably the one by which the group was usually known in Oxford.

The membership was never large; twenty-five appears to have been their highest number. Yet it is not unreasonable to suppose that the Club actually contained most of the younger Oxford men who were inclined to think seriously about religion. And it is a shocking comment upon the age and place in which they lived, that the studious, pious and philanthropic habits of those men should have provoked such an outpouring of ridicule and indignation.

The real objection to the Holy Club was the piety of its members. Such piety was an indirect but very palpable reproach to the lax clergy and lazy men of Oxford, to the deep dullness of the doctors and the general ungodliness and silliness of the place. Rough banter, the usual resource of those who feel themselves justly reproved, prepared the way for a rougher persecution. A blustering uncle threatened to cut off his nephew if he persisted in the absurd practices of the Club, and particularly in communicating once a week. Other weekly communicants were severely *admonished* by the seniors of Merton, and had to promise that they would only receive the Sacraments three times a year. We can scarcely imagine an attitude more absurd, and at the same time more odious, than the attitude of the heads of colleges and of Oxford opinion generally. It is true that Wesley's young men were High Churchmen with a liking for ritual, but they were not unorthodox. Nothing could have been further from their minds than the idea of forming a separate religious organisation, or anything which could possibly have the appearance of such an organisation; nor had they shown the least desire to question the authority of the Church of England. Even if the mysticism of Law was not entirely without effect upon their views, that effect was never shown by any practice which could have been obnoxious to ordinary people.

John Wesley assumed the leadership of the Holy Club as a matter of course. He was older than the other members; he had more learning, more experience, and a natural habit of authority. In the words of one of the Club members, "He was blessed with such activity as to be always gaining ground, and such steadfastness that he lost none." And again, "He had naturally a very clear apprehension, yet his exact prudence depended more on honesty and singleness of heart."

He had a remarkable sense of opportunity, a readiness to make use of the talents of other men and to adopt a timely suggestion, a rapid grasp of what was essential; above all, he had the great leader's gift of making others desire to follow him. He was intensely serious, and knew how to compel attention, but he was neither a bully nor a boaster. During his Oxford residence, the idea of becoming a revivalist in any wide sense of the word never occurred to him. If he thought of his future, he thought of quiet days in Oxford, with studious delights of fellowship, the gentle encouragement of piety in others, the doing of good to the sick, the poor and degraded, the improvement of his own character.

The Oxford society does not, in a literal sense, represent the "first rise of Methodism." The formal High Church practices of the Club, with a definite emphasis upon salvation by works alone, were things entirely foreign to the spirit of the later Methodism, if not opposed to the Methodist ordinance. Of all the members of the Club, none, with the exception of Charles Wesley and George Whitefield, had any part in Wesley's great mission to the English people. Most of them became ordinary, inconspicuous clergymen. As far as we know, the original Oxford society crumbled away after Wesley's departure for Georgia in 1735.

The members of Wesley's Club, though certainly distinguished by piety and courage, were for the most part rather dull young men. Kirkham was a cheerful nonentity. Morgan was a true Christian philanthropist; he might have been a useful man, had he not died so tragically, the victim of mental and bodily disease, in 1732. John Gambold, who joined the Club when he was a lad of nineteen, was a quiet soul with leanings towards mysticism; he had the living of Stanton-Harcourt in 1737, went over to the Moravians in 1742, and became a Moravian bishop. Benjamin Ingham was, for a time, more closely associated with the Wesleys. Ingham seems to have been only eighteen when he joined the Club; he, too, had a love of mysticism, with schismatic proclivities. Ingham broke away from the Methodists in 1740, became a Moravian, then founded a circuit of his own, which was finally broken up by the Scotch heresy of Sandemanianism. John Clayton, a member of the Club in 1732, was a pretty young man with a good deal of pious foppery, very neat, very regular, but a hard worker among the poor and the outcast; in religion he was orthodoxly High Church, punctual and precise, though his political views were those of a Jacobite. Thomas Broughton, another member, was also a rigid Churchman, who sternly repudiated the idea of conscious redemption, and in 1743 became the Secretary of the Society for the Promotion of Christian Knowledge. James Hervey, who joined in 1733, was a lovable, studious character. The gentle spirit of Hervey produced *Meditations among the Tombs, Thoughts in a Flower Garden, Contemplations on the Night,* and finally *Theron and Aspasio.* He made a hopeless attempt to convert Beau Nash by means of a letter; he was too mild and affectionate to quarrel with his Methodist friends, but he slipped away into the obscurity of parochial work at Weston-Favel, where he became dimly Calvinistic.

Two of the Club members were to play their shabby parts in the history of the Epworth family: lamentable John Whitelamb and the more lamentable Westley Hall. Whitelamb, trained largely at the expense of old Samuel Wesley, had assisted the rector in his great work on Job, and had actually engraved some of the plates for it; he became curate of Wroote in 1733, and married Mary Wesley. But Whitelamb "was betrayed into very great follies"; he was a weak and shiftless creature. Westley Hall was a hundred times worse. Hall married Martha Wesley, after an intermediate courtship of Kezia, and became a curate at Salisbury. Hall's religious views appear to have been as irregular as his morals, for Clarke describes him as "a Moravian, a Quietist, an Antinomian, a Deist, if not an Atheist, and a Polygamist, which last he defended in his teaching and illustrated in his practice."

Of the other members of the Holy Club whose names

have been preserved—Boyce, Chapman, Kinchin, Hutchins and Atkinson—little can be said, except that they all took Orders and faded into blameless obscurity. That astonishing man, George Whitefield, was not admitted to the Club until the last year of its existence.

The Club was neither more nor less than a society of very young and very earnest High Churchmen, with evangelistic views and a true desire to lead the lives of exemplary Christians. The members of the Club worked under the inspiration, the guidance and control of John Wesley. This young clergyman, a slender figure in his plain black cassock, led the others without seeming to do so. And as Wesley was always a man of method, of rules and regularity, the work of the Club and the personal discipline of its members were settled without ambiguity or hesitation.

In the midst of a heathen or careless Oxford, the Holy Club had the appearance of a group of missionaries. Perhaps the group was a little self-conscious, a little exclusive and superior. Lads of eighteen and nineteen — like Hervey, Ingham and Gambold when they joined the Club—must have relished the idea of setting an example to the stale, drowsy Churchmen of the University, who spent so much time over their pots at the Mitre, and so little time in Christian works. Nor is the knowledge of being persecuted in a good cause and in good company entirely disagreeable. Some of the weaker members did indeed give way to pressure, especially when the personal influence of Wesley was temporarily withdrawn, and fell back into the ordinary ways of Oxford. But the better kind stoutly persevered, stoutly performed the duties of religious men.

The Oxford Methodists, in their five years of active being (1730-1735), certainly did excellent work, even if the extent of that work was only parochial. They visited the prisoners in the Castle jail, and the poor debtors in the Bocardo. Their work in the prisons was both educational and religious. Spelling-books as well as prayer-books were distributed, for many of the prisoners did not know their alphabet. Education was always a part of Wesley's programme. An effort was made to improve the appalling social conditions of prison life, to settle disputes and to check violence.

In all these matters, it was the actual presence of Wesley, the influence of his voice, his quiet manner, his plain though gentle authority, his understanding and patience, which did the real good, and fixed the ideas of godliness and improvement in the minds of his listeners. When he was absent from Oxford for any length of time, there was always a falling-off in power and resolution and coherence, not only among the converts, but among the members of the little society. John Clayton, who was left in charge of the work in 1732, wrote to tell Wesley that "Bocardo grew worse upon his hands." The debtors, he said, "have done nothing but quarrel ever since you left us."

In addition to his work among the prisoners, Wesley helped to maintain, if indeed he did not wholly maintain, a school for children. He organised the visiting and relief of the poor, including those in St. Thomas's workhouse, collected and distributed alms, and gave to such as could use them Bibles and Prayer-books. Food, clothes, and medicine were provided for the needy; industrious men were lent money wherewith to buy the tools and materials of their humble trades.

Wesley was not the man to exhort others to practise what he himself did not practise; in charity he set the noble example of giving away all that he did not require for his mere clothing and sustenance. He managed to live on twenty-eight pounds a year, and by keeping his expenditure at the same figure, he was able to give away in one year sixty-two pounds, and in another ninety-two. There is a story of a poor, starving creature visiting him in winter in his Lincoln rooms. Wesley put his hand in his pocket, and found that he had only a few shillings left. He looked up, and his glance fell upon the pictures on the wall. The pictures were clearly unnecessary; and now they became stern accusers; with the money he had spent on them, he might have clothed the destitute girl who now stood before him. So the pictures were sold.

But the mission of the Holy Club was not by any means

limited to the instruction or relief of the poor and imprisoned. The members of the Club undertook the infinitely more difficult task of converting the young gentlemen of the University. Such an effort implied an extraordinary degree of pious optimism. It must have seemed easier to get rich men to heaven than to win these idle boys.

The Methodist overtures were never aggressive· they were rather in the nature of a friendly social advance. Young men were invited to breakfast, and there, over a dish of tea, Wesley or his colleagues would try "to fasten some good hint upon them." What is more, men like Charles and John Wesley, Ingham and Clayton, who were all excellent scholars, would assist the young men in their college work. Wesley believed that it was the duty of a good Christian to be a good scholar, if he had the means of becoming one.

But since the Holy Club was a true religious fraternity, it was necessary to have a system of personal discipline and of religious observance for the members. That system was devised by Wesley. It was, like every other product of his mind, perfectly clear and definite; its aim was to develop in each individual his capacity for pure religion. The practices of the Club were the personal practices of Wesley, and they show unmistakably his theological constitution at Oxford.

The members of the Club spent an hour, morning and evening, in private prayer. At nine, twelve and three o'clock they recited a collect, and at all times they examined themselves closely, watching for signs of grace, and trying to preserve a high degree of religious fervour. They made use of pious ejaculations, they frequently consulted their Bibles, and they noted, in cipher diaries, all the particulars of their daily employment. One hour each day was set apart for meditation. In praying for each other, they felt the mystical union of souls. They fasted twice a week, observed all the feasts of the Church, and received the Sacraments every Sunday. Before going into company they prepared their conversation, so that words might not be spoken without purpose. The Primitive Church, in so far as they had any knowledge of it, was to be taken as their pattern. Wesley showed himself not unwilling to accept the practice of regular confession, to pray for the dead, and to celebrate the Eucharist on every saint's day. And one of the principal aims of this method, in the words of Wesley, was *to cut off their retreat to the world.*

Obviously the leading idea of this method is not really evangelical; it is, on the contrary, ascetic; the end in view is personal holiness; it conduces to a kind of introspective religious egoism. The good works, even the exhortations to a holy life, were only a part of this personal pursuit; everything was done in accordance with a formal notion of pious technique. Nor does this admission, which was afterwards made by Wesley himself, detract from the noble courage of the endeavour. The limitations of mere austerity are sufficiently obvious, but no first reaction from the ungodliness of the age, and the flagrant ungodliness of Oxford, could have been anything but an austere reaction. "When I was at Oxford," wrote Wesley in 1777, "and lived almost like a hermit, I saw not how any busy man could be saved. I scarce thought it possible for a man to retain the Christian spirit, amidst the noise and bustle of the world. God taught me better by my own experience."

It would be not only ungenerous, but undiscerning, to find fault with the Oxford society because the central idea was monastic. The first impulse of Wesley and his young men was an impulse of self-preservation. Behind the line of defence, the great spiritual powers of Wesley were quietly assembling themselves; but many years of trial and discipline, of work and hard experience, were needed in order to bring those powers to glorious action.

Although his Oxford experience was turned to good account by Wesley in the actual Methodist campaign, it would be a grave mistake to regard the Club itself as the foundation of Methodism, or even as a society which had more than a local and temporary significance. The members of the Club, in so far as they openly engaged the forces of evil and indifference, were only parochial visitors. Their zeal and ambition never, for one moment, contemplated a wider field. They did not publish a single tract, nor had they any idea of appealing to the clergy or the public in general. Had it not been for the leadership of a man so remarkable as Wesley, it is unlikely that the Club would ever have been heard of outside the small regions of University gossip. And in the mind of Wesley himself, the usefulness of the association was limited to the personal improvement of the members, with excursive missionary or philanthropic work among undergraduates and paupers. Misled by romantic pictures, and by the desire to join one phase to another in a long view of glorious evolution, many writers have exaggerated the importance of the Holy Club. Its importance is limited to its influence upon the unsettled religious views and the growing religious character of John Wesley, and to a lesser extent upon the religious characters of Charles Wesley, Ingham and George Whitefield. It did not differ greatly from scores of other religious associations, except for its peculiar and unexpected position in the University of Oxford. The entire lack of any desire to produce a literature of its own, at a time when people took the keenest interest in the circulation of polemical views, may be taken as the clearest proof of the limitations of the Club, and of the absence of any strong intellectual direction. It cannot be compared with the Oxford Movement initiated in 1833 by Keble, Hurrell Froude and Newman, with the later addition of Dr. Pusey; although here again we have an association of pious young men, all, with the exception of Keble, in the early thirties. The Oxford Movement of 1833 immediately produced a series of powerful tracts, and became quickly and widely known as the Tractarian Movement. The aim of the Tractarians was not the encouragement of local piety, but a definite reform in the teaching and energies of the Church of England. Their view embraced the whole sphere of the Church's influence, and the result of their spiritual rebellion was a new chapter in ecclesiastical history. Wesley's Oxford society, therefore, from a point of view such as that of the Tractarian Movement of 1833, was only a local experiment, informally constituted, conceived with little originality, and with a range of action only slightly beyond that of a well organised body of parish workers.

We have no reason to suppose that Wesley, during his ascetic and ritualistic phase, was dry, harsh or forbidding in company. If he shut his door to those who were trivial or impertinent, and chose for his companions those who were likely to assist him in his own striving, there is evidence to show that his behaviour when he found himself in company was always delightful. One of his most notable qualities was that of a seemly cheerfulness. At no time could the bitterest of his enemies charge him with being rough or rude or surly; nor, in the most forcible of his reproaches, was there ever a trace of anger. Socially, he was charming. It was during the period of the Holy Club that he made the acquaintance of Mrs. Pendarves, and she, as we have seen, was "a truly great woman of fashion."

And we are not to believe that Wesley at Oxford was an unhappy, persecuted man. His industry and method alone would have prevented him from being unhappy. His duties at Lincoln were always congenial. He loved teaching and dissertation. He was a fine classic, a most efficient Moderator, swift and subtle in controversy. Above all, he had the consciousness of doing good and of trying to do better. Although the majority of the clergy were against him, Potter, the Bishop of Oxford, approved strongly of his work among the poor. His piety was recognised by the few who were capable of discerning piety. The honesty and fervour of his preaching were already admired. In 1732, he was elected to the Society for the Promotion of Christian Knowledge. In the same year he visited Law at Putney, and was introduced to *Theologia Germanica* and the new essays in mysticism.

Wesley was so far from being unhappy that he was not willing to change his Oxford life for any other. He was certainly not attracted by the idea of a curacy. In 1730 he had undertaken a curate's work in a parish near Oxford, but he seems to have given this up in a very short time. In 1734 he was called on to make a grave decision.

The rector of Epworth had felt, for some years, that he could no longer carry out the duties of the living. He was not a very old man, but he had been worn out by the dull resistance of his Lincolnshire boors, the chafing petulance of his own nature, and the grim cares of unrelieved poverty. In 1731 he had fallen in his chair out of the back of a wagon; when he was picked up he "looked prodigiously wild," and it is doubtful if he recovered from the effects of this accident. He felt incessant pain, he was quickly fatigued, and often had to curtail the church service. He managed to pay a visit to Oxford in 1732, where he was gladly welcomed as "the grandfather of the Holy Club," and this was probably his last journey. Yet he was not the man to call for help unless he was in real distress: he had the obstinate courage of a fighter, and according to his wife "everybody observed his decay but himself." Still, no courage could prevail indefinitely against the deadly advance of bodily weakness. In 1733 the rector appealed to his eldest son, Samuel. But Samuel had entered upon his work at Blundell's; he could not think of giving up the post.

By 1734 the forced resignation of the rector of Epworth seemed unavoidable. If Wesley resigned, the living would almost certainly pass into the ungodly hands of a fox-hunting Yahoo—or, as the rector more politely called him, "a mighty *Nimrod*." Therefore, in the face of impending calamity, the rector sent to John and begged him to apply for the living of Epworth.

John had visited Epworth on several occasions after the founding of the Holy Club. In 1731 he had walked there with his brother Charles, and walked back again. In 1733 he was there twice. When, in 1734, he received his father's appeal, he must have been familiar with the circumstances at Epworth, and he must have known that his father was broken in health and spirit and was desperately in need of assistance. He must have known, too, that the fate of the Epworth family depended in no small measure upon his decision. But John refused to make an application for the living.

The first impulse of a generous mind, without reflection, might be to condemn Wesley for this refusal. It might seem, on the face of it, to be a selfish refusal, not easy to reconcile either with much affection for his parents or with a natural sense of duty.

But Wesley, who never did anything without a reason, stated his own case in the plainest possible terms. He wrote a methodical answer to his father, displaying his argument by means of twenty-six numbered paragraphs. Before dismissing the argument as mere sophistry, it is well to remember that extraordinary men are not to be judged by ordinary standards, and that Wesley was incapable of making any decision which he himself did not consider to be the right one. And the whole intention of the twenty-six paragraphs can be put very simply:

"My one aim in life is to secure personal holiness, for without being holy myself I cannot promote real holiness in others. In Oxford, conversing only with a chosen circle of friends, I am screened from all the frivolous importunities of the world, and here I have a better chance of becoming holy than I should have in any other place. Many good works, already begun, depend upon me for their continuance. In Epworth, on the other hand, I should be of no use at all: I could not do any good to those boorish people, and I should probably fall back into habits of irregularity and indulgence. Moreover, there should be no difficulty in finding someone else, far better fitted than I am, to take the living. My present vocation is here, in Oxford, and not elsewhere."

No resounding platitude about family affection, or the duty of a son, or the duty of an ordained priest, can effectively put Wesley in the wrong. Nothing can put a man in the wrong, when he is a good man following the voice of his conscience. Wesley could find in the Scriptures an ample justification—indeed, the highest authority of all.

Apart from other considerations, there can be no question that he was right in avoiding the narrow and vexing sphere of parochial work. He could not then foresee the part he was to play, six years later, in the great revival of Protestant Christianity, a part which actually determined the whole course of that revival; but he knew that his Oxford work covered a far wider field than could ever be covered by the obscure ministrations of a rural clergyman.

He admitted, afterwards, that he was too eager in the merely personal pursuit of salvation, and thought too much about his own soul. He was passing through the formal or preparatory stages of religious experience. He felt his immediate spiritual need to be that of discipline. He could see the effects of his influence in promoting the piety of others, he could see the obviously good results of his organised work among the poor. There can be no doubt that he considered it his duty to remain at Oxford. No ordinary selfish motive, certainly no thought of ease or indulgence, led him to this decision. God had called him to a special work. He was unquestionably doing what he believed to be right when he refused to apply for the Epworth living, not because of his own religious progress alone, but also for the sake of the young men and the poor people who were looking to him for guidance or relief.

Shortly before his father's death, Wesley appears to have changed his mind, though we have no evidence which proves conclusively that he applied for the living. He himself has little to say on the subject; it is quite certain that he never regretted his refusal.

His brother Samuel reproached him with vehemence. His father patiently reproved him, saying that he thought too much of "dear self." "It is not dear self," said the old man, "but the glory of God, and the different degrees of promoting it, which should be our main consideration and direction in the choice of any course of life." "The order of the Church," observed the younger Samuel with asperity, "stakes you down, and the more you struggle you will be held the faster." But John was not to be turned from the Holy Club and the work in Oxford. And brother Samuel, who, after all, was also a clergyman "staked down" by his orders, might just as well have applied his arguments to himself.

Wesley's father died on the 25th of April 1735. He had just managed to complete his folio *Dissertationes in Librum Jobi*, with its queer engravings of Leviathan, of the whale and the crocodile, the great horse and "poor Pentapolis." The frontispiece, by Vertue, shows Mr. Wesley himself in the character of Job, sitting on a chair of antique form beneath the portcullis of an ancient gate, with a sceptre in his hand: in the distance are two pyramids. The work was dedicated to Queen Caroline; his previous works had been dedicated to Queen Mary and Queen Anne.

In 1735, many of the original members of the Holy Club had left Oxford. The new Methodism had failed. Good work had certainly been done among the poor and the prisoners, but there was no inherent vitality in the movement, there was no winning appeal, no true gesture of welcome and encouragement.

The Club lasted just long enough to receive George Whitefield, and then gradually broke up. John Wesley and his brother Charles went to London, probably in the summer of 1735, and took up residence in James Hutton's boarding-school. Dr. John Burton of Corpus met Wesley in London, and introduced him to Colonel James Oglethorpe.

James Edward Oglethorpe was a brave, benevolent man with high, twitching eyebrows, a supercilious glance, a rough temper, and a good heart. When a young soldier, he had served under Prince Eugene and the Duke of Argyll. On the recommendation of Marlborough he was appointed A.D.C. to the Prince. After a dashing career with the German army, he came back to England and brusquely devoted his energies to prison reform. He was elected to Parliament in 1722, when he was twenty-six years old, as the member for the borough of Haslemere. In 1729 he drew the attention of the House to the abominable state of debtors' prisons. A committee was appointed to inquire into the matter, and a large number of debtors were discharged. He then hit upon a plan by which military and philanthropic motives were usefully combined. He formed a body of trustees, obtained a charter, and founded the new colony of Georgia in 1732. Here he settled his debtors, and thus provided a barrier against a Spanish advance from the south. Oglethorpe in person led the settlers, planned their town of wooden houses, set up their defences, made their laws, and gave to the friendly Indians (or to those who appeared to be friendly) laced coats, tobacco, tape, powder,

bullets, and kegs of rum. He came back in 1734 with several
Indians and the chief Tomo-Chichi. He could not have
devised a better advertisement for Georgia. Tomo-Chichi
was quickly taken up by all the fashionable and curious
people in London, and everyone talked about the noble
savages and the new American settlement. Other people,
as well as discharged debtors, had gone out to Georgia.
Persecuted German Protestants had gone there from
Salzburg early in 1734, and many more were likely to
follow them.

Oglethorpe, when he met Wesley, had been looking for
an English clergyman, who could serve the English community at Savannah, and also preach to the noble Indians.
The Colonel already knew something of the Wesleys, and
he invited John Wesley to undertake this interesting and
adventurous duty.

At first Wesley hesitated. The idea of converting
Indians appealed to him with tremendous force; he pictured
them as a simple, yearning people, ready to receive gladly
the Christian message; at least they would not have the
sophisticated obstinacy of the Oxford heathens. But he did
not want to leave all his friends and his mother. He consulted Samuel, he consulted Law and Clayton, but the
question was settled by Mrs. Wesley herself: "If I had
twenty sons," she said, "I should rejoice that they were
all so employed, though I never saw them more." Wesley
therefore decided to go to Georgia. He was duly appointed
a missionary of the Society for the Propagation of the Gospel,
with a salary of fifty pounds a year.

Two members of the Holy Club were to go with him:
his brother Charles and Benjamin Ingham. Charles had
recently been ordained, and was to serve as secretary to
Oglethorpe. A young friend, Charles Delamotte, joined
the party. They were to go on board the *Simmonds* at
Gravesend in October.

Before he left, Wesley presented a copy of his father's
Dissertationes to the queen. When he was introduced to the
royal presence, the queen was romping with her maids
of honour. As the neat, grave little clergyman entered the

room, the game was stopped, and the ladies looked at him with smiling curiosity. Wesley, kneeling, presented the great folio. "It is very prettily bound," said the queen; and she put it down on a window-seat, without so much as glancing at the old rector beneath his ancient gateway. John rose, he bowed, and walked backward. The queen also bowed; she smiled graciously and gave him many kind words; and then, as John finally backed out of the room, she "resumed her sport." Unregarded in the window lay the ponderous book, with its mass of commentary and comparison, its views on the Chaldee paraphrase, on the Complutensian Polyglott and the Fragments of Aquila, its careful examination of Arius Montanus, Castello, Piscator, and the Zurich Divines.

CHAPTER V

GEORGIA

ON the 14th of October 1735, John and Charles Wesley, Ingham and Delamotte, went on board the *Simmonds*, Captain Joseph Cornish, then lying off Gravesend. They took up their quarters in the forecastle. Here they had a reasonable degree of privacy, and were able to meet and talk without interruption from the crew or the passengers. We may regard this little group as a floating detachment of the Holy Club, or indeed as the Holy Club itself, for the two Wesleys and Ingham were the only members who remained in close touch with each other. And Wesley, with his typical reliance upon method, was not long in devising their regulations.

The *Simmonds* was accompanied by the *London Merchant*, Captain Thomas, and the two ships were taking out, between them, about five hundred and seventy settlers. On board the *Simmonds* there was a party of twenty-six Moravians, under the leadership of their bishop, David Nitschmann. These good, quiet people introduced Wesley to a new religious influence. Ultimately, this influence was to be a decisive agent in his own religious evolution, and even now he was deeply impressed by a placid faith, a gentle resignation, of which he had no previous knowledge. Before he had been three days on board he began to learn German, so that he could talk more freely with his Moravian friends.

But the *Simmonds* carried emigrants of a less desirable kind. "The best people," said Southey, "are not to be looked for in new colonies." Among Oglethorpe's released debtors there were many who would have been better kept in jail. There were men ready for any sort of brutality or cunning; and there were loose, noisy and mischievous women. Some of these wretched persons were the cause of much trouble during the voyage, and of greater trouble in Georgia. Oglethorpe himself sailed with this detachment.

The *Simmonds*, with the *London Merchant*, raised anchor on the 21st of October, and got as far as the Downs. On the 2nd of November they came into Cowes road. Here, on the 19th, they were joined by the *Hawk*, sloop of war, Captain James Gascoigne. They did not get away from Cowes until the 10th of December.

From the moment of their arrival on board the ship, the Wesleys and Ingham began the work of ministry among the crew and passengers. In this work they had the cordial support of Oglethorpe. The children were taught and catechised, men and women received private instruction, Quakers were convinced of error, the sick people were fed with water-gruel and other necessary things, many were baptised, and before the end of the voyage the number of communicants had risen from five to twenty-three. Nor were they slow to apply stern methods of correction. Ingham tells how he "got a boy well whipped, by Mr. Oglethorpe's orders, for swearing and blaspheming." So, in spite of laughter and ribaldry on the quarter-deck, and the back-biting and hypocrisy of the odious Mrs. Welch and more odious Mrs. Hawkins, the ministry was quietly and effectively continued.

At no time had the austerity of Wesley risen to such a high pitch. He was at the climax of his ritualistic and ascetic period. Before the ship had left Gravesend, he and his companions renounced the use of flesh and wine, and resolved to live upon vegetables, rice and biscuit. Wesley himself abjured supper, and made up his mind to take no pleasure in eating. He drew up an exact scheme for the employment of every hour of the day. The scheme came into operation at four in the morning, and remained in force until they went to bed between nine and ten at night. Public prayers were read twice a day, and at seven Wesley attended the Moravian service. Time was methodically set apart for private study and devotion, for the instruction of the passengers, the care of the sick, and so forth.

From a nautical point of view, the voyage of the *Simmonds* was extremely adventurous. Crossing the Atlantic in those days, and especially crossing it from east to west in winter, was generally an adventure. A ship might take many days, or even weeks, in beating her way out of the Channel; and she was lucky if she got across without the loss of gear and men. Captain Cornish fell in with several heavy storms, and although he kept his reckoning with extraordinary precision, he was obliged, at least on one occasion, to let the ship drive.

That occasion was a memorable one in the life of Wesley. With all his anxious care of his soul, a storm at sea proved to Wesley that he was afraid of death. Even before they had left Cowes, he wrote in his *Journal:* "At night I was waked by the tossing of the ship and roaring of the wind, and plainly showed I was unfit, for I was unwilling to die."

Three furious gales were met in mid-Atlantic, and it was during the last of these, on the 24th and 25th of January 1736, that Cornish put up his helm and let the ship run before the wind. "The ship," says Wesley, "not only rocked to and fro with the utmost violence, but shook and jarred with so unequal, grating a motion, that one could not but with great difficulty keep one's hold of any thing, nor stand a moment without it. Every ten minutes came a shock against the stern or sides of the ship, which one would think should dash the planks in a thousand pieces." In his manuscript diary he noted, in a hand which plainly shows the unsteadiness of the ship, "Storm greater: afraid! . . . Storm high. . . . Storm v. high . . . a little less afraid." At seven o'clock he went, as usual, to the Moravians, who had quietly assembled for their service. The gale was then furious. "I observed it well," wrote Ingham; "and truly I never saw anything hitherto so solemn and majestic. The sea sparkled and smoked, as if it had been on fire. The air darted forth lightning; and the wind blew so fierce, that you could scarcely look it in the face and draw your breath." While the Moravians were singing a psalm, a great sea broke full over the ship, the mainsail split with a crack like thunder, and the water poured down between the decks. At once there was a dreadful clamour; shivered planks and falling gear crashed upon the hatches, the sailors cried out, and most of the passengers were terrified out of their senses.

But the good Moravians, after looking up for a moment, went on with their psalm.

This magnificent example of piety and courage had a profound and lasting effect upon Wesley and Ingham. "Was you not afraid?" said Wesley after the storm to one of the Germans; and he answered, "I thank God, no." "But were not your women and children afraid?" "No; our women and children are not afraid to die." Wesley himself had been afraid, had feared death; and he now saw that he could learn something from the Moravians, and something of which he stood in need.

On the 1st of February they spoke the *Pomeroy*, bound from Charleston to London, and on the 4th they got within soundings. In the afternoon of the 4th the trees of Georgia could be seen from the deck; between two or three on the afternoon of the 5th they dropped anchor near Tybee Island in the Savannah River. "The pines, palms and cedars running in rows along the shore, made an exceedingly beautiful prospect, especially to us who did not expect to see the bloom of spring in the depth of winter."

Wesley went ashore on the 6th, and on the following day he had another momentous experience. He met the young Moravian minister, August Gottlieb Spangenburg. This minister had come over with the first company of Moravians, and it was reasonable enough that Wesley should ask him for advice. Spangenburg was thirty-two, and Wesley thirty-three.

As the two young men gazed seriously at each other, Spangenburg suddenly asked: "Do you know yourself? Have you the witness within yourself? Does the Spirit of God bear witness with your spirit that you are a child of God?" This language was new to Wesley; he was instantly troubled, and did not know how to answer. Spangenburg went on: "Do you know Jesus Christ?" "I know He is the Saviour of the world," replied Wesley after a moment of painful hesitation. "True," said Spangenburg; "but do you know that He has saved *you*?" Wesley, still confused, could only say, "I hope He has died to save me." Spangenburg came back to his first searching question: "Do you know yourself?" Without conviction, Wesley quietly answered, "I do."

· This brief dialogue marks a critical phase in the history of religion. Wesley knew that his replies to Spangenburg were "vain words." Spangenburg had in his mind a vital and definite experience of which Wesley had no personal knowledge. Spangenburg had an inward sense of the presence of God, and Wesley had no such sense. Although Wesley had no idea of abandoning his ritualistic position or of changing his methods, he was now convinced of a spiritual weakness in his own character, and there is no doubt that his meeting with the young Moravian can be regarded as a decisive encounter with Providence.

Charles Wesley and Ingham went with Oglethorpe to establish the settlement of Frederica, where poor Charles found himself unable to deal with the uncertain temper of the Colonel and the vicious quarrelling of his parishioners. John Wesley began his ministry at Savannah.

He found it extremely hard to serve God without distraction in the midst of secular business. His quiet life at Oxford had not fitted him to deal with treacherous rogues, or virulent spit-fires like Mrs. Hawkins. He had very little knowledge of parochial work, and here was a parish that would have appalled the most experienced minister. People who had seemed good, gentle and religious on the ship, chastened by howling storms and the chilly fear of death, were now full of boasting, malice, jealousy and every devilment. The real heathen were not the Indians, but Oglethorpe's cargo of jailbirds.

And the Indians themselves were extremely difficult to approach: they were soft and courteous in behaviour, but Wesley could never speak to their hearts. He was too dogmatic, too superior and philosophical. He asked an old head-man, Chicali, "what he thought he was made for?" To this, Chicali replied gravely: "He that is above knows what he made us for. We know nothing. We are in the dark." Wesley could only answer by a halting reference to "the good Book."

It looks very much as though Wesley in Savannah was a

failure from the very beginning. The position was a hopeless one for the young minister, with no idea of the rough ways of the world, holding the abstracted views of a ritualist, earnestly preoccupied with the state of his own soul, and seeking salvation in a fervent profession of orthodoxy and in the strict observance of orthodox practice. He could minister effectively to those who were already pious; he could do little or nothing for the others. As for the Indians, he might as well have stayed in his Lincoln rooms. It was not long before he discovered these gentle and courteous Indians were actually "gluttons, thieves, dissemblers, liars," and promiscuous murderers. Oglethorpe told him frankly that it would be unsafe to walk alone outside the palisade.

Disillusion, disappointment, and a deep sense of spiritual inadequacy had the effect of making him even more austere. It seemed to him that he was failing because he was not sufficiently rigid. On Sundays, he held services at five, eleven and three; he had prayers in Italian at nine, and in French at one; at two o'clock he catechised the children. He lived entirely on bread, fruit and vegetables. Three days a week he fasted. Whatever his reception might be, he visited every one of his parishioners, nor could he be repelled or intimidated by threats and abuse, or even by hideous violence.

In one of his fragmentary journals there is an account of a shocking scene with Mrs. Hawkins. This woman was notoriously immoral, and Charles Wesley had made an unfortunate reference to her and to Mrs. Welch in a letter. The two incriminating words were in Greek, but John clumsily admitted to Mrs. Hawkins, "I take him to mean by those two words only two persons—you and Mrs. Welch." A few days after this admission, Mrs. Hawkins requested that Wesley would see her on a matter of importance. When he came to her room, she told him to sit down. Wesley sat down on the bed. "Sir," cried Mrs. Hawkins, who was standing with her hands behind her back, "you have wronged me, and I will shoot you through the head this moment with a brace of balls." She then advanced, with a pistol in one hand and a pair of scissors in the other. Wesley gripped her by the wrists, but she forced him down on the bed, swearing that she would have his hair or his heart's blood. The servants came in, but dared not obey either their mistress or Wesley, each of whom ordered them to take hold of the other. At last, the constable and a neighbour entered the room; but just as they were about to seize the woman, Mr. Hawkins appeared, asked "what the scoundrel was doing in his house," and told the others not to touch his wife. Mrs. Hawkins fastened upon the sleeves of Wesley's cassock with her teeth and bit them to rags; but now, seeing that other people were coming to the house, Hawkins took her by the waist and lifted her away.

Wesley had prayed for Mrs. Hawkins, he had meditated upon her case, had invoked the assistance of his brother Charles, of Nitschmann, Spangenburg, and even the fiery Oglethorpe. At most, he could only reduce her to a tearful moodiness. And this was the end of it. Well might Southey say, "The best people are not to be looked for in new colonies."

The somewhat questionable character of Mrs. Hawkins and Mrs. Welch is shown by the fact that both of them made to Charles Wesley a bogus confession of adultery with Oglethorpe, and then denounced Charles as the inventor of the scandal. That both were actually in love with Oglethorpe is fairly certain. They wanted to be the presiding queens of a licentious community, and it was for this reason that they dreaded the influence and interference of Charles and John.

We have a strange group of figures in this Georgian drama: two saintly young clergymen, terribly bewildered; the impetuous Colonel, with his tantrums, credulity and strong benevolence; those appalling creatures Welch and Hawkins; and a very dingy background of second-rate forgers, debtors and speculators, waited upon by nigger-boys and watched by prowling Indians.

But Wesley had to deal with a situation of a more dangerous kind. The chief magistrate, who was also the chief store-keeper of Savannah, was a man named Causton. His wife, Mrs. Causton, had with her a niece called Sophia Hopkey. Miss Hopkey seems to have been a pretty, artful and quite commonplace girl, without good manners or a good education.

At the time of Miss Hopkey's meeting with Wesley she was not more than eighteen. We do not know why she had gone out to Oglethorpe's benighted colony. Her aunt's husband, Causton, had cheated the revenues in England, and in 1738 he was expelled from his appointments in Savannah because he falsified his accounts. Miss Hopkey, or Miss Sophy as she was called, was being courted by a Mr. Williamson, whose character was not doubtful, but definitely bad. Sophy repelled Mr. Williamson, and then Wesley came on the scene.

The appearance of Wesley had the effect of making Sophy think in earnest about religion. It is possible, though not very probable, that she was really thinking of nothing else when she became Wesley's pupil, not only for religious instruction, but also for the improvement of her French. Sophy used to walk over to Wesley's wooden parsonage, sometimes accompanied by her friend Miss Fossett and sometimes alone, for early morning prayers. Delamotte, who had stayed with Wesley, was often present during the serious conversations which followed, but on other occasions Wesley and his pupil were left to themselves. Wesley fell sick of a fever, and for five days Miss Hopkey nursed him. She tried to please him by wearing plain white dresses, and by the gravity and seemliness of her deportment.

There is something palpably incongruous in the idea of Wesley in love. He certainly could not behave as men in love usually behave, and as they are expected to behave. A highly romantic picture of Wesley could not possibly be veracious. At the same time, he was extremely susceptible and capable of real infatuation. He was undoubtedly fascinated by Miss Hopkey, and believed eventually that he wanted to marry her. It has been suggested that Oglethorpe wished to bring about this marriage, perhaps with the idea of humanising Wesley and making him more acceptable to the settlers. Sophy herself, although she had two other suitors in the offing—Mr. Williamson and Mr. Mellichamp—clearly desired to marry John. Delamotte, who was probably jealous, tried to show Wesley that Miss Sophia was artful and designing: Wesley realised that she was "dangerous," but he could not suppress his liking for her. Charles Wesley, who was unequal to the trials of his position, left Georgia on the 26th of July, and John was thus deprived of a good counsellor.

John spent a good deal of his time among the palmetto huts of the new settlement at Frederica, a place which filled him with deeper despair than Savannah itself. He had "less and less prospect of doing good . . . many there being extremely zealous and indefatigably diligent to prevent it; and few of the rest daring to show themselves of another mind, for fear of their displeasure." Mrs. Welch and Mrs. Hawkins were in Frederica, and seemed to be having it all their own way.

Miss Hopkey also visited Frederica, and she was there on the occasion of Wesley's fourth and last excursion to that godless place. Before he left Savannah, Wesley had a strange talk with Mr. Causton. He asked Causton whether he had any message for his niece. The store-keeper said, "The girl will never be easy till she is married." "Sir," replied Wesley, "she is too much afflicted to have a thought of it." "I'll trust a woman for that," said Causton; and he added: "There is no other way." "But," said Wesley, with perfect innocence, "there are few here who you would think fit for her." Causton answered bluntly: "Let him be but an honest man, an honest, good man; I don't care whether he has a groat. I can give them a maintenance." Wesley then said, "Sir, what directions do you give me with regard to her?" and Causton replied: "I give her up to you. Do what you will with her. Take her into your own hands. Promise her what you will. I will make it good." This was in October 1736.

When he reached Frederica, Wesley found Miss Sophy changed in more than one respect. Her good resolutions had gone, she was fond of company, "scarce a shadow of what she had been," dissatisfied with her life, and anxious to return to England. He at once read to her "some of the most affecting parts of the *Serious Call* and of Ephrem Syrus."

Poor Miss Hopkey! No wonder that she often burst into floods of tears when Wesley was talking to her: it seemed as if all her little arts and all her efforts to please had come to nothing, and would always come to nothing. Oglethorpe, perhaps with a crude idea of bringing matters to a head, decided that Miss Hopkey should return to Savannah, and that she was to travel in the same boat as Wesley.

"I saw the danger to myself," wrote Wesley, "but yet had a good hope I should be delivered out of it, (1) because it was not my choice which brought me into it; (2) because I still felt in myself the same desire and design to live a single life; and (3) because I was persuaded, should my desire and design be changed, yet her resolution to live single would continue."

On the morning of the 25th of October, Wesley married Sophy's friend, Miss Fossett, to Mr. Wilson; at ten he had a brief interview with Oglethorpe, and at half-past eleven he set out in the boat with Miss Sophy, his boy Jemmy, and the usual crew.

This amazing voyage lasted for six days. Wesley prayed and sang with Miss Sophy, and read aloud his devotional books. At night, they went ashore on one of the islands, and slept under the sail of the boat. On one side of this rude tent were Miss Sophy, Wesley and the boy Jemmy; on the other, the boat's crew.

On the second morning, they crossed Doboy Sound in heavy weather, and Wesley asked his companion if she was not afraid to die. "No," said the girl wearily; "no; I don't desire to live any longer. Oh, that God would let me go now! Then I should be at rest. In this world I expect nothing but misery."

For three days the party was detained by storms on St. Katherine's Island. In this trying situation, Miss Sophy behaved with sweetness, courage and composure. "She was often in pain, which she could not hide; but it never betrayed her into impatience. She gave herself up to God, owning she suffered far less than she deserved." Whatever her designs may have been, her conduct with Wesley was irreproachable. One afternoon, after walking for some time on the island, they sat down in a little thicket by the side of a spring. Here they had a conversation upon Christian holiness, and Wesley felt that she was "much endeared to him." They tried to get away from the island on the 29th, but were driven back again by high seas, and were only able to land with difficulty. That night they lay wrapped in cloaks and blankets close to the camp fire. Wesley could not sleep, and looking across at her, he saw that Miss Sophy was also awake. Heaven knows what thoughts rushed into his mind, what deep tenderness rose protesting in the depth of his heart, as he looked at the sad, huddled form in the firelight—so infinitely pathetic, and yet so infinitely dangerous. But no thought for the safety of his own soul could prevent a startling, impulsive question:

"Miss Sophy, how far are you engaged to Mr. Mellichamp?"

She answered: "I have promised him either to marry him or to marry no one at all."

To this Wesley replied by what he calls "the expression of a sudden wish, not of any formed design." He said simply:

"Miss Sophy, I should think myself happy if I was to spend my life with you."

She burst into tears and said, "I am every way unhappy. I won't have Tommy, for he is a bad man. And I can have none else." She paused, and then added, "Sir, you don't know the danger you are in. I beg you would speak no word more on this head."

There was another silence. Wesley could say nothing. Poor Sophy ended the conversation with these words: "When others have spoke to me on the subject, I felt an aversion to them. But I don't feel any to you. We may converse on other subjects as freely as ever." So they sang a psalm and fell asleep.

Next day they landed on Bear Island, and the girl said tearfully that she could not endure the thought of living in Causton's house. Wesley told her that she was welcome to a room in the parsonage; or, better still, she might go to the good Moravians. "She made little reply." On the day following, they were back in Savannah.

Wesley now admitted that he was "much afraid" of Miss Hopkey. He consulted his friends. The friends expressed themselves so ambiguously that he could arrive at no decision, and Miss Hopkey still came to the parsonage every morning and evening: she tried to learn French, and listened with touching patience to long selections from Ephrem Syrus and to the sermons of Dean Young or Mr. Reeve. "This I began with a single eye," wrote Wesley. "But it was not long before I found it a task too hard for me to preserve the same intention with which I began, in such intimacy of conversation as ours was."

So matters went on until February 1737. At this time something like an acute crisis was taking place in Wesley's mind. He "groaned under the weight of an unholy desire." He prayed fervently and found comfort. He consulted his friends again, and found ambiguity. He drew lots, without conviction. At one time the Moravians encouraged him in the idea of marriage; at another, they told him not to think of it. Delamotte, with many tears, vowed that he could not live any longer in the parsonage if Wesley married Miss Sophy; and Wesley replied that he had no intention of marrying. On the 11th of February, as he was walking in his garden with the now distracted girl, he said, "I am resolved, Miss Sophy, if I marry at all, not to do so till I have been among the Indians." Next day she told him, "People wonder what I can do so long at your house; I am resolved not to breakfast with you any more; and I won't come to you any more alone." And on the following day she said desperately, "I don't think it signifies for me to learn French any longer." She added, "My uncle and aunt, as well as I, will be glad of your coming to our house as often as you please." Wesley said, "You know, Miss Sophy, I don't love a crowd, and there is always one there." "But we needn't be in it," replied poor Miss Sophy, with a last flutter of hope.

It is not easy to understand the final relations between Wesley and this disappointed girl. At the end of February he told her that either Ingham or he must return to England. On hearing this, she fixed her eyes on him, and changed colour several times. Mrs. Causton said cheerily, "Indeed, I think I must go too; Phiky, will you go with me?" "Yes, with all my heart," said poor Sophia. And when she was taxed with having said the very opposite, only the night before, she answered, "True; but now all the world is alike to me."

Two days later, Wesley called at Causton's house, and found Miss Sophy alone. Never before had she appeared so sweet and lovable. It was the hour of trial. "I know not what might have been the consequence had I then but touched her hand." And the next day, he was again left alone with her, and did actually take her hand, and, finding that she was not displeased, would have engaged himself for life, if he had not believed her when she said she would never marry. So the innocence of Wesley preserved him, and this extraordinary affair came to an end.

It was on the 9th of March, ten days after the decisive interview, that Mrs. Causton said to Wesley: "Sir, Mr. Causton and I are exceedingly obliged to you for all the pains you have taken about Sophy. And so is Sophy too; and she desires that you would publish the banns of marriage between her and Mr. Williamson on Sunday. . . . Sir, you don't seem to be very well pleased. . . ."

So far from being well pleased, Wesley heard of this with a swift realisation of despair. He knew now that he had really wanted to marry Miss Hopkey, and he was staggered by her apparently quick decision to marry another. She had promised to consult him before thinking of marriage; and she had broken her word. At least she had put an end to all these miserable hesitations and excuses, but it was not of the sort Wesley had imagined—if, indeed, he had imagined any at all. Instead of having smothered his desires, he had only been playing at hide-and-seek with them. Now, in one awful moment, the inhibitions broke down, and poor Wesley felt himself confounded. He was full of dreadful perplexities. There were some painful scenes with Sophy and Mr. Williamson. The marriage took place at Purysburg on the 12th of March.

The sequel to this, which had the effect of driving Welsey from Georgia, was not foreseen by anyone.

Sophy, after her marriage, neglected the duties of religion; she became altogether too gay, and vowed that she had really been all the time in love with Tom Mellichamp. Wesley admonished her on five or six occasions, in the sight or hearing of witnesses, and she promised to mend her ways. Still, she would not conform to Wesley's High Church regulations, and on Sunday, the 7th of August, he publicly expelled her from the Communion.

From a severely ecclesiastical point of view, he may have been justified in taking this course; and he himself would not admit any other than ecclesiastical considerations. But, in view of the circumstances, no action could have been more ill-timed, or more likely to provoke a scandal.

Wesley had never been popular in Savannah. He had tried to impose upon a rough and lawless people a particularly austere religious discipline. If he won, as he certainly did, the respect of the few who were religiously disposed, he incurred the enmity of the greater number, who were hostile or indifferent to religion in any form. He was incapable of policy or compromise, or of a gradual preparation. The rules were laid down by the rubric, and it was his duty to apply them. He refused the Sacraments to all who had not been episcopally baptised, nor would he bury those who were not enrolled members of the Church. He baptised by immersion, and re-baptised the children of Dissenters. He advocated fasting. One of his parishioners complained to him, "All your sermons are satires upon particular persons"—a complaint which was entirely without foundation, but which does prove that he preached with a sting. His one success had been the founding of a little society in April 1736; and we are not surprised to learn that only a few people joined it.

When Sophy was repelled from the altar, her husband and her uncle were both furious. On Williamson's instructions a warrant was issued for the arrest of Wesley on a charge of defamation. Wesley was accordingly brought before the bailiff and the recorder, and was told that he must appear at the next court. The court sat on the 22nd of August. Causton delivered to the jury a "List of Grievances," in which he tried to show that Wesley was altogether unfitted for the post of a minister. An astounding affidavit by Mrs. Sophia Williamson was also read to the court, in which she had the effrontery to say that Wesley had tried to entice her away from her relations, "and often in very pathetic terms urged to her the necessity of forsaking them and leaving their house in order to cohabit with him." She alleged, moreover, that he had "frequently made several overtures of marriage, without acquainting her relations thereof." The most charitable supposition is that Sophy had written these outrageous falsehoods under pressure from her villainous uncle and equally villainous husband. In cross-examination, her statements were amply disproved, and she admitted that "she had no objection at all to Mr. Wesley's behaviour before her marriage."

A majority found that the grievances were real: a minority of twelve "were thoroughly persuaded that the charges against Mr. Wesley were an artifice of Mr. Causton's, designed rather to blacken the character of Mr. Wesley than to free the colony from religious tyranny, as he had alleged." Williamson persisted in the civil charge, which was the only one over which the court had the right of jurisdiction, and claimed one thousand pounds damages.

Savannah was divided, but most of the people were against Wesley. He defended himself in the pulpit, though his congregation was now an extremely small one. Clearly, it was useless for him to stay in the place any longer. The one man who might have settled this murky business—Oglethorpe—had left for England more than a year before. Williamson endeavoured to prevent the accused man from getting away, but Wesley escaped by sea to Purysburg and eventually reached Charleston, whence, on the 22nd of December, he sailed for England.

As the ship, with Wesley on board, drove her way through the grey Channel seas to Deal, she passed another ship beating out westward, and taking with her a new missionary to the Indians—George Whitefield.

CHAPTER VI

SEEKING FAITH

WESLEY returned from America not only with a painful sense of having failed in his work, but with a more disturbing sense of spiritual imperfection. He felt that a true religion contained an experience of which he had yet no personal knowledge. He had merely accepted faith as a dogma, without perceiving its emotional essence, and without realising the intensely individual nature of communion with God.

It is not likely that he fretted himself with memories of Mrs. Williamson and the persecution in Savannah. Wesley was never of a brooding disposition, and no man was more readily disposed to forgive his enemies. Besides, his attention was always held by the need, the activity of the moment. He was a man running a course, thinking only of his aim and motion, and watching keenly for every signal of providence.

Writing in old age (December 1784) he said that his one idea after his return to England was "to lay his bones at Oxford." He thought, no doubt, of his familiar rooms at Lincoln, and saw himself resuming his work as a priest, a tutor and a scholar, and the head of a new Holy Club.

He arrived in London on the 3rd of February 1738, and lodged in the house of his friend, old John Hutton, in Great College Street, Westminster. Hutton was a Nonjuring clergyman, whose son, James, had been greatly influenced by the Wesleys.

On the 7th of February, Wesley met a party of Moravians at the house of Mr. Weinartz, a Dutch merchant. Two of these Moravians, Peter Boehler and George Schulius, were on their way to Georgia and South Carolina. The meeting was therefore of special interest, both to Wesley and the German missionaries.

There is no evidence of Wesley's ability as a German linguist, and it is probable that his conversations with

Boehler, Schulius and the others were in Latin. Wesley had begun to converse in Latin with his brother Charles in 1731, and they were both extremely proficient in the colloquial use of this language. We have definite proof that Boehler used Latin when he wrote and spoke to Wesley.

On three separate occasions, Moravian influence was associated with critical phases of Wesley's religious development. First, there was the striking example of Moravian quietism in the Atlantic storm, then the questioning of Spangenburg, and now the meeting with Peter Boehler.

The sect of Moravians, or Bohemian Brethren, was formed by a revival of the *Unitas Fratrum*, a religious society founded in Bohemia in 1457. This revival dating from 1722, was the work of Count Zinzendorf. Moravian doctrine laid stress on the supreme importance of a good life, carefully ordered, and always illuminated by the knowledge of God's immediate presence. Dogma was of no particular value. Faith in redemption and a consciousness of being regenerated by the operation of divine grace were essential matters, without which any pretence of religion would be altogether in vain. Dogmas could be interpreted in various ways; but faith could only be interpreted in one way—it was the certain knowledge of God. Faith was a vital, unmistakable experience, which a man either had or had not; there could be no such thing as a degree of faith. And faith could not be attained by anxious endeavour; it fell like the dew of heaven upon the soul at peace; it filled a tranquil, expectant mind, but not the mind of one who prayed with importunity. The necessary attitude was that of surrender.

Peter Boehler, at the time of his meeting with Wesley, was a young man of twenty-six. Wesley, at the same period, was thirty-five. Boehler had been a Lutheran Protestant, educated at the University of Jena. Zinzendorf persuaded him, and Professor Spangenburg, to join the Moravian Church. For some time he was the tutor of Zinzendorf's young son, and he was now an ordained Moravian minister.

Like Spangenburg, Peter Boehler saw at a glance what was the matter with Wesley. Wesley, he knew, had not yet received the inner witness, he was not a child of grace.

Wesley himself knew this, and he turned to Boehler for counsel. After the Georgia trustees and Oglethorpe had listened to his report, Wesley took Peter Boehler down to Oxford, where nothing remained of the Holy Club, and then to Gambold's rectory at Stanton-Harcourt. *"Mi frater, mi frater,"* said the young Moravian, *"excoquenda est ista tua philosophia"*—"thy philosophy must be purged away."

Wesley returned to London, but came back to Oxford on the 4th of March, where he found Boehler with his brother Charles, who was then recovering from a dangerous attack of pleurisy. On the following day, a Sunday, John Wesley was "clearly convinced of unbelief" by Peter Boehler. Here was a spiritual crisis, and one which is best understood by reading what Wesley set down in his *Journal*:

> "Immediately it struck into my mind, 'Leave off preaching. How can you preach to others who have not faith yourself?' I asked Boehler, whether he thought I should leave off, or not? He answered, 'By no means.' I asked, 'But what shall I preach?' He said 'Preach faith till you have it; and then, because you have it, you will preach faith.' Accordingly, Monday 6 [of March], I began preaching this new doctrine, though my soul started back from the work. The first person to whom I offered *salvation by faith alone* was a prisoner under sentence of death. His name was Clifford. Peter Boehler had many times desired me to speak to him before. But I could not prevail on myself to do so; being still (as I had been many years) a zealous assertor of the impossibility of a death-bed repentance."

He was now in the position of a man who, after years of research, is told that his methods are all wrong, and that nothing will save him but a radical change of system. Perhaps that is putting the case too mildly, for something more than a mere change of method was needed. There had to be a total revision, not only of religious procedure, but also of ideas concerning the very nature of faith.

This decisive change marks the end of Wesley's rigid

adherence to ritual. He could no longer maintain the attitude of exclusiveness, nor could he believe that mere observance, even mere goodness, was a sure and effective means of obtaining grace. He saw that the assurance of faith made a man literally a new creature. He saw that he had been labouring in vain, because he had not been preparing himself for the special experience of regeneration. If Spangenburg had now questioned him, as he did in Georgia, Wesley could not have answered him with even a shadow of confidence. The arrogance which had occasionally shown itself in his insistence upon sacerdotal prerogatives was now finally removed, and for a time Wesley seemed likely to touch the opposite extreme of abasement. He began to seek in earnest for what he apprehended to be the true form and experience of a vital faith. And if anything was clear, it was that such a faith could not be found by running away from the world of ordinary men.

Towards the end of April 1738, any lingering doubt was expelled by the testimony of several English Moravians, who were introduced to Wesley by Peter Boehler. After hearing their testimony, both Wesley and those with him, according to Boehler, "were as if thunderstruck."

On the 1st of May, a small religious society was founded at the house of James Hutton, the bookshop of the *Bible and Sun* in Little Wild Street, near Drury Lane.

It would be inaccurate to speak of this as the first Methodist society. Although founded on the advice of Boehler, three days before he left for America, it was emphatically a Church of England society at the beginning. The members used to meet once a week in order to pray together and to give each other religious encouragement. The persons who met were divided into *bands* or companies, having a conference every Wednesday evening at eight o'clock. No one could be admitted to the society until he, or she, had been under probation for a period of two months. Every fourth Sunday was a day of intercession, and on every fifth Sunday there was "a general love-feast." Here is the germ of Methodist organisation, and it cannot be doubted that the rules were drawn up by Wesley himself. But it was not until after the society had moved to a room in Fetter Lane that Methodism and Moravianism sharply divided the original group.

Wesley followed Boehler's advice, and began to preach on salvation by faith alone. On Sunday, the 7th of May, he wrote, "I preached at St. Lawrence's in the morning; and afterwards at St. Katherine Cree's Church. I was enabled to speak strong words at both; and was therefore the less surprised at being informed, I was not to preach any more in either of these churches." Two days later, he preached at St. Helen's: "My heart was now so enlarged to declare the love of God to all that were oppressed by the Devil, that I did not wonder in the least, when I was afterwards told, *Sir, you must preach here no more.*" And it was the same when he preached at St. Ann's, Aldersgate, at St. George's, Bloomsbury, a chapel in Long Acre, St. John's, Wapping, and St. Benet's at Paul's Wharf. It is difficult to estimate the nature of this opposition, but we may assume that Wesley had the appearance of being too *enthusiastic*.

And still the preacher himself had not found faith. He felt that he was in bondage to sin, beating the air, fighting but not conquering. He sank into "strange indifference, dullness and coldness." At last, on the 24th of May, it seemed to him that he had really found the assurance of belief. On the evening of this memorable day he went "very unwillingly" to the meeting of a religious society in Aldersgate Street, in which James Hutton appears to have been the principal figure. Someone was reading Luther's *Preface to the Epistle to the Romans*. At about a quarter to nine, while he was listening to the reader, Wesley felt a warming of the heart. He felt that he did trust in Christ, and that he was actually saved from the law of sin and death. He began to pray fervently, and more particularly for his enemies. And then, he says, "I testified openly to all there what I now first felt in my heart." But the assurance was not complete, for he did not feel the joy which he believed to be inseparable from a true knowledge of salvation. "Then was I taught that peace and victory over sin are essential to faith in the

Captain of our Salvation; but that, as to the transports of joy that usually attend the beginning of it, especially in those who have mourned deeply, God sometimes giveth, sometimes withholdeth them, according to the counsels of His own Will."

After his return home, he was "much buffeted with temptations," which returned again and again. Two days later he wrote, "My soul continued in peace, but yet in heaviness because of manifold temptations." Still, he had gained a new power; in every conflict with doubt or sin or the devils of argument he won the victory, though he was often in danger of losing ground. On the 6th of June, after a terrible encounter with his fears, he felt "a kind of soreness," and knew that he was not invulnerable. "O God," he cried, "save thou me, and all that are weak in faith, from doubtful disputations."

Conversion, in the psychological sense, consists, as we shall see later, of definite successive stages and of definite symptoms. Whatever may be the final explanation of the process, it certainly does present consistent features, not unlike those which occur in the history of disease; the attack is followed by the crisis, and the crisis either by recovery or by permanently abnormal conditions. The case of Wesley does not present a typical instance of conversion. True, the stages and the symptoms are there, but some of them are only feebly or incompletely represented. There is a real sense of unbelief and a real striving towards faith, but there is no overwhelming climax of acute despair; there is a sudden though gentle sense of relief, but no flash of blinding radiance; and above all, there is no sense of instant immunity, either from doubt or from the approach of sin. There is no physical disturbance, no voice, no vision —indeed, from Wesley's own point of view, there is a disappointing absence of emotional change.

If we are to apply the term conversion to Wesley's experience in the meeting-house, we must understand it as conversion modified by the intellectual bias of Wesley himself, conversion neutralised to a large extent by the unconscious resistance of an extremely well regulated mind. Or, if we may again compare the conversion process to the history of a disease, we must assume that Wesley could only experience conversion in a mild form. What he actually desired was a sustained emotional experience; and because he was incapable of such an experience, he fell back, again and again, into a mood of grey despondency.

Here, then, was the true nature of the conflict: it was not a conflict between a weak man and the powerful advances of evil; it was a conflict between ideals of spiritual knowledge on the one hand and the persistence of inherent characteristics on the other.

The change in Wesley's views and opinions caused serious alarm to his friends. Mrs. John Hutton wrote a letter to Samuel Wesley, informing him of the situation. John, she said, appeared to have turned into a wild enthusiast or a fanatic. On Sunday, the 28th of May, four days after the meeting in Aldersgate Street, there was a curious episode:

"Without ever acquainting Mr. Hutton with any of his notions or designs, when Mr. Hutton had ended a sermon of Bishop Blackhall's, which he had been reading in his study to a great number of people, Mr. John got up and told the people that five days before he was not a Christian. . . . Mr. Hutton was much surprised at this unexpected injudicious speech; but only said, *Have a care, Mr. Wesley, how you despise the benefits received by the two Sacraments.* I not being in the study when this speech was made, had heard nothing of it when he came into the parlour to supper, where were my two children, two or three other of his *deluded followers* . . . and two or three gentlemen of Mr. John's acquaintance, though not got into his *new notions.* He made the same wild speech again, to which I made answer—*If you was not a Christian ever since I knew you, you was a great hypocrite, for you made us all believe you was one.*"

Mrs. Hutton had no patience with all these new and dangerous notions, which only tended to unsettle the minds of weak people. She begged Samuel to "put a stop to such madness."

Samuel replied:

"Falling into *enthusiasm*, is being lost with a witness. . . . What Jack means by 'not being a Christian till last month' I understand not. . . . Perhaps it might come into his crown that he was in a state of *mortal sin*, unrepented of; and had long lived in such a course. This I do not believe; however, he must answer for himself. . . . *I heartily pray God to stop the progress of this lunacy*."

John, in the meantime, decided to visit the Moravian settlement in Germany. This decision proves clearly that he felt in need of further instruction, or desired the strengthening presence of example.

Two days before he left England, he preached to the University of Oxford in St. Mary's Church. He preached on salvation by faith: the sermon is a famous one in the history of Methodism, and was afterwards chosen by Wesley as a statement of Methodist doctrine.

Wesley, with Ingham and the minister Toeltschig, left Gravesend on the 13th of June 1738, and landed at Rotterdam two days later. He met Zinzendorf at Marienborn, and on the 1st of August, after many days of tedious travel, he reached the Moravian colony of Herrnhut in Upper Lusatia.

On the whole, the results of this visit were somewhat disappointing. Wesley, in his methodical way, observed and recorded carefully all the details of Moravian life and doctrine. He set down, at great length, the statements of Christian David, the carpenter, of Michael Linner, the eldest of the Church, and of his old friend, David Nitschmann. He felt at peace among these grave and good people, he loved their piety and industry, and he loved the trees and the cornfields. The fortnight which he spent at Herrnhut was a pleasing holiday, his immediate impressions were thoroughly congenial, and he felt that he could have spent all his life in such a place. But there was no substantial gain. Zinzendorf, with his airs of patronage, was not the man to inspire Wesley. Even the good people of Herrnhut were sometimes inclined to think too well of themselves. In a letter to Herrnhut which he wrote after his return to England, but fortunately refrained from sending, Wesley put the following questions to the Brethren: "Is not the Count [Zinzendorf] all in all among you? Do you not magnify your own Church too much? Do you not use guile and dissimulation in many cases? Are you not of a close, dark, reserved temper and behaviour?"

Wesley came back to England without having received any new spiritual benefit from his visit to Germany, but with a wholesome intention to rely upon his own work and his own efforts. He continued to preach on his new theme of salvation, and he took a leading part in the meetings of the society at Fetter Lane. But one by one the churches were closed against him. He was too irregular. He was becoming identified with the idea of a separate religious movement, to which the name of Methodism was now consistently applied. Warburton, not yet a bishop, took a delight in spreading scandalous rumours about Wesley and his views. Other clergymen preached against the dangerous teaching of the new birth. It seemed to be understood among Churchmen that nothing was more to be dreaded than a revival of piety.

Early in December 1738, George Whitefield returned from his American mission. He had been brilliantly successful.

Perhaps the work of Wesley in Savannah had borne a richer harvest than seemed likely to be the case when he was actually there. This, indeed, was the view of Whitefield himself, for within a month of his arrival at Savannah he wrote: "The good Mr. John Wesley has done in America, under God, is inexpressible. His name is very precious among the people; and he has laid such a foundation, that I hope neither men nor devils will ever be able to shake. Oh, that I may follow him, as he has Christ!" However that may be, the results of Whitefield's ministry were quickly apparent. He was extremely popular with the colonists, founded an orphanage in Savannah, and left on the understanding that he was to come back after he had collected funds for his work, assured of a cordial welcome. This young man (Whitefield was then only twenty-five) had already become a person of the first importance in the religious history of America.

Whitefield soon discovered that the churches in England were not anxious to receive him. He, like his friend Wesley, came under the suspicion of being too enthusiastic—the most awful suspicion which, in that cold, nerveless age, could fasten upon anyone. By the end of January 1739, he was barred from every London pulpit. At Bristol, where he had been so popular in 1737, things were no better. John Wesley, Charles Wesley and George Whitefield were now marked out for the official disapproval of the Church of England; the very Church to which, as loyal members, they were trying to lead back a faithless population.

A vital thing, if it is opposed (and this is what no states-man can ever learn), acquires new forces of invention and courage. Young Whitefield, seeing that he could not preach in the churches, decided to preach in the open air. This decision was one of extraordinary importance. Whitefield was now defying, not only ecclesiastical procedure, but also the letter of the law. He first preached on the 17th of February 1739, to a few hundred colliers on Kingswood Common. Three weeks later, he preached to a congrega-tion of ten thousand. A congregation of ten thousand could not have been assembled in any church, and White-field now realised the tremendous potentialities of his method. He continued to preach in open places, either in Bristol or in the surrounding country: as many as twenty thousand people gathered to hear him.

This amazing youth had kindled a blaze of religious fervour almost without parallel in the records of Christianity. The dark apathy of the Church was the more appalling by comparison.

Whitefield was anxious to extend his work, but he could not leave the awakened multitudes in Bristol without a pastor, and he wrote to Wesley. He urged Wesley to come to Bristol, and to carry on this great work. He believed that Wesley was the right man to lead a revival; the right man to organise, to *methodise*, what had every appearance of being a vast religious campaign.

Wesley himself was perplexed. He did not see the greatness of the occasion, and he hated the idea of preaching anywhere except in a church. Besides that, he seemed to be doing very well where he was; the leader of the Fetter Lane society, usefully promoting Moravianised ideas of faith in a circle of earnest acquaintances.

In times of perplexity, Wesley often had recourse to the Moravian practice of opening the Bible at hazard. He did so now; but the four passages which met his eye seemed to have little bearing on the question of going to Bristol. He therefore put the case before the society in Fetter Lane. His brother Charles was vehemently opposed to the idea; the opinion of the rest was not unanimous. At last it was agreed that the will of God might be discovered by the drawing of lots. It was thus decided that Wesley had to go to Bristol. Again the Bible was consulted, and again the passages appeared to be wholly irrelevant, though Wesley transcribed them carefully in his *Journal*: "Now there was long war between the house of Saul and the house of David. . . . When wicked men have slain a righteous person in his own house upon his bed. . . . And Ahaz slept with his fathers. . . ." But John Wesley saw clearly that God intended him to answer the call of Whitefield.

The entry in Charles Wesley's *Journal* for the 28th of March 1739, the day of the Fetter Lane decision, is extremely characteristic:

"We dissuaded my brother from going to Bristol, from an unaccountable fear that it would prove fatal to him. A great power was among us. He offered himself willingly to whatsoever the Lord should appoint. The next day he set out, commended by us to the grace of God. He left a blessing behind. I desired to die with him."

There could not be a more touching proof of the deep affection which, in spite of their occasional differences, John and Charles Wesley always felt for each other. It was probably the anxiety of Charles which made it impossible for John to make up his mind.

John arrived in Bristol on Saturday the 31st of March 1739, and met Whitefield the same day. "I could scarce reconcile myself at first," he says, "to this strange way of preaching in the fields, of which he [Whitefield] set me an example on Sunday; having been all my life (till very lately) so tenacious of every point relating to decency and order, that I should have thought the saving of souls almost a sin if it had not been done in a church."

And Whitefield, for his part, wrote in his *Journal*: 'I was much refreshed with the sight of my honoured friend Mr. John Wesley, whom God's providence has sent to Bristol. Lord, now lettest thou thy servant depart in peace." On the following day he wrote: "My heart is so knit to Bristol people, that I could not with so much submission leave them, did I not know dear Mr. Wesley was left behind to teach them the way of God more perfectly. Prosper, O Lord, the works of his hands upon him."

So, with much reluctance and with many apprehensions, Wesley began the work on which he was to be so gloriously engaged for nearly fifty-two years.

CHAPTER VII

BRISTOL AND LONDON

IN lawless violence and raw brutality few heathen men could have gone beyond the colliers of Bristol. They were treated, as colliers are often treated, like men of a separate and very undesirable race. No charity, no religion, no instruction made the least effort to reach their grimy, hideous and dejected lives. "These unhappy creatures," said a writer in the *Gentleman's Magazine* of 1791, "married and buried among themselves, and often committed murders with impunity."

They were capable of things even more repulsive than murder. In 1735 a sailor was convicted of having killed his wife in Bristol: he poisoned himself in jail, and was buried at a cross-road outside the city. The Bristol men, robbed of their prey, went to the cross-road, dug up the body, tore out the entrails and dragged them over the highway, picked out the eyes, broke the bones, and then put what was left "in a very deep grave near the gallows." These were the howling, bloody savages who were being converted in hundreds by the preaching of young George Whitefield.

The preaching of Whitefield had naturally attracted a great deal of attention. It was generally regarded as an activity of the most pernicious kind. Preaching the Gospel to working men was nearly as bad as trying to educate them; it was bound to make them discontented and to lessen their industrial value. This view was crudely expressed in the *Gentleman's Magazine*:

"The Industry of the inferior People in a Society is the great Source of its Prosperity. But if one Man, like the Rev. Mr. Whitefield, should have it in his Power, by his Preaching, to detain five or six thousands of the Vulgar from their daily Labour, what a Loss, in a little Time, may this bring to the Publick! For my part, I shall expect to hear of a prodigious Rise in the Price of Coals about the City of *Bristol*, if this Gentleman proceeds, as he has begun, with his charitable Lectures to the Colliers of *Kingswood*."

In taking up the new work of evangelism, Wesley saw that he would have to face the most formidable opposition. There was not merely a chance, but a positive certainty, of being persecuted with violence. But Wesley, though at times he appeared to hesitate, was a man of unswerving purpose, with all the courage of a soldier and all the fervour of a saint. Organised Methodism dates from the arrival of Wesley in Bristol. He saw at once the need of a system. Nothing of permanent value could be achieved without a centre of control, a recognised form of discipline. Religious societies were not the invention of Wesley; they had naturally come into existence when there was so little religion in the churches; but Wesley saw in these societies the essential units of the new organisation. Societies were founded in Nicholas Street and Baldwin Street, and on the 9th of May a piece of ground was taken on the site of the Horse Fair, for the building of the first Methodist meeting-house. But the chief thing, after all, was the preaching. Wesley's first sermon in the open air was preached two days after his arrival to a congregation of about three thousand. He stood on "a little eminence" in a brickyard. For the first few weeks his preaching does not seem to have drawn together such large congregations as those which had come to hear Whitefield, but it was accompanied by the most extraordinary results. Those results, which we may categorically define as the true phenomena of conversion, had first shown themselves in London; but now, in Bristol, they rapidly became more frequent and more disturbing. People dropped to the ground as though felled by a sudden blow, they roared aloud, and were agitated by cruel, unsightly convulsions. After continuing in this deplorable state for a few minutes or a few hours, they came to themselves with a happy sensation of joy and relief; the weight of sin was lifted, and the wandering soul was called back to a knowledge of God.

These experiences are of such importance in the early history of Methodism that it seems necessary to examine them more fully in another chapter. It is very singular that Whitefield, whose preaching was loud, vigorous and emotional, had not yet produced these results, and seldom produced them in his later ministry; while John Wesley, who preached with quiet deliberation in a plain, unrhetorical manner, produced them almost immediately. No one could charge Wesley with extravagance; but Whitefield exposed himself to this charge on every occasion. Whitefield exemplified the popular notion of a wild revivalist; Wesley had only the appearance of a straying clergyman who ought to have known better; yet Wesley could pierce his listeners to the very heart, and shake them as they had never been shaken by the boisterous evangelism of Whitefield.

Wesley preached, as Whitefield had preached already, on the consciousness of salvation. No theme could have been more distasteful to the prevailing doctrinal ideas of the Church. "Sir," said Bishop Butler to Wesley, "the pretending to extraordinary revelations and gifts of the Holy Ghost is a horrid thing; yes, sir, it is *a very horrid thing.*" And he added: "Sir, you have no business here; you are not commissioned to preach in this diocese: therefore I advise you to go hence."

Butler (*Analogy* Butler) was appointed Bishop of Bristol in 1738 and he was very much disturbed by the scenes of conversion which were taking place within his diocese. Yet Butler was one of the few conspicuously pious Churchmen of his period: his prim, jealous orthodoxy was not insincere, and his view of the Holy Ghost among the colliers was that of a man who truly believed that he was protesting against a form of irreligious fanaticism. He reflected, though in a more dignified way, the opinions of the *Gentleman's Magazine.* The idea of a special revelation to the vulgar was entirely beyond his comprehension, nor could he believe that any true religion could work without ecclesiastical patronage.

Wesley remained in Bristol, or in its neighbourhood, until June. When he was not preaching, he was organising.

He was unceasingly active. His religious societies grew rapidly and required fresh accommodation. Men who felt the need of revival came to hear him, and to study his methods.

Among these men was the Welsh revivalist, Howell Harris of Trevecca. Harris, in a little book which is now exceedingly rare, gives his impressions of the new teacher: "He preached on Isaiah xlv, 22 ('Look unto me, and be ye saved, all the ends of the earth'), and so excellently and clearly held forth free justification by faith, without the works of the Law . . . and the Spirit of God attended his discourse to my soul in such a manner, that much of the Lord's glory broke in upon my soul, and my prejudice against him fell away, and I was convinced that he was a faithful minister of Jesus Christ." Harris, at this time, was twenty-five.

Another young man, John Cennick, became associated with Wesley at about the same period. He was a native of Reading. In his early days he "fell into frivolity and sin," and was "convicted" suddenly as he was walking down Cheapside. After a phase of ineffectual asceticism, his agony of mind became so acute that he gave way to despair. In 1737 (when he was nineteen) he "found peace with God." Cennick was probably introduced to Wesley by Kinchin, who had been a member of the Holy Club. The part played by Cennick in the history of Methodism is not of great importance, but he was one of the first of Wesley's lay preachers, the first master of the Methodist school at Kingswood, and the author of a small volume of hymns. He was a theological Proteus; in 1740 his views were strongly Calvinistic, he was already at variance with John and Charles Wesley, and he was calling for help, like a solitary Eli (for so he described himself) to Whitefield in America. He finally turned Moravian.

Thomas Maxfield, a young man of Bristol, was converted in 1739, and began to help Wesley. He, too, though many years later, passed over to the Calvinist group.

On the 24th of April, Wesley visited Bath and preached to about a thousand people in the open air. Here he formed two Methodist "bands," one of men and one of women. He went to Bath on several occasions between this date and the 11th of June, when he set out for London.

Lady Huntingdon had not yet made Methodism a fashionable amusement, and it was natural enough that Wesley should be opposed by the gay society of Bath. There were even rumours of intended violence. On the 5th of June, after he had been expressly warned of what might occur, Wesley encountered Beau Nash.

Nash, who personified in the most disagreeable manner the arrogance, the elegance and the grinning depravity of the age, was then sixty-five. He was the Master of the Ceremonies, the King of Bath. A more stupid, a more worthless old man never strolled in fine clothes. He ruled by an assertion of tremendous triviality, which pleased the lazy and foolish crowds who filled the Pump Room. His large white hat and his coarse red face were greeted everywhere; his rudeness passed for wit; his ostentatious charity was accepted as the proof of benevolence; and his ridiculous pretensions were taken as a mark of authority. That even royalty could thus be ruled by the son of a Welsh glass-blower, so rakish that Oxford had expelled him, illustrates in a very striking way the social ethic of the period.

As Wesley was preaching to rather more than a thousand people, "among whom were many of the rich and the great," Nash came up to him. We can imagine with what curiosity the "rich and the great" must have observed this encounter. There was the little, neat clergyman in his black dress, and there was the hideous old man, smothered in finery. No two people could have been more opposed in every sense of the word: Wesley, placid, immovable and patient; Nash, ruffling and puffing with monstrous emptiness and sour impertinence. But Nash, like the poor thing he was, crumbled away after a very brief dialogue.

"By what authority," said the King of Bath, "do you do these things?" "By the authority of Jesus Christ. . . ." "Nay; but this is contrary to Act of Parliament: this is a conventicle." "Sir, the conventicles mentioned in that Act are seditious meetings; but this is not such . . . therefore

97

it is not contrary to that Act." "I say it is," replied Nash, with the desperate inconsequence of a fool. "And besides," he added, "your preaching frightens people out of their wits." "Sir, did you ever hear me preach?" "No." "How, then, can you judge of what you never heard?" "Sir, by common report." Wesley saw the opening: "Common report is not enough. Give me leave, Sir, to ask, Is not your name Nash?" "My name is Nash." "*Sir, I dare not judge you by common report*: I think it is not enough to judge by."

At this point, there must have been a muffled merriment, even among the genteel, and Nash, after an awful pause, could only splutter, "I desire to know what this people comes here for." Before Wesley could answer, an old woman said, "Sir, leave him to me.—You, Mr. Nash, take care of your body; we take care of our souls; and for the food of our souls we come here." Beau Nash had nothing more to say: the red face, still redder with angry confusion, passed through the crowd like a flaming sign of defeat.

Wesley found himself notorious. The streets of Bath were full of people "hurrying to and fro, and speaking great words." Some idle ladies followed him into a house and said they wanted to speak to him. "I believe, ladies," said Wesley "the maid mistook: you only wanted to look at me."

In the meantime George Whitefield had been preaching with unexampled effect in London. He had been travelling from place to place, and reached London on the 26th of May. On the evening of his arrival he preached on Kennington Common to fifteen thousand people. At Moorfields, as many as sixty thousand are said to have listened to him, or at least to have looked at him; and when, on the 1st of June, he preached at "a place called Mayfair, near Hyde Park Corner," his congregation was estimated at the stupendous figure of eighty thousand. There were not boats enough to take the people across the river to Kennington, or coaches enough to carry them to the Park. No such preaching had been known since the beginning of the world. And yet there was not much to show for it in the way of permanent change. It would be worse than inaccurate to say that Whitefield was only an orator; he was a man of burning zeal and the most vital conviction; but his method certainly had many of the drawbacks of a purely sensational eloquence. Probably more than half of his congregations went to see him merely because he was much talked about. Grave Dr. Watts raised a warning forefinger, and spoke of religious irregularity.

On the 13th of June, Wesley came back to London, in response to an earnest appeal from the Fetter Lane society, which was falling to pieces without him. On the following day he accompanied Whitefield to Blackheath, where they found "twelve or fourteen thousand people." Here, to the astonishment of Wesley, he was requested by Whitefield to preach. He did so, "greatly moved with compassion for the rich that were there." "After sermon," wrote Whitefield in his *Journal*, "we spent the evening most agreeably, together with many Christian friends, at the Green Man."

Wesley spent most of the remainder of 1739 between Bristol and London, but he visited other places, often preaching to large congregations, and paid his first visit to South Wales. Scenes resembling those of the Bristol conversions occurred in London, but not frequently, and apparently not elsewhere.

The first time Wesley preached at Moorfields, there stood among his congregation a sturdy man who was to become one of the bravest of the new missionaries. His name was John Nelson; he was a stone-mason from Yorkshire. Nelson had lived for many years in gloomy apprehension of divine wrath. He was not, like Cennick, a frivolous creature; on the contrary, he was a pattern of honesty, of manly virtue and goodness. But he fell so far short of what he desired to be, his resolves were so far in advance of his performance, that he believed himself damned. Without finding help or encouragement, he listened to Catholics and Dissenters, to Quakers and clergymen. When Whitefield began to preach in London, Nelson went to hear him. He listened to Whitefield, and compared him to "a man that could play well upon an instrument." Nelson felt a warm admiration for Whitefield; he felt, like a stout, generous fellow, that he was ready to fight anyone who offered to disturb him; but Whitefield could not touch his heart. Then he went again to Moorfields to hear Wesley. "Oh! that was a blessed morning for my soul! As soon as he got up upon the stand, he stroked back his hair and turned his face towards where I stood, and I thought he fixed his eyes on me. His countenance struck such an awful dread upon me before I heard him speak, that it made my heart beat like the pendulum of a clock; and when he did speak, I thought his whole discourse was aimed at me." Here was the essential difference between the preaching of Wesley and the preaching of Whitefield, very strikingly illustrated by the experience of the same listener. Whitefield had the air of a man "playing well upon an instrument"—a man producing the impersonal effect of genius. But Wesley stroked back his hair and looked into your eyes; his grave, penetrating words were meant for you personally; you had the sense of being directly apprehended by the mind of the preacher. It was this illusion of direct personal contact, appearing to place the listener and the preacher in a field of mutual experience where the rest of the congregation counted for nothing, which gave the words of Wesley such tremendous power.

Whitefield left for America at the beginning of August. John Wesley, "insensibly led," was now at the head of the new religious movement, though he himself would never have described it as a new movement, nor did he then measure the forces and possibilities of a grand revival. One of his chief concerns was the trouble in the Fetter Lane society. In this particular group, the Moravian influence was becoming dominant. Such an influence was incompatible with the active diffusionist principles of the two Wesleys. Quietism was the very opposite of the energetic policy which Wesley had now adopted, and a breach with Moravian teaching was clearly inevitable.

In this country, Moravian views had never been widely acceptable. The first *Diaspora* or missionary group had been established in London in 1728, on the suggestion of a lady of Queen Caroline's court. But the Brethren had not been successful. Moravian doctrine had the forlorn appearance of an importation; it was never congenial to England; and there is little doubt that the Moravians were not well represented in London in 1739. There was a sullen turbulence in the Fetter Lane society which was not in keeping with the usual gentleness of Moravian behaviour. Wesley was closely associated with the Fetter Lane society, and had certainly considered himself its leader; otherwise it is difficult to see why he should have been concerned with a difference of opinions that could scarcely have had more than a local importance.

Towards the end of 1739, a number of people in London came to Wesley and told him they wanted to form a society of their own, and to place themselves under his guidance. He agreed to meet them every Thursday evening, as long as it was possible for him to do so. The first evening, about twelve came; and the next week, thirty or forty. "When they were increased to about an hundred," he says, "I took down their names and places of abode, intending, as often as it was convenient, to call upon them at their houses. Thus, *without any previous plan*, began the Methodist Society in England; a company of people associating together to help each other to work out their own salvation." And soon after this new society had been formed, a building was acquired, eminently suitable to become the first headquarters of Methodism.

It was obviously difficult to carry on the field-preaching campaign in winter, though Wesley could gather congregations of seven or eight thousand on the coldest of November days. His attention was directed to "a vast, uncouth heap of ruins"—the Foundry at Moorfields. He preached there on the 11th of November, and soon afterwards borrowed money for the purchase, repair and alteration of the building.

We do not know the date of the original Foundry. It stood in Windmill Street (now Tabernacle Street) close to Finsbury Square. In 1716, people were invited there to view the interesting process of re-casting the guns taken by Marlborough from the French. Andrew Schalch, a young

Swiss engineer, had been specially invited. Schalch, looking
about him with a practised eye, observed traces of moisture
in the moulds. He warned the Surveyor-General that the
probable result of running hot metal into these moulds
would be a violent explosion. The Surveyor, instead of
putting a stop to the work, advised the people to be careful,
and himself prudently withdrew, together with Schalch
and a few others. An explosion took place, blowing off part
of the roof, wrecking the galleries, and killing, maiming and
burning the spectators and the workmen.

Such were the immediate results of pouring hot metal
into wet moulds, but the ultimate consequences were of much
greater importance: Schalch was asked to choose another
place for the casting of the king's ordnance; he chose a
rabbit-warren at Woolwich, and thus founded the Arsenal:
Wesley bought the abandoned ruins at Moorfields, and
thus established the first administrative centre of Methodism. So much may depend upon an error of judgment in
making cannon; a thing which, at first sight, has no appearance of being a useful or constructive process.

When the Foundry was re-built, it had a plain chapel
which could accommodate about fifteen hundred people.
There were no pews in the chapel, but about a dozen benches
with rails for the women. There were ordinary benches on
the floor and in the galleries. The men and women sat
apart, "as they always did in the primitive church." Behind
the chapel was a meeting-room for the classes, where the
five o'clock morning service was held in winter. One end
of this room was fitted as a school; at the other end there
was a book department for the sale of Wesley's publica-
tions. Wesley's own quarters were above the meeting-room.
There was a separate house for attendants and preachers,
and there was a small coach-house with a stable. It was
probably soon after the repair of the building that Wesley's
mother, then in her seventy-first year, took up residence at
the Foundry. She died there in 1742.

Charles Wesley, during his brother's absence in London,
in the autumn and winter of 1739, had gone to Bristol.
Charles worked manfully to save the Kingswood men from

their "Egyptian bondage." He dined with happy George the collier, he preached and prayed in the lanes and streets of the city, he expounded "with great freedom and power" at Baptist Mills or the Bowling Green. The devil "set up his throat in Benjamin Rutter," or whispered to Francis Hurd, but Charles beat him in every encounter.

The Church not only refused to recognise Methodism as an activity in any way related to its own, but attacked it with peculiar bitterness. Eminent clergymen, in sermons and pamphlets, denounced Methodists as "restless deceivers of the people," "insolent pretenders," "rapturous enthusiasts, assuming the language of the Holy Ghost," and charged them with making "indecent, false and unchristian reflections on the clergy," "boasting of immediate inspiration," "gathering tumultuous assemblies to the disturbance of the public peace," "encouraging abstinence, prayer and other religious exercizes, *to the neglect of the duties of our station.*" Dr. Trapp went so far as to accuse them of "teaching such absurd doctrines, and seconding them with such absurd practices, as to give countenance to the lewd and debauched, the irreligious and profane." "Can it promote the Christian religion," cried Dr. Trapp in a noble frenzy, "to turn it into riot, tumult and confusion? to make it ridiculous and contemptible, and expose it to the scoffs of infidels and atheists? . . . Our prospect is very sad and melancholy. Go not after these impostors and seducers; but shun them as you would the plague."

Even with some knowledge of the ecclesiastical position in the eighteenth century, it is not easy to explain the attitude of the Church. But there are certain elements of the opposition which are clear enough. Sympathy with Tillotson's views on the one hand and with the policy of Walpole on the other had brought upon the Church a mood of general quiescence. Zeal, sentiment or emotion were equally out of favour. When Johnson said that you could not tell where you were with a man who pretended to have the inner light, he was expressing the current idea of his period. Orthodoxy of a coy, prudish kind had succeeded to the stern fervour of the Puritans. Warburton discovered that the Regicides were all "enthusiasts," and also "of the same kind with the Methodists." The danger of a new Puritanism was evident. New religions had the odour of conspiracy. It was also supposed that a popular movement might very well develop on Jacobite lines, even if it did not veer suddenly in the direction of Popery. Church and State were both uneasy, and they desired nothing more than a continuance of placid repose. Even in 1740, the Methodists were making too much noise; they were offensive to the gravity and composure of a drowsy but still dignified Establishment. Nor was the offence wholly imaginary. The apologist of Methodism has to admit the extravagance, the folly or disorder of the weaker brethren, and such extravagance gave the opposition reasonable grounds for complaint. It cannot be denied that the preaching of Whitefield, however sincere and effective it may have been, was not often of the kind that would make a good impression upon a man of taste and learning. Nor can it be denied that the words and behaviour of other Methodist preachers too frequently resembled the gesture and accent of the most revolting hypocrisy. In addition to this, the scenes of popular conversion, with their cries and raptures, were intensely disagreeable to those who believed them to be signs of imposture or madness. There were thus many symptoms in early Methodism which must have been not merely distasteful but alarming to representative churchmen, and even to those who were not to be suspected of prejudice or insincerity. It is quite possible, too, that professional jealousy was accountable for a large part of this hostile attitude. Very few people went to church, and those who did so were usually careless, irreverent or sleepy. On the other hand, people flocked in vast numbers to listen attentively to the Methodist preachers in the open fields. And finally there was the Methodist appeal to a new sort of religious experience which seemed to place people on terms of unbecoming familiarity with their Creator. It looked as though emotions of a doubtful kind were to take the place of duty and obedience; there was too great a readiness to dispense with the blessings and services of the one true and respectable Church.

The attack of the clergy was reinforced by all the filthy devices of journalism. Pamphleteers and versifiers outdid each other in the bald indecency of their cumbrous inventions. And it is observable that the personal target of most of this ribaldry was not Wesley, but Whitefield. Wesley was rarely attacked in person; and when he was attacked, it was usually in order to point out to him that a man of scholarship and breeding ought to know better than to associate with disorderly fanatics.

In all this frothy opposition, the only valid charge was that of irregularity. Speaking of the Methodists in a dull nonsensical romance called *The Spiritual Quixote*, Richard Graves observed: "I know of no new opinions which they maintain, except that of the lawfulness of preaching without a legal call; and of assembling in conventicles or in the open fields, in direct opposition to the laws of the land."

No doubt the real offence lay in the missionary aspect of Methodism. While the Gospel was being preached to the poor and the vulgar, the churches were half empty; and the Church believed, not only in the unquestioning servitude of the poor and the vulgar, but in the simple policy of leaving them alone. Any religion the Church could still offer was a religion of learning and elegance; it was reserved, like all the luxuries and benefits of those times, for those who were rich, noble, or at least genteel. The Methodist was therefore guilty of a social treason. The eighteenth-century God had obviously ordained the subjection of the labouring masses, and such men as Wesley and Whitefield, with dangerous notions of free graces and spiritual equality, were disregarding the wise designs of Providence.

It was also supposed that a new religious fervour in the multitude would lead to riots and confusion. Any cause of popular excitement would be likely to have such a result, and to bring about a general state of uneasiness.

Wesley did not concern himself with reply or defence. He needed no *apologia*. He was entirely without malice. In the whole mass of his writings there are only a few pieces which are of a purely defensive character. His life was emphatically a life of action; his one business, the diffusion of a true knowledge of God.

Early in 1740, the school at Kingswood, proposed by Whitefield for the education of poor children and classes of adults, was completed. Cennick was appointed the head-master. Thus, with a school and meeting-houses of its own, Methodism had more and more the appearance of being an independent sect.

A far more important thing than the establishment of schools and meeting-houses was the institution of lay preachers. This, like all the decisive steps in the history of the movement, was not the outcome of a deliberate plan.

In the spring of 1740, Wesley, who was in Bristol, heard that Maxfield had been preaching to the people at the Foundry; that is, he had not been reading approved sermons, but composing and delivering sermons of his own. It has been suggested that Cennick had already been preaching at Kingswood with the consent of Wesley, but this is hardly probable. The only authority for the statement would appear to be the word of Cennick himself, which, in view of his consuming self-importance, is hardly enough. It has also been pointed out that a person named Joseph Humphreys was described by Wesley as "the first lay preacher that assisted me in England in 1738." The assumption in this latter case is that Humphreys was really a Morav an, and was not appointed by Wesley to preach to any group under his own charge—the mere fact of "assistance" is certainly ambiguous.

What is clear is that as soon as Wesley heard of the preaching of Maxfield, he hurried off to London to put a stop to what he regarded as a most presumptuous and dangerous proceeding. Having arrived at the Foundry, he first consulted his mother. "My son," said the old lady, "I charge you before God, beware what you do; for Thomas Maxfield is as much called to preach the Gospel as ever you were!" And yet Mrs. Wesley was always a woman of High Church principles. John hesitated. He felt that he was being giddily hustled from all the safe and comfortable forms of orthodoxy on which he had placed an absolute reliance. He listened to the preaching of Maxfield. "It is the Lord's doing," he said; "let Him do what seemeth good. What am I, that I should withstand God?" He formally approved of Maxfield as a lay preacher. Before the year came to an end, he had appointed twenty others.

This was obviously a vital decision. Two or three men, even men with the energy of Whitefield and the Wesleys, however rapidly they might have travelled and however forcibly they might have preached, could never have consolidated a vast popular religious movement without the assistance of laymen. The lay preachers gave to Methodism a steady and sustained impulse. They were often labouring men, able to teach with a form and accent familiar to their fellows, and to set before them attainable examples of true piety. They were essential, not merely to the organisation, but to the spirit of the movement. They gave a conformity to what might have otherwise been sporadic and fortuitous; they were the active ranks in the army of revival.

As far as the opposition was concerned, this was the culminating grievance. Making the poor preach to the poor was making the blind leaders of the blind. The idea of men in shabby clothes expounding the Scriptures in a vulgar dialect was too horrible, if it was not too ridiculous. No one could profitably point the way to heaven unless he wore a surplice, and knew the parts of a Latin verb when he saw them. It was a dastardly filching of prerogative. True, the first apostles were humble men; but things had changed enormously since the days of the apostles; every one agreed that there could be no such thing as grace without education.

The Bishop of Armagh met Charles Wesley at the Clifton Hotwells. "I knew your brother well," said his lordship with serene condescension; "I could never credit all I heard respecting him and you; but one thing I could *never* account for—the employment of laymen." "Well, my Lord," said Charles, "the fault is with you and your brethren." "How so? how so?" replied my Lord. "Because you hold your peace," said Charles boldly, "and the stones cry out." "But I am told," said the Bishop, avoiding the awkward point, "that these fellows are quite un-learned." "Some of them are," Charles answered; "and so the dumb ass rebukes the prophet."

There is little in the family history of Wesley at this time (1739-1740) that is of essential importance. His brother Samuel died at Tiverton on the 6th of November 1739, in his fiftieth year. But Samuel, whatever his dry excellence may have been, is a purely negative figure in the history of Methodism. His only contribution is that of a formal protest.

CHAPTER VIII

GEORGE WHITEFIELD

IN its early days, the Methodist movement was not so much associated in the popular mind with John Wesley as with the very conspicuous and remarkable personality of Whitefield. His easily observable peculiarities made Whitefield the obvious target of satire and abuse. His fame as a preacher exposed him to the scurrilous attacks of popular journalism.

It has been said that Whitefield, by his own unaided efforts, could have revived Christianity in England. That is a very questionable proposition; but it would not be unreasonable to say that Wesley's earlier campaign would have been infinitely less effective if he had not been supported by the tremendous activity of Whitefield. Without knowing something of George Whitefield, we cannot properly understand the history of John Wesley.

Whitefield, like Wesley, was descended from a line of clergymen. His earliest known ancestor is William Whytfield, vicar of Mayfield, Sussex, in 1605. Thomas, the son of William, became the vicar of Liddiard Melicent in Wiltshire, and then of Rockingham. Thomas was succeeded in this living by his son Samuel, and he, in his turn, was followed by a second Samuel. Andrew Whitefield, brother of the second Samuel, had fourteen children, one of whom, Thomas, became the father of George Whitefield. Thomas was trained to be a wine-merchant in Bristol, but later became the landlord of the Bell Inn at Gloucester. We know practically nothing of Whitefield's mother, except that she was a Bristol woman named Elizabeth Edwards, related to the families of Blackwell and Dimour. He was brought up by his mother alone, for his father died when he was two years old.

In 1740, Whitefield published an extraordinary account of himself which he had written during his first voyage to America. He seems to have composed it with the earnest desire of revealing himself as an example of penitence, and, since he wanted to show the original depravity of his nature, he morbidly exaggerated the importance of his infantile failings.

"I can truly say, I was froward from my mother's womb. I was so brutish as to hate instruction, and used purposely to shun all opportunities of receiving it. . . . Lying, filthy talking and foolish jesting I was much addicted to. . . . Stealing from my mother I thought no theft at all, and used to make no scruple of taking money out of her pocket before she was up."

He behaved irreverently in church, he liked to see the players, he liked a game of cards. He never looked at his Bible, but he was quick enough to turn the pages of a silly romance. Then, at the age of twelve (that is, in 1726), this desperate sinner began to think about religion. He was sent to the school of St. Mary de Crypt in Gloucester. Already he displayed the gift of oratory, and took delight in playing in the school theatricals. Up to the age of sixteen he helped his mother in the work of the public house. Assisted by charity, and notably by that of Lady Betty Hastings, the sister of the Earl of Huntingdon, he was entered as a servitor at Pembroke College, Oxford. He matriculated in 1732. He describes an acute religious experience at Oxford which took place in 1735:

"One day, perceiving an uncommon drought and a disagreeable clamminess in my mouth, and using things to allay my thirst, but in vain, it was suggested to me than when Jesus Christ cried out 'I thirst,' His sufferings were near at an end. Upon which I cast myself down on the bed, crying out 'I thirst! I thirst!' Soon after this, I found and felt in myself that I was delivered from the burden that had so heavily oppressed me."

He was admitted to Wesley's Holy Club in 1735, and was ordained a deacon on the 20th of June 1736. In July, he graduated Bachelor of Arts. He is said to have first preached on the 8th of August 1736, at St. Botolph's,

Bishopsgate. But an early sermon, delivered in the same year at the church of St. Mary de Crypt in Gloucester gave the first proof of his ability; at least fifteen people were "driven mad."

From the very start, he preached on the new birth, or conscious salvation, and in 1736 it was already his ambition to become a missionary. When he embarked on his first voyage to America in 1737, the following verses appeared in the *Gentleman's Magazine:*

"How great, how just thy zeal, advent'rous Youth!
To spread, in heathen climes, the Light of Truth!
Go, loved of heaven! with every grace refined,
Inform, enrapture each dark Indian's mind;
Grateful, as when to realms long hid from day,
The cheerful dawn foreshows the solar ray."

In America, he was received with cordiality. His approach to the red and white men of Georgia was not like that of the excessively sacerdotal Wesley; it was more ingratiating, more humane. Whitefield came provided with tape, buttons, buckles, powder and shot, pewter porringers, tools and fishing tackle, drugs, cheeses, wine, lemons, and stationery. He had plenty of Bibles and good books; he had also shirts and coats and excellent stockings. Even the bawdy, unmannerly and sullen people of Frederica, where John Wesley had beaten the air in vain, gave him a sort of welcome. Savannah became his parish. When he left, after a stay of little more than three months, he was accompanied to his embarkation by tears and prayers, by gifts and every imaginable kind wish. And as long as he remained in the pleasing perspective of a missionary to eager and distant heathen, no one in England thought anything but well of him. When he returned, and worked among the heathen of his own country, the situation was completely reversed.

After the London preaching of 1738, the chief vehemence of the popular attack on Methodism was concentrated, with savage delight, upon the person of Whitefield. His figure, his manners, his incessant use of a vivid religious phrase-

ology, and above all his extraordinary power in preaching,
exposed him at once to the fiercest kind of ridicule. He was
the arch-Methodist. "I do not know whether you have
heard of a new sect," wrote the Countess of Hertford at this
time: "there is one Whitefield at the head of them."

George Whitefield, in youth, was agile and slender, with
a natural grace of movement. He was above the average in
height. The most noteworthy peculiarity of his face was a
terrible squint; but this, we are told, rather increased than
lessened the effect of an uncommon sweetness of expression.
In colour, he was fresh and fair. His voice was probably
one of the finest ever heard in public oratory; it was a voice
of amazing compass and volume. Franklin believed that
Whitefield could easily make himself heard by thirty thousand people, and yet the sound he produced was always
melodious, rich, and controlled by appropriate modulations.
He never stumbled over a word, and was never at a loss.
"By hearing him often," said Franklin, "I came to distinguish between sermons newly composed, and those which
he had often preached in the course of his travels. His
delivery of the latter was so improved by frequent repetition, that every accent, every emphasis, every modulation
of voice, was so perfectly well turned . . . that, *without
being interested in the subject*, one could not help being pleased
with the discourse: a pleasure of much the same kind with
that received from an excellent piece of music." His fame
is still that of the most celebrated of English preachers.

Whitefield could certainly hold the attention and raise
the emotions of his audience in an almost incredible way.
He could make them entirely forgetful of place and circumstance. He could produce a most complete illusion. Once,
he was using the metaphor of a blind man tottering towards
the crumbling edge of a precipice; Chesterfield was present,
and at the critical point of the illustration his lordship
sprang from his chair—"By God!" he cried: "he's over!"
To have this effect upon a creature of such reptilian coldness
as Chesterfield was not far short of a miracle.

Again, when preaching at New York, he compared the
stricken soul to a ship in distress: the masts have gone; she

is on her beam ends; what is to be done? Two or three sailors jumped up: "The long boat, Sir!—take to the long boat!"

A ship-builder was asked his opinion of Whitefield. "I tell you," he answered, "every Sunday that I go to my parish church, I can build a ship from stem to stern under the sermon; but, to save my soul, under Mr. Whitefield, I can't lay a single plank."

And even greater miracles were performed by this irresistible oratory. Whitefield could raise money in Scotland. He could induce the cautious Franklin to fish out of his pockets, first all the copper, then all the silver, and finally the pieces of gold. "I'd give a hundred guineas," said Garrick, "if I could say Oh! like Mr. Whitefield"; and he protested that Mr. Whitefield could make people cry by the moving way in which he pronounced the single word *Mesopotamia*.

Exact accounts of his preaching are not very numerous. David Hume gives a description of an effect which was used more than once. Towards the end of a sermon, Whitefield paused, with a sudden gesture commanding attention and silence: "The attendant angel," he said, "is about to leave the threshold of this sanctuary and ascend to heaven. . . ." He stamped on the floor of the pulpit and raised his eyes. "Stop, Gabriel!—stop!—and carry with you the news of yet one more sinner converted to God!" Or again, he would abruptly stretch out his hand and turn his head: "Look yonder, look yonder! What is it that I see? It is my agonising Lord. Hark! . . . Do you not hear?" And when he spoke of Peter weeping bitterly, he would hide his own face in a fold of his gown. The impression made by these devices, flat enough in mere print, was overpowering.

It is said that he spoke always as one preaching *for the last time*. In a little while, it might be too late. The hour in which he was talking might be the last hour of the world; he met his listeners under the awful imminence of judgment. He was choked with tears. His physical effort was often tremendous; he appeared like a man being killed by fervour. Sometimes he seemed to lose all control; sometimes he was near complete exhaustion.

In every way, his methods differed from those of Wesley. The power of Whitefield lay in word and gesture, in vigour of delivery, often in coarse vehemence; the power of Wesley was of a more penetrating, spiritual kind. Yet both men were equally necessary to the great revival. "Even the little improprieties both of his language and manner," said Wesley of Whitefield, "were a means of profiting many who would not have been touched by a more correct discourse, or a more calm and regular way of speaking."

His manner and theology were caricatured in verses, plays and pamphlets. The industry of Tyerman has produced a list of forty-nine pamphlets, for and against Whitefield, printed in one year alone. Few of these caricatures have a literary value; their tendency (or rather, their less objectionable tendency) is shown in the verses of Evan Lloyd:

> "He knows his Master's realm so well,
> His sermons are a Map of Hell,
> An Ollio made of Conflagration
> Of Gulphs of Brimstone, and Damnation,
> Eternal Torments, Furnace, Worm. . . ."

Or we may take two other popular lines, often quoted:

> "Hail, O Saint Whitefield, Ape of Grace,
> Thou holy Sinner with a Formal Face."

The satire of Chatterton is more ingenious more violent, and naturally of more interest. Chatterton hated the Methodists. When he was only eleven, he wrote the poem of *Apostate Will*, and before the eighteen years of his tragic life were over he had made many slighting references to the Methodist revival. In his journal for 1769, the year before his death, there is a portrait of Whitefield:

> "Now he raves like brindled cat,
> Now 'tis thunder,
> Rowling,
> Growling,
> Rumbling,
> Grumbling,

Noise and nonsense, jest and blunder;
Now he chats of this and that,—
No more the soul jobber,
No more the sly robber.
He's now an old woman who talks to her cat."

It was undoubtedly the mere singularity of Whitefield, and his extraordinary success as a preacher, which attracted a fashionable following. Lady Betty Hastings was his first patron; by 1739 he was in touch with a patron of far greater importance—the Countess of Huntingdon. Lady Huntingdon made Whitefield one of her domestic chaplains in 1748, and it was with her assistance that Calvinistic Methodism was established, with George Whitefield as one of the leaders. It was in the drawing-rooms and chapels of Lady Huntingdon that Whitefield preached to high society, and even won a few superior souls.

The Calvinism of Whitefield, the cause of a doctrinal rupture with Wesley, seems to have been in evidence as far back as 1737, and was developed in the course of his earlier visits to America.

It is doubtful if Whitefield ever had a very clear apprehension of Calvinistic theology. The essence of Calvinism is the doctrine of absolute predestination, and the acceptance of predestinarian views must logically paralyse all evangelical effort. If men are damned or saved from the moment of birth, what is the use of preaching to them? If predestination is absolute (as Calvin positively affirms), there can be no acquired salvation; if it is not absolute, there can be no Calvinism. We have to suppose that Whitefield, who was an evangelist and nothing else, must have made ample reservations, he must have believed in limited election or in the revocable nature of divine decrees. Perhaps he was ready to maintain, as later theologians have maintained, that people who were not elect were merely left to "the operation of exact justice"—a more comfortable proposition, but quite inconsistent with the views of Calvin. At all events, his Calvinism was hazy, elastic, tenuous, and often impalpable. He declared the universality of redeeming love, and the willingness of Christ to save all. "The man's heart," says Tyerman, "was larger than his creed." It was also larger than his head.

The unflinching personal courage of Whitefield was equal to that of Wesley himself. He could face a murderous mob, even the Irish mob, without a sign of fear. He undertook a ministry in America, and crossed the Atlantic thirteen times.

In 1741, after making extremely formal proposals of marriage to Miss Delamotte, Whitefield married Mrs. James of Abergavenny.

Not much is known of Mrs. James, except that she was a widow, that her original name was Barnell, and that she was supposed to have a fortune of about ten thousand pounds. Wesley saw Mrs. James in 1741, and described her as "a woman of candour and humanity." Howell Harris tried to persuade her to write Calvinist pamphlets. According to Whitefield, she was between thirty and forty at the time of her marriage—"Once gay; but for three years past a despised follower of the Lamb of God . . . neither rich in fortune nor beautiful as to her person, but, I believe, a true child of God."

There appears to be no reason for believing Cornelius Winter, who says that Whitefield's married life was unhappy; had it been unhappy, we should have known more about it; but as it is, we know practically nothing at all. Within a week of his marriage, Whitefield left his bride and continued in the active service of evangelism.

Methodism in Wales was finally organised on a Calvinistic basis in 1743, with Howell Harris the Superintendent, and Whitefield the perpetual Moderator.

The non-residence of Whitefield in Savannah was justified by his work in collecting funds for his parish and orphanage during his itinerancy in England. He spent more than three and a half years in America between 1744 and 1748. In the winter of 1748 he drew large fashionable audiences to Lady Huntingdon's house in Chelsea. His new Tabernacle in Moorfields, close to the Foundry, was built in 1753. In June 1756 he laid the foundation stone of the more famous Tabernacle in the Tottenham Court Road.

The "spiritual routs" at Lady Huntingdon's, conducted by Venn, Romaine, Madan and Whitefield, were important social gatherings in 1758; they were supposed to have a serious effect upon theatrical revenues. "It were no wonder," said the *Monthly Review*, "that a Whitefield or a Wesley should be jealous of so powerful a rival as a Garrick; or even a Woodward, a Shuter, or a Yates." There was a bitter attack on Whitefield by the players in 1760, culminating in the raw buffoonery of *The Minor*. Whitefield was displayed as a lewd, canting hypocrite, under the name of *Parson Squintum*, in scores of indecent pamphlets, as well as in the ribald comedy of Samuel Foote. But new champions were rising. Lady Huntingdon's group was reinforced by more than one noble convert. Captain Scott of the 7th Dragoons, a Minden fighter, preached Methodism to his men in full regimentals. "This red coat," said Fletcher of Madeley, "will shame many a black one." The Earl of Buchan, his son, and Lord Dartmouth, became zealous members of the Methodist connection. Lady Chesterfield and other women of rank listened eagerly to the new preachers. It would have been hard to say whether Lady Huntingdon entertained her guests more agreeably in her drawing-room than she did in her chapel.

Whitefield consumed himself by the incessant play of his own energies. John Wesley met him in Edinburgh in 1763, and wrote in his *Journal*, "Humanly speaking, he is worn out." Yet Whitefield, at that time, was only forty-nine years old. He had become slow in motion, corpulent, with heavy breathing. Within a month of this meeting, he set out on his sixth voyage to America.

Wesley met him again on the 28th of October 1765. He wrote: "I breakfasted with Mr. Whitefield, who seemed to be an old, old man, being fairly worn out in his Master's service, though he has hardly seen fifty years." Again, in 1769, Wesley set down: "I had one more agreeable conversation with my old friend and fellow labourer, George Whitefield. His soul appeared to be vigorous still, but his body was sinking apace; and unless God interposes with His mighty hand, he must soon finish his labours."

He was now at the height of his fame, and the noisier kind of opposition had died down. In August 1769, there were nearly two thousand communicants on one Sunday at the Moorfields Tabernacle. In September of the same year, Whitefield started on his thirteenth and last voyage. He left England with certain misgivings. "I expect many trials on board," he said. "Satan always meets me there."

He died on the 30th of September 1770, in his fifty-seventh year, and was buried at Newburyport in Massachusetts. He bequeathed to Lady Huntingdon the orphan house at Savannah, other lands and buildings, *and all his negroes.*

The most striking testimony in favour of George Whitefield is that of John Wesley himself. In the quality of his mind, in his manners and movement, Wesley was the very opposite of Whitefield; he disliked extravagance, loudness and familiarity almost as much as he disliked the devil. Yet, in spite of difference and disagreement and the occasional vehemence of the Calvinist controversy, Wesley always regarded Whitefield as one of the dearest of his friends. "He breathes nothing but peace and love," he said. "Bigotry cannot stand before him, but hides its head wherever he comes." Both John and Charles Wesley perceived in Whitefield the power of the spirit, and recognised his immense value in the religious awakening of the people. In such a work as that on which all three were engaged, there could be no shadow of rivalry. "Lord, grant," said George Whitefield in speaking of Wesley, "that he may be preferred before me wherever he goes!"

In one respect, that of theological tolerance, Whitefield was perhaps superior to the Wesleys. It is true that he defended hotly what he believed to be the principles of Calvin, but his attitude to other denominations was never hostile. He would preach anywhere, or for any cause, except in a Popish church or for a Popish enterprise. And in this respect, his views were merely those of any orthodox English

Churchman: he believed, like Wesley, that Roman priests were "blind leaders of the blind,"' and that Rome was the mother of abominations, the harlot of the Seven Hills. When the atrocities of the anti-Methodist Cork riots of 1750 were brought to the notice of the public, one of the most vehement champions of the persecuted, all of them Wesleyans, was George Whitefield.

His disposition was amiable. He wished to love all men, and thought himself one of the least worthy. "I know no reason," he said to his followers, "why you should be solicitous about anything that happens to such a dead dog as I am." He was glad when he was called on to endure pain, slander or persecution. "How good is God thus to prepare me by sufferings, that so His blessings may not be my ruin." An occasional petulance appears to have been the worst of his failings, and perhaps an occasional sharpness in rejoinder.

He deplored, as much as Wesley or any other good man, the lethargy and depression of the Church. "Lord, the Christian world is cast into a deep sleep." But no man was more loyal to the Establishment. He said categorically:

"I am, and profess myself, a member of the Church of England. . . . I keep close to her articles and homilies, which, if my opposers did, we should not have so many dissenters from her; but it is most notorious that for the moralising iniquity of the priests the land mourns. We have preached and lived many sincere persons out of our communion. . . . Speak therefore I must, and will, and will not spare; God look to the event. Whatever becomes of the pastors who feed themselves, and not the flock, I have borne my testimony, I have delivered my own soul."

It has been said that Whitefield's power, like that of other great orators, resided entirely in the effect of his immediate presence, and that his writings are insufferably dull. A statement of this kind ought certainly to be qualified. It is easy enough to magnify the orator at the expense of the writer, and to make the glory of the one all the greater by contrast with the insufficiency of the other. But Whitefield was by no means an inferior writer. We are not likely to read his sermons, or any sermons of that prosy period, with an extraordinary degree of pleasure; but if we do read them, we find them well constructed, clear, forcible and manly in expression. The style of his early *Journal* is neat, exact, and often peculiarly vivid. He did not possess the admirable literary talent and the learning of Wesley, but he could write with vigour and distinction.

Still, his eminence in the Methodist revival is that of a great popular preacher, not that of a man who could make any serious contribution to theology or appeal in any subtle way to the stubborn intelligence. And as a preacher to the multitude his record is probably unique in the history of the Christian Church. Unlike the placid image of Wesley, so gentle in gesture and yet so luminous with spiritual meaning, the mental image of Whitefield presents itself with a stormy movement of uplifted arms and of black draperies, hanging like a cloud over the bowing heads of the nful.

But with all his dark fervour, Whitefield was a very natural, a very conversable and pleasing man. He could "laugh heartily." Some of his repartees are excellent. In Boston, as he was walking in the street, he met a certain Doctor of Divinity. "Ah!" said the Doctor, "I am sorry to see *you* here." "So is the devil," answered Whitefield. Again, when the episcopal minister of Charleston taxed him with using gay tunes, commonly associated with trivial or profane words, Whitefield replied: "Very true, Sir; very true. But pray, Sir, can you assign a good reason why the devil should always have the best tunes?"

Of contemporary opinions concerning Whitefield, we may single out that of Samuel Johnson, not as one of the least prejudiced, but as one of the most representative. "His popularity," said Johnson, "is chiefly owing to the peculiarity of his manner. He would be followed by crowds were he to wear a night-cap in the pulpit, or were he to preach from a tree." And on another occasion, he said: "I take it he was at the height of what his abilities could do, and was sensible of it. He had the ordinary advantages of education; but he chose to pursue that oratory which is for the mob." Boswell observed that he had a great effect on the passions (which was one of his favourite remarks), and Johnson replied: "I don't think so. He could not represent a succession of pathetick images. He vociferated, and made an impression. There again was a mind like a hammer."

In modern literature, the most convincing estimate of Whitefield is still, apart from an unduly severe censure of his language and writings, that of Lecky:

"Unlike Wesley, whose strongest enthusiasm was always curbed by a powerful will, and who manifested at all times and on all subjects an even exaggerated passion for reasoning, Whitefield was chiefly a creature of impulse and emotion. He had very little logical skill, no depth or range of knowledge, nothing of the commanding and organising talent . . . so conspicuous in his colleague. At the same time, a more zealous, a more single-minded, a more truly amiable, a more purely unselfish man it would be difficult to conceive. He lived perpetually in the sight of eternity, and a desire to save souls was the single passion of his life. . . . His failings were chiefly those of a somewhat weak nature, of overstrung nerves, and of a half-educated and very defective taste. He was a little irritable and occasionally a little vain. . . . His devotional language is marked by an utter absence of reticence, dignity, or measure."

But if the language of Whitefield was marked by an absence of dignity and measure, it was not marked by an absence of effect. In the work of construction, Whitefield must rank below the Wesleys: he does not rank below them in amplitude of spirit. To appreciate the meaning of the English revival of religion in the eighteenth century, it is necessary to see beyond the limits of Wesleyan Methodism. Whitefield, certainly, was no organiser. He was, in a sense, the assistant of Lady Huntingdon: it was her Ladyship, and not Whitefield, who controlled the Calvinistic Methodist societies. Yet his influence cannot be measured by the growth of Lady Huntingdon's Connection, by his institutional designs in America, or even by the spread of Methodism as a whole. It was the boundless, though unequal influence of a man who, almost entirely by the gift of oratory, set himself to lead a godless people into the way of salvation.

CHAPTER IX

RELIGIOUS EXPERIENCE

EVERY great religious revival is accompanied by personal experiences of a special kind, not peculiar to revivals, but appearing at revival periods in greatly intensified forms and in greatly increased numbers. Such experiences are generally described as those of conversion.

Whether used in a scientific or a theological sense, the term conversion is appropriate; for what actually occurs as a result of the experience is a total change of mental outlook, with a corresponding re-arrangement of the entire personal complex. The moment of conversion may occur at any time in the life of an individual who is accessible to the influences which produce it, nor is it always religious in character. In the wider sense of the term, it simply implies a more or less permanent psychological or spiritual change, in which new groups of controlling ideas take charge of the mind, and govern the thought and behaviour of the transformed personality.

During revival conditions, the whole process of conversion may be exceedingly rapid, particularly at crowded meetings. In typical cases, the change is preceded by a state of uneasiness which tends to produce a climax of agonising despair, and is followed by a state of tranquillity, joy and assurance. Most of these typical cases occur among people in whom the inhibitory action of a well-disciplined mind is not present, and whose ordinary mental activities are of limited range; above all, among people with little faculty for expression. The same process among highly intellectual types, as in the case of Luther, Pascal, or Wesley himself, is not usually marked by a phase of acute crisis or by violent physical symptoms, as it is in the familiar examples of revival; yet the difference here is not in the process, or in the results, but only in the form of the individual reaction.

Those who are religious naturally wish to see in this

process the special operation of divine grace. No one can say that such a view is mistaken; though conversion, in the wider sense, is of many kinds, and may amount to nothing more than a sudden explosion of hitherto concealed personal ingredients. Rousseau on the road to Vincennes, dazzled by the rush of new ideas into his mind, may be said to have been converted by the discovery of his own genius.

But in the ordinary sense, conversion is a religious experience, accompanied by a real newness of being. The natural man, we may say, is conquered by the spiritual man. Billy Bray, speaking of his conversion in 1823, said, "Everything looked new to me—the people, the fields, the cattle, the trees."

It is assumed, and the assumption is borne out by evidence, that conversion of the sort we are here considering is limited to individuals of a certain type. According to Professor Coe, you must have emotional sensibility, a tendency to automatisms, and suggestibility of the passive kind. James describes the predisposition in a simple diagrammatic or mechanistic way by assuming a large peripheral area of the mind, in which groups of ideas accumulate (ideas of a religious nature), until, at the moment of surrender or saturation, they invade and occupy completely the centre of the primary consciousness, and thus become the dictators and controllers of the transformed life. From this we may infer, and rightly, that conversions, or sudden changes in the personal equilibrium, are especially likely to take place at adolescence; and we may also infer that women, and particularly those who are subject to nervous or circulatory disorders, are more readily disposed to this experience than men; and that such phenomena will be almost wholly restricted to a definite social environment.

The occurrence of sudden conversions during the Methodist revival is of extraordinary interest, and we propose to examine, first some of the most remarkable cases, and afterwards their effect upon Wesley, and his interpretation, not always consistent, of their meaning.

The first noteworthy instance of conversion phenomena in which Wesley himself was concerned is to be found in the *Journal*, under the date of New Year's Day, 1739. Charles and John Wesley, Ingham and Whitefield were present at a love-feast in Fetter Lane. "About three in the morning, as we were continuing instant in prayer, the power of God came mightily upon us, insomuch that many cried out for exceeding joy, and many fell to the ground."

Three weeks later, as John Wesley was "expounding in the Minories," there was a striking individual case. "A well-dressed, middle-aged woman suddenly cried out, as in the agonies of death. She continued to do so for some time, with all the signs of the sharpest agony of spirit. When she was a little recovered, I desired her to call upon me the next day."

In April 1739, at the beginning of Wesley's ministry in Bristol, conversions of a violent and highly sensational kind took place in large numbers, but only when John Wesley was present. He had not anticipated such happenings. When, at a meeting in Baldwin Street, "one that stood cried out aloud with the utmost vehemence, even as in the agonies of death," Wesley was filled with astonishment. On the same occasion, several others cried out, but were presently relieved of their distress and began to praise God with a happy mind.

Under the preaching of Wesley, these occurrences became more and more frequent, accompanied often by physical symptoms of a very painful and disturbing kind. A large proportion of the people thus affected were young women.

Towards the end of the month (April 1739), Wesley began his work among the prisoners in the Bristol Newgate. Extraordinary scenes of conversion were recorded. Here is the entry in Wesley's *Journal* for the 25th of April:

"While I was preaching in Newgate . . . I was insensibly led, without any previous design, to declare strongly and explicitly that God willeth all men to be thus saved; and to pray that *If this were not the truth of God, He would not suffer the blind to go out of the way; but, if it were, He would bear witness to His Word.* Immediately one, and another, and another sunk to the earth: they dropped on every side as thunderstruck. One of them cried aloud. We besought God on her behalf, and He turned her heaviness into joy. A second being in the same agony, we called upon God for her also; and He spoke peace unto her soul. In the evening, I was again pressed in spirit to declare that *Christ gave Himself a ransom for all.* And almost before we called upon Him, to set to His seal, He answered. One was so wounded by the sword of the spirit, that you would have imagined she could not live a moment. But immediately His abundant kindness was showed, and she loudly sung of His righteousness."

On the following day: "*All Newgate rang* with the cries of those whom the Word of God cut to the heart; two of whom were in a moment filled with joy, to the astonishment of those that beheld them."

News of what was happening spread rapidly in Bristol. "Many were offended." Men spoke angrily or scornfully of imposture, of trickery and devilment. A certain doctor was particularly defiant, and came to Newgate in order to see for himself. He closely observed a woman who, as Wesley preached, "broke out into strong cries and tears." "He went and stood close to her, and observed every symptom, till great drops of sweat ran down her face, and all her bones shook. He then knew not what to think, being clearly convinced it was not fraud, nor yet any natural disorder. But when both her soul and body were healed in a moment, he acknowledged the finger of God."

A similar case of incredulity vanquished took place at the Baldwin Street meeting on the 1st of May. Wesley could hardly make himself heard for the cries and groanings of his congregation. "A Quaker who stood by was not a little displeased at the *dissimulation* of those creatures, and was biting his lips and knitting his brows, when he dropped down as thunderstruck. The agony he was in was terrible to behold. We besought God not to lay folly to his charge; he soon lifted up his heart and cried aloud, 'Now I know thou art a prophet of the Lord.'"

Before considering the more general aspect of these occurrences, we will reproduce Wesley's own account of two individual cases, in which the physical and mental experiences reach the highest degree of violence and horror. The first is that of John Haydon, a weaver, who was present at the Baldwin Street meeting when the Quaker was overpowered.

Haydon was apparently a godly man; he was a zealous Churchman, regular in behaviour, leading a life without reproach. He had come to the meeting out of curiosity, and afterwards went about among his friends "till one in the morning," trying passionately to persuade them "it was a delusion of the devil." But, as Wesley was returning to his lodging, he was met in the street by some people who told him that "John Haydon was fallen raving mad." The unhappy weaver had been resisting the invasive ideas which implied that he was not as righteous as he had imagined himself to be, he was trying to oppose the inward process, and now the flood came tumbling in upon the wreckage of a broken personality. Wesley thus describes the conversion:

"It seems he [John Haydon] had sat down to dinner, but had a mind first to end a sermon he had borrowed on Salvation by Faith. In reading the last page, he changed colour, fell off his chair, and began screaming terribly, and beating himself against the ground. The neighbours were alarmed, and flocked to the house. Between one and two I came in, and found him on the floor, the room being full of people, whom his wife would have kept without; but he cried aloud, 'No; let them all come; let all the world see the judgment of God.' Two or three men were holding him as well as they could. He immediately fixed his eyes on me, and stretching out his hand, cried, 'Aye, this is he, who I said was a deceiver of the people. But God has overtaken me. I said it was all a delusion. But this is no delusion.' He then roared out, 'O thou devil! thou cursed devil! yea, thou legion of devils! thou canst not stay. Christ will cast thee out.

I know His work is begun. Tear me in pieces if thou wilt; but thou canst not hurt me.' He then beat himself against the ground again; his breast heaving at the same time as in the pangs of death, and great drops of sweat trickling down his face. We all betook ourselves to prayer. His pangs ceased, and both his body and soul were set at liberty."

The second case is that of Sally Jones, a young woman at Kingswood. The description is under the date of the 23rd of October 1739:

"Returning in the evening, I was exceedingly pressed to go back to a young woman in Kingswood. The fact I nakedly relate, and leave every man to his own judgment of it. I went. She was nineteen or twenty years old; but, it seems, could not write or read. I found her on the bed, two or three persons holding her. It was a terrible sight. Anguish, horror and despair, above all description, appeared on her pale face. The thousand distortions of her whole body showed how the dogs of hell were gnawing her heart. The shrieks intermixed were scarce to be endured. But her stony eyes could not weep. She screamed out, as soon as words could find their way, 'I am damned; lost for ever. Six days ago you might have helped me. But it is past. I am the devil's now. I have given myself to him. His I am. Him I must serve. With him I must go to hell. I will be his. I will serve him. I will go with him to hell. I cannot be saved. I will not be saved. I must, I will, I will be damned.' She then began praying to the devil. We began
　　　　'Arm of the Lord, awake, awake!'
She immediately sunk down as asleep; but as soon as we left off, broke out again, with inexpressible vehemence: 'Stony hearts, break! I am a warning to you. Break, break, poor stony hearts! Will you not. break? What can be done more for stony hearts? I am damned, that you may be saved. Now break, now break, poor stony hearts! You need not be damned, though I must.' She then fixed her eyes on the corner of the ceiling, and said, 'There

he is; aye, there he is. Come, good devil, come. Take me away. You said that you would dash my brains out; come, do it quickly. I am yours. Come just now. Take me away.' We interrupted her by calling again upon God; on which she sunk down as before, and another young woman began to roar out as loud as she had done. My brother now came in, it being about nine o'clock. We continued in prayer till past eleven; when God in a moment spoke peace unto the soul, first of the first tormented, and then of the other. And they both joined in singing praise to Him who had 'stilled the enemy and the avenger.'"

It seems necessary, at this point, to refute the idea that Wesley produced his conversions by invoking the terrors of divine wrath, and thus working upon the fears of the feeble-minded. Ignorant people still believe that Wesley habitually preached against a lurid background of eternal conflagration. No idea of the man or his method could be more villainously false. It was only in extremely rare cases that Wesley appealed to the "terrors of the Lord"—indeed that phrase hardly ever occurs in his *Journal.* "He preached," says Winchester, "the love of God to man, because his own heart was filled with a great love and pity for his sinning and suffering fellows." Faith and salvation were his principal themes. He spoke always in the plainest manner, with measure, deliberation and gravity; but never with the intention of frightening people into repentance.

The appearance of conversion phenomena under the preaching of Wesley, and indeed the wider effect of his preaching, was therefore due to something which a theologian would readily describe as the operation of heavenly grace. Those who saw Wesley, if they saw clearly, received at once the impression of holiness and power. A condescending Catholic has described him as "the shadow of a saint." And it was by virtue of intrinsic personal qualities that Wesley could turn men into the path of righteousness.

The cases we have given were among the most remarkable of the scores which occurred in the period 1739-1740, principally at Bristol. In every example, the sense of relief is instantaneous, though the phase of despair may be prolonged for several hours, or even for several days. The majority of those converted are women.

At one time, there was a curious prevalence of uncontrollable laughter among women, exceedingly painful, and accompanied by a shocking violence of movement. We do not know of any cases in which the conversion experience was followed by death or madness, although the charge of driving people mad was one commonly directed against Methodist preachers. The experience was followed, as a rule, by a state of religious well-being, of happiness and composure; nor was there any difficulty in resuming the ordinary business of life. Together with the authentic instances of conversion, there were some that were wholly fraudulent, and others in which the conversion impulse was met half way by the desire for notoriety.

Charles Wesley, who was invariably repelled by emotional scenes, and under whose preaching they seldom occurred, always suspected the presence of these fraudulent cases. The *outward affections*, he said, could be readily imitated. By 1743, he took up an attitude that was almost hostile in regard to what he brusquely called "the fits." He had detected many counterfeits, and many rogueries. On a certain day, "One who came from the ale-house, drunk, was pleased to fall into a fit for my entertainment, and beat himself heartily. I thought it a pity to hinder him," said Charles drily; "so, instead of singing over him . . . we left him to recover at his leisure. Another, a girl, as she began her cry, I ordered to be carried out. Her convulsion was so violent as to take away the use of her limbs, till they left her without the door. Then immediately she found her legs, and walked off." He announced that anyone who cried out so as to drown the preacher's voice would be gently carried to the farthest corner of the room, and left there. After this, he was rarely troubled with such disturbances. Yet, in the earlier days of his preaching, he appears to have been convinced that such things proved "the power of the Lord." On the 12th of March 1739, he recorded how "A woman cried out as in an agony— another sunk down overpowered—all were moved and melted as wax before the fire." Again, in September of the same year (at Bristol): "The breath of God attended His word. A man sunk down under it. A woman screamed for mercy. . . . Never did I see the like power among us." On the other hand, his earliest impulse was to repudiate energetically the idea of sudden conversion. He noted in his *Journal* a meeting which took place at five in the morning. "We fell into a dispute whether conversion was gradual or instantaneous. My brother was very positive for the latter, and very *shocking*. . . . I was much offended at his worse than unedifying discourse. Mrs. Delamotte left us abruptly." The quotation is of importance as showing the original belief of John and the original incredulity of Charles.

The scenes which accompanied the preaching of John Wesley at Bristol also occurred once or twice under the ministry of Cennick. But since the evidence for these depends mainly upon a letter written by Cennick himself, a man essentially weak and vain and highly emotional, it is evidence which cannot be accepted without reserve; and Cennick, on his own showing, was greatly assisted by the opportune arrival of a thunderstorm.

Many of the lay preachers of Wesley experienced the most violent forms of conversion.

Thomas Maxfield was converted during the Bristol revival in 1739. He was listening to Wesley at a meeting in Nicholas Street, when he saw a young man and then a little boy fall into convulsions. Maxfield fixed his eyes on the child, and "sunk down himself as one dead." He roared and beat himself on the ground, so that six men were hardly able to hold him. "Except John Haydon," said Wesley, "I never saw one so torn of the evil one."

John Pawson was converted by an unknown Methodist preacher: the change took place in the twinkling of an eye, and he was "brought out of darkness into marvellous light, out of miserable bondage into glorious liberty, out of the most bitter distress into unspeakable happiness."

Thomas Olivers, walking towards his house in Bradford, saw a ray of light descending "through a small opening in the heavens," and at that moment "his burden fell off."

The case of John Haime, perhaps the bravest and the most sorely tried of all the lay preachers, is remarkable for the prolongation and the acuteness of a state of despair. He was a soldier, pursued by the devil from his youth. He had visions of the world on fire; he saw the demon like a great bird, flying at him in broad daylight, and then standing in his way and glaring at him with dreadful red eyes. Southey would have us believe that the great bird of John Haime was only a bustard; but who ever heard of a bustard behaving like this? It is much more likely that it was really the devil. The fears of John Haime brought him to the verge of palpable insanity. Before his regiment left for Flanders, he had the good fortune to meet Charles Wesley at Colchester, and Charles Wesley spoke words of peace and encouragement. Haime fought at Dettingen, and faced the fire of the enemy for seven hours with extraordinary joy, and a somewhat incongruous feeling of love and goodwill. Soon after this, while yet unconverted in the true sense, he formed the first Methodist society in the army. At Fontenoy, the Methodist dragoons went into action rather desiring than avoiding death, and fighting with a new kind of wild bravery. But not long afterwards, Haime fell back into "his old miserable state." "The roads, the hedges, the trees, everything seemed cursed of God," he wrote in his own statement. "Nature appeared void of God, and in the possession of the Devil. The fowls of the air, and the beasts of the field, all appeared in a league against me. I was one day drawn out into the woods, lamenting my forlorn state, and on a sudden I began to weep bitterly: from weeping I fell to howling like a wild beast, so that the woods resounded. . . . Very frequently Judas was represented as hanging just before me. So great was the displeasure of God against me, that He, in great measure, took away the sight of my eyes: I could not see the sun for more than eight months: even in the clearest summer days, it always appeared to me like a mass of blood. At the same time I lost the use of my knees. . . . I was often as hot as if I was burning to death: many times I looked to see if my clothes were not on fire." Blasts of hot brimstone struck him in the face; he was tripped by an invisible power and thrown to the ground. Illusions of heat, flames and fire were continually in his mind. One night he was in hell; then he was on a volcano in the midst of a blazing lake. Still he preached, and after his discharge from the army he was appointed as a travelling preacher by Wesley. In 1766, Wesley, who understood his case, sent him to live with a family at St. Ives in Cornwall. Here, in one instant, the torments of twenty years came to an end. His affliction left him. He was a new man, a witness of God's infinite mercy.

After the Bristol revival of 1739-1740, conversion scenes under the direct preaching of Wesley became less frequent. For many years, indeed, conversions of the sort we are describing ceased altogether.

In 1758, not long before the famous revival conducted by John Berridge at Everton, there were a few cases, generally isolated. In 1761, there was a single case. At Stroud in 1765, three young men fell into convulsions; and in the case of two of these, Wesley observes that, as it was growing late, they *had not time* "to wrestle with God for their full deliverance." In 1772, a revival took place at Weardale in Durham, but the most typical scenes occurred when Wesley was not present. It is not clear that the Warrington cases, mentioned in 1780, occurred under the immediate preaching of Wesley. The *Journal* records typical conversions at Newcastle in 1786, when Wesley was eighty-three years old. In the same year, he noted "extravagances" at Chapel-in-le-Frith.

An endeavour should be made to separate cases of mere emotional disturbance from those of real conversion. The extraordinary scenes among the children and the maids at Kingswood School in 1768 and in 1770 presumably belong, in the main, to the former category.

Wesley himself was naturally interested in the happenings at Kingswood, and he set down carefully the accounts which he received from the masters in charge. A total failure to grasp the nature of a child was a weakness not peculiar to Wesley, but evident in the general outlook of his age. The Kingswood scenes, to us inexpressibly hideous, were accepted by Wesley as "the work of God upon children." At the present day our views, both of God and of children, are very different. Wesley saw nothing horrible in taking parties of infants to see a dead body, and nothing revolting in the idea of maids and little boys running up and down the dark stairs at night in frenzies of tearful apprehension.

James Hindmarsh, the master at Kingswood, first drew Wesley's attention to the events in the school in a letter written on the 27th of April 1768. "On Wednesday, the 20th," said Mr. Hindmarsh, "God broke in upon our boys in a surprising manner." His surprise, at least, was reasonable. Poor little creatures, from eight to fourteen years old, cried out for mercy all night in the darkness of "their several apartments." Even as Mr. Hindmarsh wrote, new cries were ringing in his ears. Some of the children "found peace," and others were "under a deep conviction."

In September 1770, a more dreadful visitation took place. Wesley himself had preached to the school, and had noticed "a very uncommon concern." About ten days after his preaching, the disturbances rose to their climax. Terrified children ran to the master in the playground, asking "what they must do to be saved." All night they cried and prayed, jumping out of their beds and falling on their knees. When the maid Betty was sent up to them, a boy called Jacky Brown caught hold of her and cried frantically, "Oh, Betty, seek the salvation of your soul!" At this, Betty "burst out into tears and strong cries," and was presently joined by the two other maids, Mary and Diana. On the following day, the three maids and many of the boys, "worn out as to bodily strength, and so hoarse that they were scarce able to speak," were "full of love, and of joy and peace in believing."

Wesley, in his *Short History of the Methodists*, gives many other cases of infantile conversion. In 1772 he produced something like a repetition of the Kingswood scenes in a charity school at Hertford. He recorded other examples, reported to him by the leaders. Yet, when he visited Kingswood in the autumn of 1771, he set down in his *Journal*: "It is strange! How long shall we be constrained to weave Penelope's web? What is become of the wonderful work of grace which God wrought in them [the children] last September? It is gone! It is lost! It is vanished away! . . . Then we must begin again; and in due time we shall reap, if we faint not."

The typical sudden conversions which took place in the actual presence of Wesley are most thickly grouped in the first year (1739) of the Methodist revival. In the fifty-one following years of his work they are relatively infrequent. There is thus no progressive relationship between the incidence of sudden conversions under the immediate personal influence of Wesley and the tremendous growth of the Methodist movement and of the new experience of religion as a whole. And we may naturally ask whether the peculiar distribution of these cases is due to a change in Wesley's attitude or to a change in general conditions. Probably there was a change in both. Religious fits were not popular; they were often regarded as a sign of weakness or hypocrisy. The charge of enthusiasm and of driving people mad was damaging to the prestige of the movement. In the course of time there was an obvious tendency, on the one hand to resist mere excitement, and on the other to avoid a technique which produced emotional symptoms. When spectacular conversion no longer attracted favourable or profitable notice, there must have been a falling-off in the number of self-induced or spurious cases; it is impossible to say to what extent the absence of such cases reduced the general statistics of alleged conversions. And we must also take into account a natural limitation in the number of genuine convertible types. That number must, sooner or later, have been exhausted in any given district.

Whitefield at Cambuslang in Lanarkshire in 1742, and Berridge at Everton in 1759 (new fields in both cases) produced violent conversions on a large scale. Whitefield spoke of people seeming to be "slain in scores," and being carried off like casualties in a battle. Berridge conducted one of the most extraordinary revivals ever seen in this country. But in neither case were the effects produced over a long period. The supply of convertible types was apparently exhausted.

But Wesley, after 1742, was breaking fresh ground. He had every chance of producing revival scenes comparable to those of Bristol; and yet they hardly ever occurred. It is necessary to discover his own views on the subject of these religious transformations.

When he described the instances of conversion which came under his own notice, he always chose words calculated to give the idea of a sudden, painful and violent process. People were "cut to the heart"; they were "struck by lightning," "wounded by the sword of the spirit," "in the pangs of death." God was "making bare His arm" and "showing His power," breaking the stony heart and subduing the proud. The Word came "like a fire or a hammer." The effect was that of a shock, assault or collision. The convert fell as though he was knocked over by the blow of a cudgel: one moment he was gaping at the preacher, and the next, he was down on the floor, with two or three stout fellows trying to keep him quiet.

It seemed to Wesley, at first, that such drastic experiences were partly, if not wholly, miraculous. They could not be referred to "natural causes." They might be divine or diabolical, but they were certainly brought about by some invasive power. Wesley did not understand the extreme suggestibility of the ignorant; he did not observe that the most violent scenes nearly always took place in crowded rooms, where every kind of suggestion was obviously at work; indeed, he was anxious to prove that they took place just as frequently in the open air, which was not the case. To begin with, he was not willing to admit the possibility of fraud. When he was eventually convinced that fraud sometimes occurred, he was discouraged and disappointed, but his views in regard to a true spiritual intervention in the majority of cases was unchanged. It would be incorrect to say that he tried to induce sudden conversions, or that he regarded them as necessary experiences. He admitted that the only real test of conversion was the change of life. When he heard of cases which had not come under his personal notice, he anxiously inquired for the fullest particulars.

With reference to the Bristol cases, he wrote: "Perhaps it might be because of the hardness of our hearts, unready to receive anything unless we see it with our eyes and hear it with our ears, that God, in tender condescension to our weakness, suffered so many outward signs . . . yet many would not believe." A little later, he said, "I have seen many hysterical and many epileptic fits: but none of them were like these, in many respects." He was ready to see, in the violence of the symptoms, the expulsion of "the son of wickedness." A case of mere enthusiasm was altogether different. He quotes such a case in 1742, when a man came riding through Newcastle, "hallooing and shouting, and driving all the people before him, telling them God had told him he should be a king, and should tread all his enemies under his feet." The man was treated by Wesley with proper firmness. "I sent him home immediately to his work." In the same year (1742) he "carefully examined those who had lately cried out in the congregation" at Tanfield. The result of this examination proved the sincerity of the converts, most of whom had "a piercing sense of their sins." In 1743, after examining the Newcastle cases, he said: "These symptoms I can no more impute to any natural cause, than to the spirit of God. I can make no doubt but it was *Satan* tearing them as they were coming to Christ." Here, for some reason, he saw, no longer the power of God, but the power of the devil.

In 1759, the year of the Everton revival, Wesley expressed a more critical opinion of these cases:

"The danger was to regard extraordinary circumstances too much . . . as if these were essential to the inward work, so that it could not go on without them. Perhaps the danger [now] is to regard them too little, to condemn them altogether, to imagine they had nothing of God in them, and were a hindrance to His work. Whereas the truth is, (1) God suddenly and strongly convinced many . . . the natural consequences whereof were sudden outcries and strong bodily convulsions: (2) To strengthen and encourage them that believed . . . He favoured several of them with divine dreams. . . . (3) In some of these instances, after a time, *nature mixed with grace*: (4) Satan likewise mimicked this work of God, in order to discredit the whole work. . . . *At first it was doubtless wholly from God*. It is *partly* so at this day. And He will enable us to discern how far, in every case, the work is pure, and where it mixes or degenerates."

Here, the attitude is critical and judicious. The possibility of counterfeit, and of "nature mixing with grace" is admitted; while the fact of true conversion remains unaltered. In 1786, five years before his death, Wesley speaks of Satan pushing the "lively people" of Chapel-in-le-Frith to "extravagance." "Just so," he says, "did the French Prophets, and very lately the Jumpers in Wales, bring the real work into contempt. Yet whenever we reprove them, it should be in the most mild and gentle manner possible."

The "real work," the conversion of tens of thousands, was wholly independent of these cases. Yet it must be admitted that the behaviour of the people at Chapel-in-le-Frith in 1786 does not appear to have differed greatly, if at all, from the behaviour of the Bristol people in 1739. They cried out, dropped as though dead, and then loudly proclaimed their salvation. But this was now looked on as "extravagance," begotten of the Father of Lies.

It would be too much to say that Wesley's views on sudden visible conversions had changed radically before the end of his life; but they had certainly changed in some degree. He was inclined to regard physical disturbance with increasing suspicion; he was not prepared to maintain that the only true conversion must be instantaneous. Yet the sudden conversions, and especially those of 1739, had a deep effect on his views and his teaching throughout the whole of the fifty years of revival. Whatever his last opinions may have been, he was greatly encouraged and greatly influenced by these phenomena. We can hardly doubt that the majority of the recorded cases may be allowed to have been varieties of religious experience, in the sense in which the psychologist makes use of that term. Their effect upon the mind of Wesley was incalculable, and they must have given a peculiar zeal and impetus to his earlier mission. No one who reads the *Journal* intelligently can doubt this for a moment.

Wesley never regarded these experiences as the crowning proof of regeneration, or as the most valuable results of his preaching. So far is that from being the case, that he expressly states the opposite. Writing to his brother Samuel he appeals to his "living arguments"—the lion become a lamb, the drunkard sober, the whoremonger detesting the very lusts of the flesh. He was willing to believe, as the Christian must believe, that God does not always go about His work in the same manner. And he concluded, wisely, that because a thing can be simulated, it does not follow that it is never real.

CHAPTER X

PREACHING AND PERSECUTION

IN 1740, Wesley definitely separated from the Moravians,
and at the same time vigorously repudiated the doctrines
of Calvin. His action was inevitable. No two things could
have been more opposed to his own teaching, to the entire
purpose of his life, than the quietism of Zinzendorf and the
Calvinistic theory of election.

The Fetter Lane society was now virtually ruled by a
Moravian named Molther, and in July 1740 Wesley was
told that he could no longer preach in their rooms. He
therefore read a paper to the society, explaining the differences between them, and then, announcing his withdrawal,
called on those who believed in the Methodist views to
follow him out of the building. Some eighteen or nineteen
people, mostly women, and probably including the Countess
of Huntingdon, got up and went with him. The Methodist
elements were now clearly severed from the Moravian group,
and those who left the society in Fetter Lane joined the
organisation at the Foundry. By the close of 1740, there
were Methodist societies in London, Bristol, Kingswood
and Bath.

Wesley abjured the Moravian doctrines; yet, in May
1741, he wrote: "I had a long conversation with Peter
Boehler. I marvel how I refrain from joining these men;
I scarce ever see any of them but my heart burns within
me; I long to be with them, and yet I am kept from them."

The immediate effect of the denial of Calvinism was an
open disagreement between Wesley and Whitefield.

An exchange of views on this matter had already begun
during Whitefield's absence in America in 1739. In 1740,
when the disagreement had become evident, Whitefield
wrote to a friend: "For Christ's sake desire dear brother
Wesley to avoid disputing with me. I think I had rather die
than see a division between us; and yet how can we walk
together if we oppose each other?"

This personal controversy became acute in 1741, accompanied by hasty printing and preaching, and by most unhappy recriminations. Yet it would be wrong to say that the friendship between the two leaders was ever broken. After Whitefield had returned from America in 1741 he wrote to Wesley, criticising the management of the society at Bristol. Wesley replied with gentle firmness: "Would you have me deal plainly with you, my brother? I believe you would: then by the grace of God I will. Of many things I find you are not rightly informed; of others you speak of what you have not well weighed. The Society Room at Bristol, you say, is adorned. How? Why, with a piece of green cloth nailed to the desk; two sconces for eight candles each in the middle; and—nay, I know of no more."

At the time of this unfortunate difference, with its profitless arguments about faith and election, green cloth and tallow candles, Methodism was never in greater need of unity. The Bristol clergy were refusing the Sacraments to the Methodist colliers of Kingswood. Virulent pamphlets, mainly directed against Whitefield, but attacking the Methodist position generally, were produced by the dozen. Fantastic accusations were levelled against Wesley, as that he had been fined for selling Geneva without a licence, and that he had large remittances from Spain in order to raise an army of twenty thousand men who would join the forces of a Spanish invasion and set a Popish king on the throne of England.

The first indications of mob violence appeared at Bengeworth, where Henry Seward pulled the nose of Charles Wesley, and at Upton in Gloucestershire, where Cennick's followers were beaten on the head with brass pans. In September 1740, a number of men forced their way into the Foundry, and began to speak "big, swelling words."

In the autumn of 1741, a far uglier sort of violence showed itself in South Wales. William Seward, a native of Bardsey near Evesham, and a man of some wealth, was at that time on a preaching tour with Howell Harris. At Caerleon, he was struck in the eye, and a few days later lost his sight. At Hay, on the Welsh border, he was brutally

struck on the head and killed. He was buried in the churchyard of Cusop. Seward had accompanied Whitefield on his
second voyage to America, and was a man for whom Whitefield had the highest admiration.

Wesley himself was first called on to face angry mobs
in 1741, during his open-air preaching in London. Stones
were flung at him in Marylebone Fields, and at Hoxton the
rabble tried to drive an ox among the congregation. Wesley
never compromised with a mob. He faced it with steady
composure, with pity, or with vigorous retort. On the 4th
of January 1742, he wrote: "On Saturday, while I was
preaching at Long Lane, a rude rout lift up their voices
on high. I fell upon them without delay. Some pulled off
their hats, and opened their mouth no more; the rest stole
out one after another. All that remained were quiet and
attentive."

By insensible degrees, he became an itinerant preacher.
We see him more and more frequently riding upon the highways of England; not upon such roads as we ride over to-
day, but on ways muddy, rocky and wet; grassy or marshy
tracks, full of pits, deep-rutted, narrow, abounding in quags,
covered with loose flint-stones, or not covered at all, darkened
by overhanging, unlopped trees, or washed away on the
open moors. On these highways, coaches were stranded,
broken or overturned frequently; trees for the Chatham
shipyards were sometimes two or three years on their way
from Sussex; old ladies were hauled laboriously to the parish
church in winter by teams of oxen. The account of the
journey of a prince and his retinue, travelling in carriages
from Windsor to Petworth, reads like the voyage of a
convoy in rough weather, with many wrecks.

Sometimes accompanied by a servant, Wesley rode hired
horses. He could ride from London to Oxford in one day,
in 1741, changing horses twice. In his later travels he
covered much greater distances between morning and
night; but a day for Wesley never meant less than eighteen
hours. Probably no man—not even the most venerable and
ferocious fox-hunter—rode over more English miles than
Wesley in the course of his lifetime. If his carriage travelling

is included, he journeyed over more than a quarter of a million miles between 1738 and 1790. But he was never a good horseman. He used to read books while riding, and as this meant holding his hands close to his face and letting the reins drop on the horse's neck, it is not surprising that the horse occasionally fell down or ran away. Wesley was often bruised by these falls, but the application of warm treacle on brown paper generally restored him. It is difficult to estimate his average speed on a journey; it would seem to work out at something like five miles an hour. His longest ride—ninety miles in one day—took about twenty hours.

No man, since Paul of Tarsus, had ever set out with a more burning desire to bring a knowledge of the Gospel to ignorant or heedless men. And like Paul, Wesley could not content himself with preaching alone. He left behind him organised groups of religious people, he appointed leaders, he made a parish of the greater part of Britain, a parish to which he attended with scrupulous and regular care.

He toiled with the unwavering zeal of a primitive Christian, with a new revelation of the apostolic fervour. He was no dreaming visionary. On the contrary, he was cool, orderly and practical. A spiritual impulse of the noblest kind was joined, in him, to a masterly sense of administration and a clear perception of the value of method. He was the gentlest and the most humble of men; but he spoke as one having authority under God. He was never bewildered by the extent of his work, or made impatient by the claims of detail. The salvation of a single sinner—a chance acquaintance of the road, an hostler, the serving-maid of an inn—would occupy the whole of his energy. No man was less capricious, less impulsive. His travelling was controlled by a carefully prepared schedule; his rare moods of irritation were almost invariably caused by loss of time. "There," he would say, with a shade of petulance, "are ten minutes lost for ever!" He always tried to avoid foolish people who might delay him by their trivial stories or their idle curiosity.

In the autumn of 1741 and the spring of 1742 he visited South Wales.

It is probable that a tradition of field-preaching in Wales had been handed down from the time of that strange irregular, Vavasor Powell (1617-1670). Griffith Jones of Llandowror, a Welsh clergyman, had also preached in every part of Wales, and had instituted a wonderful system of "circulating schools" before the end of 1740. Jones and his pious teachers had unquestionably prepared the Welsh mind for the approach of Methodism. Williams of Pantycelyn, another itinerant clergyman and the writer of some fine revivalist hymns, had also done much to extend the idea of field-preaching.

And yet Wesley was not conspicuously successful in Wales. There was something in the nature of the Welsh people (possibly their delight in dramatic situations) which led them towards the spiritual aristocracy of Calvin, and they were more attracted by the preaching of their own countryman, Howell Harris of Trevecca. Harris was a man of large views, in spite of his doctrine, and of larger sympathies; he tried to keep the peace between Wesley and the Calvinist group, and he regarded Wesley himself with the warmest affection. The name of Daniel Rowlands, the Methodist vicar of Llangeitho, and perhaps the most eloquent of Welsh preachers, must be associated with that of Harris.

A far more important move on the part of Wesley was his first visit to the North of England in May 1742. He reached Birstall, near Leeds, on the 26th of May, and there he met John Nelson. Nelson was a burly, plain-speaking man (we have already seen him listening to Wesley at Moorfields) who was now the leader of a Methodist group at Birstall. The uncouthness of his language brought upon him the disapproval of Benjamin Ingham, who was now living at his home at Ossett near Wakefield, and was conducting a revival of his own among the people of the West Riding. Ingham was under the spell of Moravian stillness, and, although he was a clergyman, the doors of the Yorkshire churches were shut in his face.

After preaching on Birstall Hill, Wesley proceeded to

Newcastle. He left Birstall on the 27th of May, and reached Newcastle on the following day. The road distance between these two places is not far short of a hundred miles; so this was good going.

Wesley was accompanied on this journey by his servant, John Taylor.

After they had found an inn, put up their horses, and refreshed themselves with a cup of tea, they went out to look at the town. It was not the immense place that it is to-day; indeed, it was not a town of great size. But Wesley had never seen such a rabble of squalid, noisy, drunken, blaspheming wretches. Even the grubby children cursed and swore and fought and tumbled in the gutters. Filth, misery and degradation showed that a prosperous England was already laying the base of her new industrial greatness. Enterprising men had perceived the blessings of cheap labour. Five churches, a Catholic chapel and a Quaker meeting-house indicated a thoughtful provision for religious needs. And yet there seemed little religion in Newcastle.

On Sunday morning at seven o'clock, John Wesley and John Taylor stood in the Sandgate and began to sing the hundredth psalm. "Three or four people came out to see what was the matter, who soon increased to four or five hundred. I suppose there might be twelve or fifteen hundred before I had done preaching."

Wesley had lighted the torch. There is nothing in the whole splendid history of Methodism which equals the sudden blaze of the Newcastle revival. Nor is there anything in Wesley's *Journal* more beautifully eloquent than his simple account of this preaching:

"Observing the people when I had done to stand gaping and staring upon me, with the most profound astonishment, I told them, 'If you desire to know who I am, my name is John Wesley; at five in the evening, with God's help, I design to preach here again.' At five, the hill on which I designed to preach was covered from the top to the bottom. I never saw so large a number of people together, either at Moorfields or at Kennington

Common. I knew it was not possible for the one half to hear, although my voice was then strong and clear, and I stood so as to have them all in view, as they were ranged on the side of the hill."

He was pressed to stay in Newcastle, but he could not do so, because he was due at Birstall again on Tuesday evening. Newcastle, now awakened, became soon the strong centre of Methodism in the north.

On the 5th of June, travelling by shorter stages, Wesley came to Epworth. He had not been there for many years. His father's church was now in the hands of a curate, Mr. Romley—a man of a sullen, formal and bigoted disposition, but no doubt extremely loyal to his bishop. Romley at once rejected Wesley's offer of assistance, and himself preached a loud and sour sermon upon the character of an *enthusiast*. This, of course, was a challenge. As the people came away from the church, they found John Taylor standing at the gate, and telling them: "Mr. Wesley, not being permitted to preach in the church, designs to preach here at six o'clock."

A great concourse of people, perhaps wondering if Mr. Romley would make a scene, came to the churchyard at six o'clock, and saw John Wesley standing upon his father's tombstone. Such a large congregation, he said, had never before gathered at Epworth. We must remember that Wesley was becoming celebrated, and the people of a man's birthplace are generally proud of his celebrity, even if they disapprove of him. He chose for his text: "The kingdom of heaven is not meat and drink; but righteousness, and peace, and joy in the Holy Ghost."

He stayed in Epworth for eight days, preaching there and in the neighbouring villages; and every evening he stood on the tombstone and addressed the people. On the sixth day of his preaching in the churchyard, several "dropped down as dead." A well-known unbelieving gentleman stood motionless, with gaping mouth, and fixed eyes looking upwards. The sermon was ended, but the poor gentleman was still there, gaping and staring like one struck by a sort of perpendicular paralysis. Wesley went up to him. "Sir,

are you a sinner?" "Sinner enough," he replied in a deep
and broken voice, but without moving. His wife and servants, all in tears, put him into his chaise and drove him
home.

Dejected Whitelamb, that feeble and pallid creature, was
living apathetically at Wroote. He sent a maundering letter
to Wesley, in which he said: "Your presence creates an
awe, as if you were an inhabitant of another world. . . . I
am quite forgotten. None of the family ever honours me
with a line. . . . I have been passionate, fickle, a fool;
but I hope I shall never be ungrateful." Wesley hastened
to Wroote, and preached in the church there. And poor
Whitelamb wrote to Charles: "I had the honour and happiness of seeing and conversing with my brother John. He
behaved to me truly like himself. I found in him what I
have always experienced heretofore—the gentleman, the
friend, the brother, and the Christian."

On the 28th of June, Wesley returned to Bristol. On the
18th of July, hearing of his mother's illness, he set out for
London. Mrs. Wesley died at the Foundry on the 23rd of
July, and was buried in the presence of "an almost innumerable company" at Bunhill Fields.

At the beginning of November he was in Newcastle
again, greeted with affection by the "wild, loving, staring
Society" of sailors, colliers and keelmen. His brother
Charles had been there some weeks before. Immense
multitudes came to hear him, but Wesley was at first disappointed by the absence of spectacular conversions. He
still regarded these conversions as a test of the depth and
power of a revival. He was therefore glad to observe, a few
days after he had arrived, that some people "dropped down
as dead" in the usual manner. He also observed "that here
the very best people, so-called, were as deeply convinced
as open sinners." Indeed, some of the very best people were
"constrained to roar aloud for the disquietness of their
hearts; and these generally not young (as in other places),
but either middle-aged or well stricken in years."

At Wickham, three miles from Newcastle, he was not
successful. "I spoke strong rough words; but I did not

perceive that any regarded what was spoken. The people indeed were exceeding quiet, and the cold kept them from falling asleep."

The task of consolidating his work in Newcastle kept Wesley there for about six weeks. It was necessary to obtain a house to accomodate the large society which was now in existence, and to serve as a headquarters for future administration and development. No such house could be found, so Wesley decided to build one. He secured a piece of ground outside the gate of Pilgrim Street, and on the 20th of December laid the foundation stone of a building which was estimated to cost seven hundred pounds. Wesley, after paying the deposit on the land, had twenty-six shillings left to go towards the building fund. It is characteristic of his sublime confidence that he ordered the work to proceed without delay. So was built one of the largest and most famous of Methodist centres, the "Orphan House" of Newcastle.

In 1742, the societies at Bristol, Kingswood and the Foundry were greatly increased, and new societies were founded, not only at Newcastle, but at various places in Warwick, Leicester, Somerset, Gloucester, and Wiltshire.

As the Methodist movement grew, Wesley created, or rather adopted, a simple though extremely efficient form of organisation. The people were divided into "classes," each with a supervisor or leader. A subscription of a penny a week was collected from each member, and thus a considerable revenue was raised to meet the current expenses. At the same time the discipline of the societies was tightened. Those who walked unworthily were dismissed, and none was admitted without giving a proof of religious intentions. No lay preacher was appointed except by the sanction of Wesley himself. A sectarian appearance was undoubtedly given to the movement by these regulations, and the hostility against the Methodists became of a more general kind.

The first serious outbreak of violence occurred in the Walsall district of Staffordshire. Charles Wesley had preached at Wednesbury in November 1742, and John had followed him in January 1743. A society of about one hundred members was then formed. Eggington, the vicar of Wednesbury, was at that time extremely well disposed towards Wesley and the Methodists. But after Wesley came a noisy Welshman, who called the clergy dumb dogs, and then some ignorant fellows from London. The Methodists, exhilarated by the language of these uncouth leaders, loudly asserted that all Church people were damned. It is not surprising that, in view of such a statement, Eggington changed his opinion of the Wednesbury society, and preached against Methodism "with great bitterness of voice and manner." Wesley came to the place in April, and tried to restore order, and Charles visited the district in May. By this time, ferocious mobs, openly encouraged by the local magistrates and clergy, had established a reign of violence. The houses of the Wednesbury Methodists were wrecked, even pregnant women were villainously abused, men were beaten till they were nearly dead, and the flinging of stones and mud was an ordinary daily procedure.

John Wesley, as soon as he heard of these riots, hurried to the assistance of his people. He arrived at Wednesbury on the 22nd of June, and found that matters were a little easier. He came again in the autumn. On the 20th of October, he rode from Birmingham to Wednesbury. Here he was forced by the Wednesbury rioters to go with them to the houses of two magistrates in succession, but as it was now night, the magistrates refused to get out of bed. A pitched battle took place between the mobs of Wednesbury and Walsall, and Wesley was taken prisoner by the latter. It seemed as though nothing could save him from death. He was in the hands of a murderous rabble, in the open fields, on a dark, rainy night. Yet he was all the time as perfectly composed as if he was sitting in his study. He escaped; and we may see in this escape, as Wesley saw in it, the hand of God.

Wesley's behaviour in the face of mobs must be treated of in a separate chapter. His immense courage, and above all his calmness and wonderful restraint, deeply impressed the popular mind and gave him the reputation of a man set apart by providence.

Charles, following his brother's example, had also become a travelling evangelist. In order to obtain a maximum result, it was agreed that the two brothers should not travel together. Charles visited Cornwall, for the first time, in July 1743.

The Cornish mobs raised against Methodism equalled in mere stupidity and brutality those of Staffordshire. Men who were capable of battering to death the survivors of wrecked vessels, or of cutting off their hands as they clung to the rocks, could not be described as choice examples of civilisation. A certain roughness might be expected from such men. But the attitude of the clergy and the landowners (they can hardly be called the gentlefolk) was even more shocking. It is deplorable to find a man of culture like Dr. Borlase, one of the most respectable inventors of Druid antiquities, persecuting the Wesleys and their preachers with idiotic anger and a villainous disregard of justice. Yet Borlase was both a magistrate and a clergyman.

A mob at St. Ives, on the 22nd of July, broke into the meeting-house where Charles Wesley was preaching, completely wrecked all the furniture, beat down the women and trampled upon them, and finally fought and quarrelled among themselves. They were led by the town clerk. Stone-throwing and assaults upon women became frequent. It was only after the energetic intervention of the mayor that something like order was restored in the town.

John Wesley came to Cornwall at the end of August 1743. He spent about three weeks in the county. In places (as at St. Ives) he met with a mixed reception; in others, the people were glad to see him; in others, they were hostile. He first preached in or near the green pit of Gwennap, near Redruth, on the 3rd of September. At St. Just, his preaching seems to have been always acceptable, and there he found a large and attentive congregation. On the 13th of September, he went to the Scilly Isles. On the 20th of the same month, he preached again at Gwennap; this time to a congregation of ten thousand. The "natural amphitheatre" of Gwennap, a great hollow among the fields, was to become the most famous of his open-air meeting-places.

In 1774 there was "a hot persecution" of Methodists in Cornwall, and the preaching-house at St. Ives was pulled down. Preachers and other Methodists were illegally pressed for the army, John Nelson among them. Nelson was eventually discharged through the influence of Lady Huntingdon; but Thomas Beard, another pressed man, died in hospital at Newcastle.

Persecution, like war, and indeed like every sort of violence, ultimately recoils upon the aggressor and strengthens the cause of the persecuted. Wesleyan Methodism became, within twenty years, the most vital religious force, and hence the most vital agent of civilisation, in Cornwall. Dr. Borlase fumed impotently against those he was pleased to call "a parcel of mad, crazy-headed fellows."

The first Methodist Conference was begun at the Foundry on the 25th of June 1744. Wesley recorded this with curious brevity: "Monday the 25th and the following days we spent in conference with many of our brethren (come from several parts), who desire nothing but to save their own souls, and those that hear them." Yet here was the institution of the controlling executive, which still remains the central administrative body of the Wesleyan Church.

It is important to notice that four clergymen, in addition to the Wesleys, were present at this Conference: Hodges, of Wenvoe in Glamorganshire; Piers, of Bexley; Taylor, of Quinton in Gloucestershire; and Meriton from the Isle of Man. Four of Wesley's lay preachers were also present. The Conference was therefore presided over by a majority of clergymen of the Church of England.

At this Conference, as at those which followed annually, matters of policy, discipline and administration were carefully discussed, and rules were drawn up for the guidance or control of the workers. It was decided that Methodists were to defend the doctrines of the Church of England; that their purpose, by the will of God, was to reform the nation, and more particularly the Church; that lay assistants were only to be used in cases of necessity; that tickets of admission were only to be issued to candidates for membership after they had been on probation for three months; and that it was lawful for Methodists to bear arms. Lay preachers were instructed to avoid affectation or wild gestures, and not to introduce hymns of their own composing: they were advised, after preaching, to take lemonade, candied orange-peel, or soft warm ale; but at all costs to have no late supper or egg and wine. And here it may be profitable to give a few of the excellent maxims which Wesley afterwards drew up for his preachers:

"Endeavour to speak in public just as you do in common conversation.

"Labour to avoid the odious custom of coughing and spitting while you are speaking. And if at some times you cannot wholly avoid it, yet take care you do not stop in the middle of a sentence, but only at such times as will least interrupt the sense of what you are delivering.

"To drawl is worse than to hurry.

"The good and honourable actions of men should be described with a full and lofty accent; wicked and infamous actions, with a strong and earnest voice, and such a tone as expresses horror and detestation.

"The mouth must never be turned awry; neither must you bite or lick your lips, or shrug your shoulders, or lean upon your elbow; all which give just offence to the spectators.

"Never clap your hands, nor thump the pulpit.

"Your hands are not to be in perpetual motion: this the ancients called the babbling of the hands.

"And when, by such assistances as these, you have acquired a good habit of speaking, you will no more need any tedious reflections upon this art, but will speak as easily as gracefully."

Methodism was essentially a democratic organisation; the lay preachers were simple, fervent, rough men, working chiefly among the industrial classes. The first large Methodist communities were established among the sailors and keelmen of Newcastle, the Bristol colliers, and the tinners of Cornwall.

In addition to the unquestioned value of popular preaching, there was another factor of vital importance: the Methodist congregation was a singing congregation, with a vast repertory of original hymns. These hymns, sung often to lively and well-known tunes, brought into the movement that cheering element of concerted praise which has always been a strong and attractive feature in Protestant churches. Pious rhymes are readily memorised; pious rhymes with good tunes are the marching music of a church, and the happy, familiar music of pious families. Nothing tends more to unite a simple people in loyalty and affection than the common knowledge of a chorus. And the merit of a hymn, or at least its peculiar social merit, is that all the people sing it together—it is all chorus. You can measure the fervour of a revolution, or a religious movement, by the fervour of its popular music. A new kind of hymnal, full of gay, comforting, solemn or militant verses, became one of the treasured books of Methodism. The author of the greatest number of these verses was Charles Wesley.

CHAPTER XI

BROTHER CHARLES

HIS brother Charles was the man for whom John Wesley felt the deepest personal affection, even if they differed a little sharply at times. This alone would make the character of Charles a matter of interest. But Charles Wesley, though he was not the director of the Methodist revival, played a part in the earlier campaign nearly as important as that of John himself. Not only was he a fighter and administrator of the first rank; he wrote the great songs and lyrics of revival which gave to the new spirit a form so cheerful, so living, friendly and harmonious.

Charles was born at Epworth in 1707, two years before the fire at the rectory. He was a sickly child. When he was five years old, his mother firmly undertook his instruction, and it is interesting to find the regular singing of psalms included in her schedule.

Although he was a delicate boy, Charles had a gay spirit, he loved fun, and was apt to be somewhat quarrelsome. Susannah Wesley, if she "broke the wills" of her children, certainly did not break the character of her sons. When he went up to Westminster at the age of nine, Charles proved his ability at fisticuffs. He was jolly, quick and pugnacious, and fond of acting. In 1721 he was a King's Scholar. In 1726 he was admitted to Christ Church, Oxford.

Neither the affectionate firmness of his mother at Epworth, nor the prim severity of his brother Samuel at Westminster, had lessened the buoyant liveliness of Charles. At Oxford he met the serious and ascetic but always kindly John, who had only recently obtained the dignity of his Fellowship. Charles was not by any means disposed to take things too seriously. He was going to have a bit of a fling in his own way; he was no rake, no idler; but he saw no harm in amusement. "My first year in College," he says, "I lost in diversions: the next I set myself to study." Like John, he became a good classic, and a very fine Latinist.

We have already seen how, in 1729, he was the virtual founder of the Holy Club. In 1730, he graduated, and took pupils. At the beginning of this year his father wrote to him: "You are now launched fairly, *Charles*; hold up your head, and swim like a man; and when you cuff the wave beneath you, say to it, much as another hero did,

Carolum vehis, et *Caroli* fortunam.

But always keep your eye fixed above the pole star, and so God send you a good voyage through the troublesome sea of life, which is the hearty prayer of your loving father."

In 1733 Charles Wesley took his degree of Master of Arts. He was a steady, religious young man, clearly influenced by the High Church views of John, but with no wish to enter Holy Orders. On the contrary, he was extremely averse to the idea of becoming a clergyman. He was ordained—it would not be incorrect to say that he consented to be ordained—on the eve of the mission to Georgia.

Poor Charles was unsuccessful, both as a minister and a secretary. No one, not even saintly John, could have been less fitted to deal with the rogues and the harlots of Oglethorpe's new colony. He tried to settle disputes among the spitfire women, to whom his piety and zeal were equally offensive. He tried to carry out his duties as assistant to Oglethorpe. And Oglethorpe, listening to the stories of mischievous brutes (soldiers are always the most credulous of men), accused Charles Wesley of interference—nay, of downright mutiny and sedition. Charles, when he was ill, was left alone lying on the floor-boards. A shot was fired at him as he walked in a myrtle grove. His resignation was demanded, but the accusers could not prove their case, even with the fullest resources of hardy lying, and things were patched up. There seemed to be no end to his troubles. Never had a righteous young man been more horridly persecuted. Remembering what we know of Mrs. Welch and Mrs. Hawkins, who had plagued John in the same fashion, we can guess the nature of some of the troubles. In a *Journal* entry under the date of the 28th of March 1736, he says: "Both myself and the congregation (at Frederica) were struck with the first lesson: Joseph and Potiphar's wife." He resolved gloomily to starve to death, sooner than beg from his enemies. John came to Frederica and put an end to this folly; and Charles eventually regained the affection and the esteem of the moody and gullible Oglethorpe. In July 1736 he set off for England, full of dissatisfaction with himself, and full of despair at the cruelty, the rascality and the vice of the settlers. He was particularly revolted by the outrages on negroes, several of whom were tortured to death every year by Colonel Lynch.

He was in a state of extreme dejection after his return to England, and even felt "a cowardly desire of death." All his buoyancy had gone. It seemed as if, for a time, he had even lost his natural courage. A too early acquaintance with the cruelty and cunning of men had thrown him off his balance. But soon he was swimming like a man again, cuffing the wave beneath him, and raising his eyes to the pole star.

Like his brother John, Charles was a short man, neat, presentable and pleasing. He was fuller in body and softer in feature than John, and he did not possess John's tranquil charm of manner.

Soon after his return from America, and while he was in the lower deep of melancholy, he called on John's Aspasia, Mrs. Pendarves. She was at that very moment reading a letter which contained the false report of his death. "Happy for me had the news been true!" said Charles. That was in January 1737. By August, he had come to a more reasonable state of mind. On the 26th of that month he was chosen to present the University Address to the king at Hampton Court: he dined with the royal party, and the next day he waited on the Prince of Wales and dined at St. James's. Four days later, he was arguing with Law at Putney. On his second visit, Law ended their talk with churlish impatience. "Nothing I can either speak or write," he said, "will do you any good."

In 1738, Charles met Peter Boehler, and began to teach him English. Boehler was a more congenial guide than

Law; he taught Charles, as he taught John, that faith was a matter of personal experience.

On Sunday, the 21st of May, lying ill in the house of a humble London tradesman, Charles Wesley "found himself at peace with God." Three days later, he says, "Towards ten, my brother was brought in triumph by a troop of our friends, and declared 'I believe.'" Yet neither Charles nor John was wholly freed from doubt: at the beginning of June, poor Charles found that he was "utterly dead at the Sacrament," and three days later he "rose exceeding heavy and averse to prayer, and almost resolved not to go to church."

The experience of Charles, which resembled very closely that of John, was not the experience of a sudden complete conversion, but he still had to struggle with "the devil and his own heart."

Charles was now a believer in present salvation through faith. He began to preach this doctrine on Sunday, the 2nd of July, first at Basingshaw, and again "at London Wall." On the 10th, he preached to the men under sentence of death in Newgate.

Hangings were then so frequent as to be reckoned among the ordinary amusements of the public. People were hanged for pilfering a few shillings or stealing a piece of sarcenet; they were hanged for destroying ornamental trees or forging a seaman's ticket. There were considerably more than one hundred capital offences. Children were hanged. Women who had killed their husbands were condemned to be burnt alive, but the exquisite humanity of the English law permitted them to be strangled before the fire was lit. On a good morning at Tyburn, you might have seen as many as twenty people "turned off." On other occasions there might be only two or three. We remember the disappointed gentleman who came home to breakfast, and complained that "hardly any fellows were hanged this morning."

In ministering to the poor creatures in the condemned cells at Newgate, Charles Wesley was doing a noble work. True, they had the Ordinary; but the Ordinary was only a prison official, and he was not often popular. The exhortations of Charles, on the other hand, brought peace and comfort, and even happiness. We cannot read without a feeling of cold horror his plain account of scenes at Newgate or at Tyburn. He prayed in the cells with a sick negro, who was to die because he had robbed his master. He went with the negro, and nine other men, to the Tyburn gallows. "At half-hour past nine their irons were knocked off and their hands tied. . . . By half-hour past ten we came to Tyburn, waited till eleven: *then were brought the children appointed to die.*" The executions took place simultaneously at twelve o'clock:

> "The Black had spied me coming out of the coach, and saluted me with his looks. As often as his eyes met mine, he smiled with the most composed, delightful countenance I ever saw. Read caught hold of my hand in a transport of joy. . . . None showed any natural terror of death: no fear, or crying or tears. . . . We sang several hymns. . . . When the cart drew off, not one stirred, or struggled for life, but meekly gave up their spirits. Exactly at twelve they were turned off. I spoke a few suitable words to the crowd; and returned, full of peace and confidence in our friend's happiness. That hour under the gallows was the most blessed hour of my life."

It was not long before Charles, like John, was barred from the churches. In June 1739 he was summoned before the Archbishop of Canterbury, on a charge of preaching in churches where he had no appointment. The Archbishop forbade his clergy to admit the Wesleys. Charles began open-air preaching at Broadoaks in May 1739; in June he preached to ten thousand people at Moorfields. In August he set out as an itinerant preacher, and in the autumn he took his brother's place at Bristol. During the greater part of 1740 he travelled with Thomas Maxfield. In 1741 he was in peril of being misled by Moravian stillness. "The Philistines are upon thee, Samson," said John; "but the Lord is not departed from thee. . . . O my brother, my soul is grieved for you! The poison is in you, fair words have stolen away your heart." Charles was not long in error. He wanted to be an evangelist, and he saw that no true evangelist could hold the doctrine of quietism. For seventeen years he travelled and preached, at first preparing the way for his brother, and afterwards helping to consolidate his work.

The preaching of Charles was of a more cordial, familiar kind than the preaching of John. He was not an eloquent man, but he spoke with heartiness and bluff persuasion. His sermons, judged as mere performances, are mediocre. His effect as a preacher varied greatly at different times and in different places. For instance, John gives an account of a scene at Bristol in 1741: "I was a little surprised when I came into the room, just after he [Charles] had ended his sermon. Some wept aloud; some clapped their hands; some shouted, and the rest sang praise." But Charles, writing of his own preaching at Tavistock in 1746, says: "The word rebounded as from a wall of brass. So great a bar I have seldom felt; and was therefore forced in a quarter of an hour to dismiss them." And he observed on the 9th of August 1751: "I preached, but very feebly, on 'The third part I will bring through the fire.' Preaching, I perceive, is not now my principal business." His earlier discourses appear to have had a strong effect upon women, but he was never, like his brother or George Whitefield, a preacher of real eminence.

Charles Wesley's principal contribution to the Methodist revival must be looked for in the hymns which he composed with such facility, and often with such a true poetic impulse. Many of these hymns are well known to every one. "Hark how all the welkin rings," afterwards changed to "Hark the herald angels sing," was one of his earliest hymns, written in 1739. Others which are extremely popular in Protestant churches are "Jesu, lover of my soul," "Come, let us join our friends above," "Love divine," and "Soldiers of Christ arise." In general, the hymns of Charles Wesley are bright, happy and simple, with bounding gaiety of rhythm or the vigour of a quick march. He is more often in a mood of praise and cheerfulness than in one of sorrow or severity. He does not often turn to the spectacle of divine wrath, as in the following energetic lines:

> "Lo! it comes, *Jehova's* Day
> Of flaming vengeance comes,
> Seizes on its ready prey,
> And all the proud consumes;
> Root and branch the wicked burns,
> Fit fewel for Thy righteous ire!
> *Then* Thy wrath inkindled turns
> To everlasting fire."

And here he is illustrating *Select Passages* from the Scriptures, and the treatment has to fit the selection.

Popular hymns must be simple, easily remembered and easily sung; they must not exceed the proper dimensions of their form. But Charles could write poems of another kind. He could write satirically as in *The Man of Fashion*; he could sing with rending pathos, as he does in the verses on his dead child. Or again, in the *Mother's Hymn*, he could strike a full chord, in a way that almost anticipates the lyrical richness of Blake:

> "What follies abound
> When reason is drowned
> By a heathenish Nurse in a torrent of sound!
> When, by Satan beguiled,
> With sonnets defiled
> She angers her Maker to quiet her Child!"

Charles Wesley married, in 1749, Sarah Gwynne, the daughter of Marmaduke Gwynne of Garth in Breconshire. Gwynne was a man of very considerable wealth, a magistrate, and a man of high standing in the county. He kept twenty servants and a resident chaplain. He had been offended by the irregular preaching of Howell Harris, but Harris converted him, and Gwynne became a Methodist, or at any rate a patron of the Methodists. In 1745 he came to Bristol, and assisted the Wesleys at their second Conference. Both Charles and John Wesley were afterwards entertained at Garth.

Sarah Gwynne was much younger than Charles Wesley; she was good, amiable and pious, and well fitted to be his wife. We are told that she was a neat performer on the harpsichord. Gwynne, who might have endowed his daughter handsomely, insisted upon Charles producing an income of a hundred a year, and this was arranged by John out of the profits from the sales of their books.

The marriage took place at Garth on the 8th of April 1749. John was the officiating clergyman. Charles, John, Sarah and her sister Becky (or Betty), rose at four in the morning and spent nearly four hours in prayer and the singing of hymns, some of which had been specially composed by the bridegroom. After their marriage, Charles and Sarah travelled together for some time, but in the autumn they took a small house at Stokes Croft in Bristol, moving, later, to a new house in Charles Street. For over twenty years the Bristol house was their home, but Charles spent a large part of his time, up to 1756, in travelling; and from 1756 to 1770 he was frequently in London. In 1771, the Wesleys moved from Bristol to London, where they lived in a commodious house at number one Chesterfield Street, Marylebone. This house, with twenty years' lease to run, and cellars well stocked "with wine and abundance of table beer," was provided for them by the generosity of Mrs. Gumley, the aunt of Lady Robert Manners.

The marriage of Charles Wesley was an extremely happy one. Charles was not a man with an irresistible vocation for the work of a field-preacher. He was homely and affectionate, and liked the comfort and the sweet associations of his own rooms and his own fireside. After a final tour through the counties of Staffordshire, Yorkshire and Lancashire in 1756, he settled down to the more placid labours of the study and the meeting-house. He still preached regularly, when his health allowed him to, and assisted in the administration of the Methodist movement, but it may be said that he retired from active service in 1756. When he was established in Chesterfield Street, he used to ride every day to the Foundry, or to the New Chapel. He rode a white pony: the reins were dropped on the pony's neck, and Charles ambled along the quiet green highways from Marylebone, reading books or scribbling verses.

It was in the Marylebone House that the two sons of Charles Wesley, Charles and Samuel, gave their famous concerts. Both these young men were extremely gifted, and were admirable performers of the music of Bach or of Mr. Handel. Charles Wesley junior became the organist of St. George's, Hanover Square: he was introduced to George III by Dr. Shepherd, and often played to the king. Samuel was more of an artist—indeed, he was too much of an artist for his father's liking. Samuel had a scarlet court suit provided by the Earl of Mornington, his distant relative; he was rather a wild fellow, and joined the Roman Church, though he afterwards recanted.

The Wesley concerts were organised on a subscription basis: three guineas for a series of twelve recitals. Daines Barrington, and many cultivated and fashionable people, bought tickets; and it is interesting and pleasing to find among them old General Oglethorpe. John Wesley disapproved of this: he saw in these brilliant assemblies the danger of worldliness, and his worst fears were realised when Samuel joined the Romans. He has an entry relating to one of these musical evenings in his *Journal* for 1780: "I spent an agreeable hour at a concert of my nephews. But I was a little out of my element among lords and ladies. I love plain music and plain company best."

In his old age, Charles Wesley met many of the celebrated people of his day. He met young Wilberforce in the house of Hannah More, and gave him a blessing. In his concert-room he made a great variety of acquaintances. His little oddities of manner, his absence of mind and occasional sallies of temper were small disadvantages compared with his wide benevolence, his charity and piety and cheerfulness. He died on the 29th of March 1788 at the age of eighty-one. "He had no transports of joy," said Whitehead, who attended him, "but solid hope and unshaken confidence in Christ, which kept his mind in perfect peace." The last verses which he wrote were composed not many days before his death:

"In age and feebleness extreme,
Who shall a sinful soul redeem?
Jesus, my only hope Thou art,
Strength of my failing flesh and heart:
O could I catch a smile from Thee,
And drop into Eternity!"

Charles Wesley was not a great man, but he was a man
who rose, in every sense, very far above the common level.
In more than one respect he differed from his brother. He
did not approve cordially of the lay preachers and he disliked the effect of separation from the Church which was
manifest in the unification of the Methodist societies. But
he was not consistent. At one time he was more than two-
thirds Moravian. At another, and in spite of his repudiation
of the "Horrible Decree," he could assist Lady Huntingdon
and her chaplains in the special work of Calvinistic Methodism. Nor did his zealous churchmanship prevent him
from renouncing the orthodox views of the episcopacy:
and yet he was profoundly shocked by the ordination of
Coke in 1784.

On many occasions we find in Charles the qualities which
made him the fighting boy of Westminster. He was capable,
not merely of rocky opposition, but of headstrong violence
in attack. His anger was of the gusty kind; he was quickly
made calm again; and was nearly always restored to his
habitual serenity by an appeal to his affections. We see in
him traces of the alternate mutability and obstinacy which
we associate with emotional people: we have seen the same
qualities in the old rector of Epworth. He was certainly
more emotional than John, and yet he had sometimes a
greater degree of ordinary common sense. John would see a
miracle where Charles saw only a vulgar delusion, or a more
vulgar fraud. Charles differed from John, also, in being a
more sociable person, in having more time for drinking a
dish of tea or listening to a good tune on the harpsichord.
He was readier for the harmless amenities of life; a more
leisurely, indeed, in Johnson's phrase, a more "stationary
man." But in matters which seemed to him of importance,

Charles was anything but stationary. His violent intervention prevented John, in 1749, from marrying Grace Murray, and practically forced Grace to marry another man. It is impossible to say what would have happened to John if Charles had remained stationary in this case, but the methods of Charles, as we shall see in Chapter XIV, were not those of a very prudent or a very generous man.

Perhaps the chief spiritual difference between the brothers was, that Charles was led by solid convictions resting upon a purely doctrinal basis, and John was led by a true vision of divine truth. Charles we think of as a dear, homely fellow, responsive to little cares and great affections; and John as a man who walked upon the higher ways of saintliness, often, in spite of his practical mind, with a perplexing indifference to the joys or tribulations of ordinary people.

But John could not escape the penetrating sorrow of bereavement. He was an old man of eighty-five when his brother died. When he received the news, he was on a preaching tour in the central and northern counties. At Bolton, as he read aloud the verse of a hymn to his chapel congregation, he came on the words:

"My company before is gone,
And I am left alone with Thee."

The words were those of his brother Charles. For the first time in a ministry of fifty years, Wesley broke down in public under the stress of a personal emotion. He burst into a flood of tears, sat down in the pulpit, and covered his face with his hands.

At that time, John Wesley was probably the best loved man in England, with friends in nearly every town and village in the kingdom; but no friend could take the place of brother Charles, the warm-hearted man who had shared in all the trials and dangers of the early work, and whose very mistakes were so often due to his impulsive loyalty.

CHAPTER XII

LADY SELINA

IN the England of Chesterfield, Bolingbroke and Horace Walpole, religious ladies were generally supposed to be mad. When we look at Lady Huntingdon's portrait, and observe the lines and angles of her thin, hard face, and the curious intentness of her sunken eyes, we may wonder if her piety was entirely without fanaticism or the desire to command. We remind ourselves that a woman who is wealthy, a widow and a countess, is not likely to meet with serious opposition. Titles meant a great deal more in the eighteenth century than they do now; and not merely vulgar interest, but even piety and common sense and learning thought it proper to make obeisance to rank. Lordships and ladyships floated serenely in the clear skies of privilege, raised very far above the eye-level of the herd, and looking down with airs that might be affable, but were always patronising.

Lady Huntingdon enters the field of Wesley's life in two ways: first, as a source of revivalist energy, helping to make Methodism known to people of rank; and second, as the patroness and financier of the Calvinist party. Her part in reducing the hostility of the upper classes towards Methodism in general has never been properly appreciated.

She was apparently a member of Hutton's society in 1738. Her long life (1707 to 1791) enabled her to watch the progress of Methodism from the rise of the Fetter Lane society to the year of Wesley's death: she died on the 17th of June 1791, at the age of eighty-four; Wesley died on the 2nd of March in the same year, at the age of eighty-eight. Lady Huntingdon and Wesley were therefore two of the oldest survivors of the group which, in 1738 and 1739, had prepared the way for the great revival.

Selina, Lady Huntingdon, was the daughter of the second Earl Ferrars. She married Theophilus Hastings, the ninth Earl of Huntingdon, in June 1728. Their principal residence was Donnington Park in Leicestershire.

Even in her youth, the Countess of Huntingdon must have been exceedingly plain. The haggard face we see in her late portrait could never have made a claim to beauty. "Lady Huntingdon," says Walpole of an earlier portrait, "looks like an old basket-woman trampling on her coronet at the mouth of a cavern. . . . Poor Whitefield! If he was forced to do the honours of the *spelunca*." Nor does the exquisite anonymous person, who wrote her life so adoringly and with such fulsome flowing superlatives, ever suggest that she was personally attractive. But she was a lady, a really tremendous lady, whose thin lips and beaky nose helped to give her an air of authority and high birth. She turned away sternly from the follies or fun of youth, and even from the ordinary social amusements; she had "awful convictions of the certainty and eternal duration of a future state." From her earliest years, she appears to have been cold, reserved and pious. When she was a gloomy little girl, she had been profoundly impressed by a funeral, and at once began to think of her own approaching death.

It was natural for her to find herself in opposition to the distracted emptiness of the age in which she lived. She can hardly have doubted that most of the people she met were likely to spend their future state in a most disagreeable manner. Such a thought, far from giving her satisfaction, filled her with pity. Even Chesterfield, she believed, had a soul worth saving beneath his dry, composed elegance. Even a smirking ape, like Walpole, might be snatched from ultimate perdition.

Lady Selina was introduced to the new religious views by her sister-in-law, Lady Margaret Hastings. (It was Lady Margaret who afterwards married the Yorkshire evangelist, Benjamin Ingham.) A dangerous illness had the effect of concentrating her entire attention upon the religious life.

It is said that Lady Huntingdon, after this illness, sent a message to John and Charles Wesley. "Now the day began to dawn," we are told. "Viewing herself as a brand plucked from the burning, she could not but stand astonished at the mighty power of that grace which saved her from destruction just when she stood upon its very brink"—surely an exaggerated view of the case.

The Hastings ladies, Frances, Catherine and Margaret, were especially attracted by Ingham, and attended the meetings of the London societies. They had first listened to Ingham when they were on a visit to Ledstone Hall in the West Riding, and Ingham was preaching in a neighbouring parish. The effect of this preaching is thus pleasantly and respectfully described by Lady Huntingdon's biographer: "Under the ministry of Mr. Ingham, the Lord met these exalted females with all the blessings of His grace. They heard with pleasure, and drank in, like thirsty travellers, the refreshing streams of consolation; they made an open profession of the faith, and exhibited a bright example of female excellence to the world. . . . They were amiably condescending to all their inferiors, even to the poorest, and more especially to the pious poor." See what it was to be well-bred and religious at the same time. If they had not listened to Mr. Ingham, these "exalted females" might never have acquired the lovely merit of condescension.

Theophilus Hastings himself had a turn for religion. He accompanied his wife to the meetings of the Fetter Lane society in 1738, and was capable of asking intelligent questions about doctrine. His Lordship did not condescend to become a Methodist, but he was always well disposed towards the preachers, even to the point of inviting them to dinner. Donnington Park, says Tyerman, "became a sort of rallying place for Christian ministers and Christian people." Perhaps the Earl belonged to Wesley's category of "almost Christians."

But Lady Huntingdon was a member of the first Methodist society. She was in the meeting-house in Fetter Lane when John Wesley broke away from the Moravians, and she was probably one of the small company that rose and followed him out of the room. Lady Huntingdon was never as deeply impressed by Wesley as she was by George Whitefield, whom she first heard, presumably, during his London preaching in 1738. She must have heard a good deal about him from one of her friends, Lady Anne Frankland, one of his early converts, and it will be remembered that White-field had been assisted in his Oxford days by Lady Betty Hastings. A very delightful proof of Lady Selina's early admiration for Whitefield is contained in a letter to her from that stirring and sturdy old woman, Sarah Jennings, Duchess of Marlborough:

"I must accept your very obliging invitation to hear Mr. Whitefield. . . . Your concern for my improvement in religious knowledge is very obliging, and I hope that I shall be the better for your excellent advice. God knows we all need mending, and none more than myself. . . . The Duchess of Ancaster, Lady Townshend and Lady Cobham were exceedingly pleased with my observations on Mr. Whitefield's sermon at St. Sepulchre's Church. . . . Women of wit, beauty and quality cannot bear too many humiliating truths—they shock our pride. But we must die; we must converse with earth and worms."

Sarah Jennings was ready to admit that she might possibly learn something from the Methodist preachers. The Duchess of Buckingham, to whom Lady Selina had presumably sent a similar invitation, replied in a style more consonant with a proper sense of superiority:

"I thank Your Ladyship for the information concerning the *Methodist* preachers: their doctrines are most repulsive, strongly tinctured with Impertinence and Disrespect towards their Superiors, in perpetually endeavouring to level all Ranks, and do away with all Distinctions. It is monstrous to be told that you have a heart as *sinful* as the Common Wretches that crawl on the Earth. This is highly *offensive* and *insulting*; and I cannot but wonder that Your Ladyship should relish any Sentiment so much at variance with High Rank and Good Breeding."

And a few years later, Howell Harris wrote to Charles Wesley: "The Gentlemen in part of Breconshire and

Carmarthenshire hunt us like *Partridges*, but still the work prospers." Still the work prospered, in spite of the staggering impertinence of those who dared to suggest that lords and ladies might be as effectively damned as draymen or fishwives. The Duchess of Buckingham, in defending rank from the implications of such a rude theology, believed that she was only pointing out what must have been as clear as day to any person of sense. Lords and ladies, if they did not find their way to reserved mansions in paradise, were gently extinguished by an easy method of painless annihilation; and common wretches might take their chance of the brimstone pit or the burning sea. The Duchess of Queensberry, Prior's fair Kitty, in all the exuberance of beauty and youth, had wavered; she had listened with momentary alarm to the preaching of Charles Wesley and Ingham; but she had come back to the world again.

To people who wished, like Lady Huntingdon, to retain the privilege of aristocracy, and at the same time to enjoy the benefits of religion, there was something particularly attractive in the doctrine of John Calvin. According to this doctrine, all effects were contained in the first cause, whatever happened was simply the manifestation of a divine purpose, and there was no will outside the supreme will of God. Such a doctrine, abolishing at one stroke the possibility of individual choice, is the spiritual counterpart of the mechanistic theory. The supreme will fixes, at the very beginning of time and energy, an absolute order which cannot be changed. Conversion, therefore, could only be a revelation of destiny, and not even a sure revelation at that.

The strict religious application of a mechanistic theory can have only one result: you have to assume that every human soul is either elect or damned from the beginning of time. The true Calvinist does not hesitate to affirm that such is the case. And although the doctrine of free will cannot be thus abandoned without committing the Christian to a series of inexplicable contradictions, the teaching of predestination has the advantage of setting up a spiritual aristocracy. A person who is elect is palpably superior to a person who is damned. It is not so easy to discover why the elect should preach, either to the elect or to the damned; or how you can be sure that the damned are not preaching to the elect. Be that as it may, the possibility of "advancement" is not denied, and the chosen people, however illogically, do not believe in merely leaving well alone.

Lady Huntingdon found, in this individualistic religion, a form entirely suited to her way of thinking. It is impossible to say whether she adopted those views at the same time as Whitefield, or at a later date under his influence. Judging from her attitude towards the Wesleys before 1749, it seems probable that she was not a professed Calvinist until she had become closely associated with Whitefield. Huntingdon, no doubt, endeavoured to check any eccentricity on the part of his wife; but after his death in 1746 (the occasion of ninety-eight polite elegies) she was free to do as she pleased.

Whitefield was in America from October 1744 to June 1748. Soon after his return, he was frequently in the company of Lady Huntingdon. If Lady Huntingdon deserved her title of Pope Joan Huntingdon or the Queen of the Methodists, it would be proper enough to describe Whitefield as her favourite cardinal or her prime minister. For twenty years Whitefield, with his powerful and persuasive oratory, assisted Lady Selina and her party in building up the edifice of Calvinistic Methodism.

That Lady Huntingdon lost no time in getting to work is proved by a graceful letter from Lord Chesterfield, dated the 18th of June 1749:

"Really there is no resisting Your Ladyship's importunities. It would ill become me to censure your enthusiastic admiration of Mr. Whitefield. His eloquence is unrivalled, his zeal inexhaustible; and not to admire both would argue a total absence of taste, and an insensibility not to be coveted by anybody. Your Ladyship is a powerful auxiliary to the Methodist Cabinet; and I confess, notwithstanding my own private feelings and sentiments, I am infinitely pleased at your zeal in so good a cause. You must have twenty pounds for this new Tabernacle whenever you may think proper to demand it—but I must beg my name not to appear in any way."

The Tabernacle he refers to was the new Bristol Tabernacle for Whitefield.

For more than forty years, this grim, vehement and zealous lady, professing herself a worm and yet striving to rule in the most autocratic manner, built her chapels and launched her preachers. As a peeress, she had the right to appoint any number of domestic chaplains. She gathered round her a group of evangelical clergymen, some of them men of extraordinary ability, and most of them ready to accept the doctrines of Calvin.

Henry Venn, a Fellow of Queen's College, Cambridge, became associated with her in 1756. He was appointed to the living of Huddersfield in 1759; his health broke down, and he retired to the small parish of Yelling in Huntingdon. Venn is remembered as the author of the *Compleat Duty of Man*.

William Romaine, the best known of Lady Selina's chaplains after Whitefield, was the son of a French Protestant who had fled to England after the revocation of the Edict of Nantes. He matriculated at Hart Hall (afterwards Hertford College) Oxford, and became the curate of Lew Trenchard in Devonshire. In 1750, Romaine was the morning preacher at St. George's, Hanover Square, where his fiery democratic orations were the cause of much resentment. Crowds of ragged people came to hear him, to the discomfort of the genteel congregation, who liked to have the church to themselves. There was trouble of the same kind when he preached at St. Dunstan's-in-the-West. In 1755, Romaine became the follower of Whitefield and a subscriber to the doctrine of election. After his appointment as chaplain to the Countess, he preached frequently, both in her kitchen and in her drawing-room, with excellent results. He was the curate and morning preacher at St. Olave's, Southwark, and held appointments, from time to time, in other London parishes. Romaine was vulgarly supposed to have an accurate geographical knowledge of hell; he was actually a man of learning, not bitter in doctrinal disputes, and a strange example of theological hybridism. He took a great interest in astronomy.

Martin Madan, another of Lady Huntingdon's men, was an extremely popular preacher, with a passion for the oratorios of Handel. He had been bred for the law, but was persuaded by Lady Huntingdon, Romaine, and other pious friends, to enter the Church instead. Another influence had turned his thoughts towards Methodism. He was spending the evening with some gay fellows at a coffee-house, when it was suggested that it would be good fun if he ran out to hear John Wesley, who was preaching in the neighbourhood, and then came back and amused the coffee-house with an imitation of the preacher. Madan agreed that it would be an excellent diversion. He ran off, wickedly chuckling, to the preaching-room. But when he came back to his friends, he looked uncommonly serious. "Well!" said the expectant company, "have you taken off the old Methodist?" "No," replied Madan; "but he has taken me off," and he began to think less of the law and of coffee-houses, and the idle ways of the world. Martin Madan became one of the most celebrated of Lady Huntingdon's preachers: he had a fine presence, a big voice, good manners, and ponderous eloquence. He was a musical amateur of some skill, and wrote several choral pieces. His optimism and courage were such that he took charge of Lady Huntingdon's work in Brighton for more than a year.

Fletcher of Madeley, a man equal in piety and beauty of character to John Wesley himself, became known to the Countess in 1758. In a letter dated the 19th of March 1758, Lady Huntingdon, said "I have seen Mr. Fletcher, and was both pleased and refreshed by the interview." And Fletcher, in the simplicity of his heart, wrote with admiration to his friend Wesley, telling him that he had met "a modern prodigy—a pious and humble *Countess!*" Fletcher became the visiting principal of Lady Huntingdon's college at Trevecca, but resigned the post in consequence of the dispute over the anti-Calvinist Minutes of Wesley in

1770. He remained the friend of Lady Huntingdon and wrote many long letters to her.

Assisted by these, and other men who were less remarkable but not less in earnest, Lady Huntingdon brought into existence the straggling organisation of her special cult. Her leading intention was that of converting well-bred people to a clear apprehension of the advantages of Calvinistic theology. For this purpose, she planted chapels in Bath, Brighton and Tunbridge Wells. But it would be inaccurate to say that she did not take a wider view of revival. Her attempts to win the "poor heathen" in America and to bring the Gospel to "poor wicked Ireland" were at least sincere. And when she set out in rather a stately way upon her "preaching tours," with horses and coaches and the travelling pomp of a great lady, she did seriously believe that she was doing unspeakable good to the masses. Yet the tangible results which can be credited to her own initiative are surprisingly small. The Calvinistic Methodism of Wales owed its foundation to the labours of Harris and Whitefield, and in no small measure to the Welsh evangelistic clergymen, long before Lady Huntingdon became active. It cannot be said that the Countess gained any considerable ground for Calvin in the territorial sense. Her college at Trevecca was an isolated experiment; her chapels were isolated centres of endeavour. She never exercised that vigorous personal superintendence which gave Wesley's organisation such tremendous vitality. She was not really the Queen of the Methodists. She was only a patron. Nor was there anyone among her lieutenants who had a marked faculty for administration. Whitefield had no such faculty; Venn, Madan and Romaine were effective preachers, but with views on control and discipline which did not go beyond the boundaries of a parish. Associated clergymen, such as Grimshaw, Berridge and Fletcher, were naturally restrained by their own parochial duties. And although Lady Huntingdon was fond of devising codes and manifestos, she could only impose her will upon the domestic chaplains and the men who were employed to serve her chapels. The final secession of her preachers from the

Church of England, and their refuge under the Toleration
Act in 1779, affected only a very small body of men, and
emphasised very clearly the limited range and the limited
powers of her "Connexion."

We have to remember, therefore, that Lady Huntingdon's
value was essentially that of a patron, not lacking enthusiasm
or material resources—indeed, with a profusion of both—
but in no sense a great founder or a great revivalist. That
she was actually regarded in this light by the men who
worked for her is abundantly clear from their letters.

Take, as an example, the attitude of Whitefield in a
letter written to Lady Selina soon after his return from
America in 1748:

> "Ever since reading Your Ladyship's condescending
> letter, my soul has been overpowered with His presence,
> who is all in all. When Your Ladyship styled me *your
> friend*, I was amazed at your condescension; but when I
> thought that Jesus was my friend, it quite overcame
> me. . . . I just now rose from the ground, after praying
> the Lord of all lords to water your Soul, honoured Madam,
> every moment. As there seems to be a door opening for
> the Nobility to hear the Gospel, I will defer my journey
> and preach at Your Ladyship's. Oh that God may be
> with me and make me humble! I am ashamed to think
> Your Ladyship will admit me under your roof; much
> more am I amazed that the Lord Jesus will make use of
> such a Creature as I am—quite astonished at Your
> Ladyship's condescension, and the unmerited super-
> abounding Grace and Goodness of Him who has loved
> me."

This language, at first glance nauseous enough, is comprehensible if we bear in mind the conventional language
addressed to patrons in the eighteenth century. Whitefield
understood the position. He saw in the patronage of a great
lady not merely an example of condescension, but a first-
rate opportunity for extending his own work.

The Brighton chapel was paid for by the sale of Lady
Huntingdon's jewels, or of some of them; it was opened

in 1761. The more famous chapel at Bath was dedicated on the 6th of October 1765. In this chapel, the most elegant congregations came to hear Whitefield or Wesley or Romaine. People used to form parties, such as they formed for a rout or the opera, to attend the preaching of some fashionable Methodist. Whether the preacher was Madan or the godly Fletcher, Walter Shirley or one of the greater leaders, he was sure of a smart, critical and curious audience.

When the young Earl and Countess of Sutherland were both carried off by a "putrid fever" at Bath, the funeral orations at the chapel drew all the nobility in the city. Even more impressive scenes took place when that noble Methodist, the Earl of Buchan, died at Bath in 1767. The body of the Earl was taken to the chapel, and there it lay in state, "covered with black baize, and the usual funeral concomitants, except escutcheons." Tickets, signed by the heir, were issued to the nobility and gentry, and three hundred were thus admitted. Whitefield was the preacher. It may be doubted whether, at any funeral, there could have been better taste, or a more splendid oration.

Horace Walpole, who could not let slip an opportunity for gossip or sly observation, visited the Bath chapel, and wrote an account of it: "They have boys and girls with charming voices that sing hymns in parts to Scotch ballad tunes; but indeed so long, that one would think they were already in eternity, and knew how much time they had before them. The Chapel is very neat, with true Gothick windows (yet I was not converted); I am glad to see that luxury is creeping in upon them before persecution. They have very neat mahogany stands for branches, and brackets of the same in taste. At the upper end is the *hautpas* of four steps, advancing in the middle; at each end of the broadest part are two of *my* eagles with red cushions for the parson and clerk. Behind them rise three more steps, in the midst of which is a third eagle for pulpit. Scarlet arm chairs to all three. On either hand a balcony for elect ladies. The rest of the congregation sit on forms. Behind the pit, in a dark niche, is a plain table with rails; so you see the throne is for the apostle. Wesley is a lean, elderly man, fresh coloured, his hair smoothly combed, but with a *soupçon* of curl at the ends. Wondrous clean, but as evidently an actor as Garrick." And at the end of the letter is the memorable portrait of the Countess of Buchan, "who is carrying a pure rosy vulgar face to heaven, and who asked Miss Rich, *if that was the author of the poets.*"

The college of Trevecca, standing in the glorious landscape of the Breconshire hills, is more famous than any of Lady Huntingdon's many chapels. It was well situated for the experiment, close to the little town of Talgarth, but rural, quiet and pleasantly secluded. Trevecca House (now College Farm), suitably altered for her purpose, was opened by the Countess on her birthday, the 24th of August 1768. Whitefield preached at the opening; Fletcher was made president; Easterbrook was the headmaster, soon to be followed by Benson.

In this College, Lady Huntingdon proposed to train young men, ostensibly for any religious career, but by preference for the ministry of Calvinistic Methodism. Here she spent much of her time, and here, at each anniversary period, came an immense concourse of people to whom the students chanted their songs of pious greeting.

We need not follow the vicissitudes, theological, architectural and social, of this curious establishment. Its present condition is deplorable. It was the most successful of all Lady Huntingdon's private ventures, and the most original. We like to think of her walking by the green banks of the Llynfi or over the rising pasture-land with her melodious companies of earnest young men; always rather a grim lady, and a grey lady now, a trifle patronising, yet abundantly pious, with a strange mystical intentness in her sunken eyes.

But Lady Huntingdon had not retired indefinitely to this pleasant green vale of Trevecca. Her new chapel at Tunbridge Wells was opened in 1769. Her "preaching excursions" were continued. She gave most popular religious entertainments in her great house at Chelsea.

The most distinguished people came to the Chelsea house, to see Pope Joan or hear the preachers. Chesterfield

came, and Horace Walpole, the Duchess of Argyll, Lady
Betty Campbell, Lady Ferrars, Bubb Dodington (the friend
of Voltaire), George Selwyn, Lord Holderness, the Duchess
of Montagu, Lady Cardigan, Charles Townshend, Pitt,
Lord North, Mrs. Boscawen, the Countess of Rockingham,
the Duchess of Queensberry, Lord March, Lord Sandwich,
the Duchess of Manchester, and a multitude of others. It
must have been grand to hear Mr. Whitefield "improving
the awful providence" when Lady Essex and Mrs. Charles
Yorke "died rather suddenly of sore throats."

Few of these fashionable and eminent people were converted. The most notable gain was that of Lord Dartmouth,
who was the sole representative of Methodism at the Court.
But we are not to suppose that all these wits and fine ladies
came simply to be amused: Townshend, Walpole and
Selwyn probably came for no other reason; others were more
serious, and to many the eloquence of Whitefield was profoundly moving.

The death of Whitefield in America in 1770 deprived
Lady Huntingdon not only of a personal friend, but of the
man who gave to her religious crusade its peculiar force and
character. The great period of Lady Huntingdon's revival
undoubtedly coincides with the period of Whitefield's
residence in England between June 1755, and the summer
of 1763. During the last four years of his work in England,
from the summer of 1765 to the autumn of 1769, Whitefield was tired and broken, and he was no longer capable of
the prodigious oratory of his prime.

Lady Huntingdon pluckily endeavoured to carry on the
work in America. She inherited from Whitefield the estate
of the Orphan House at Savannah, with its profitable rice
and indigo plantations. Whitefield saw no harm in pur-
chasing "a large number of negroes" to work in the
plantations and thus to augment the revenues of the Orphan
House, or, as he preferred to call it, the College. He
considered it impossible for white people to work hard in
"so hot a country." In 1770 there were fifty slaves on
the establishment of the Orphan House, men, women and
children. One of the first acts of Lady Huntingdon as

the inheritor of Savannah College was to remit a bill to the agents, requesting that the amount should be spent in the purchase of a female slave, to be named *Selina*, "in order best to establish that period of my only receipt of money during the whole course of my possessing the trust . . . and that in your accounts it may fully fix and determine the time of this remittance, taking care that it may appear as by my special appointment of it."

But, with all the advantages of cheap slaves and a fertile estate, the work in Savannah did not prosper.

In 1772 a number of Trevecca students embarked at Blackwall for America, after a most touching ceremony of farewell. The ship lay for some days in the Downs, waiting for a fair wind; most of the students went ashore at Dover, and the ship sailed without them.

The agents at Savannah were not trustworthy. Heaven knows what became of the negroes and the plantations. The Orphan House was totally destroyed by fire. During the War of Independence, everything disappears in a dark chaos of muddle. In 1784 Lady Huntingdon could think of nothing better than to liquidate the affairs of the Orphan House estate and to sink the proceeds in a fund for a mission to the Indians "on a grand scale." With this object, she wrote two letters to George Washington. We do not know of any reply from Washington; the scheme came to nothing, and the estates of Savannah passed into other hands.

In her personal relations with John and Charles Wesley, at any rate up to the time of the Calvinistic broils of 1771, Lady Huntingdon was generally cordial. In 1741 she wrote anxiously to John concerning the Moravian tendencies of his brother. She invited the members of Wesley's first Conference (in 1744) to her town house, and received them with much hospitality. Her interest in the greater Methodist revival was not lessened by any ideas of emulation or comparison. She attended Wesley's Conference at Leeds in 1762, and followed carefully the development of his work, polity and discipline.

Charles Wesley, writing to his wife in August 1766, said: "On Tuesday next my brother is to preach in Lady Huntingdon's chapel at Bath. That and all her chapels (not to say, as I might, herself also) are now put into the hands of us three [the two Wesleys and Whitefield]." In 1769 Lady Selina paid a visit to the school at Kingswood. And in the same year the Countess wrote frankly to John Wesley, "I find something wanting, and that is, a meeting now and then agreed upon, that you, your brother, Mr. Whitefield and I should, at regular times, be glad to communicate our observations upon the general state of the work." The intention of this muddled sentence is clear, but the proposed regular conferences did not take place.

The attitude of John Wesley towards the Countess was courtly and generous, but always a little reserved. He said that she "was much devoted to God, and had a thousand valuable and amiable qualities." He could not often speak of her younger preachers with approval. He noted, in a *Journal* entry dated the 28th of August 1778, at St. Ives: "Those who style themselves My Lady's Preachers, who screamed and railed and threatened to swallow us up, are vanished away. I cannot learn that they have made one convert: a plain proof that God did not send them." Writing from Grimsby on the 2nd of July 1779, he said: "In this, and many other parts of the kingdom, those striplings who call themselves Lady Huntingdon's Preachers have greatly hindered the work of God. They have neither sense, courage, nor grace, to go and beat up the Devil's quarters in any place where Christ has not been named; but wherever we have entered as by storm . . . they creep in, and by doubtful disputations set every one's sword against his brother." So much for Wesley's opinion of the young men from Trevecca.

Lady Huntingdon certainly had a real affection for Charles Wesley and his family. In 1752 she nursed Mrs. Charles Wesley through an attack of smallpox in Bristol, and did all she could to lessen the anxiety of Charles, who was in London.

John Wesley preached for the last time for Lady Huntingdon at her house in Portland Row in February 1770. Not long afterwards, the Countess denounced Wesley's

Conference Minutes as "popery unmasked," and now, with no Whitefield to pour oil on the troubled waters, this precarious alliance was broken. Yet one of the last letters of Wesley to the Countess (June 1771) is written in a spirit of gentle reproach and with a warm assurance of esteem. In his final paragraph he says:

"Such as I am, I love you well. You have one of the first places in my esteem and affection; and you once had some regard for me. But it cannot continue if it depends upon my seeing with your eyes, or on my being in no mistake. . . . My dear Friend, you seem not to have well learned yet the meaning of those Words, which I desire to have continually written upon my heart, 'Whosoever doeth the Will of My Father which is in Heaven, the same is My brother and sister and mother.'"

Lady Selina died on the 17th of June 1791. She left behind her the reputation of an extraordinary character, whose piety and benevolence were more conspicuous than her understanding. Southey draws attention to the presence of insanity in her family, and it is impossible to forget that she was the kinswoman of the demented Earl Ferrars, who shot his steward with a pistol ball, and then came up to stand his trial in the dress of a jockey. Yet she was far more than a merely eccentric person, and her influence was actually considerable.

When Dr. Cornwallis, the Archbishop of Canterbury, gave balls and routs in his episcopal palace, and Mrs. Cornwallis astonished the world by a blaze of costly splendour, Lady Huntingdon went to Court and personally complained to the king of this ugly scandal in the Church. The king, professing his admiration for the brave lady and her good works, sent a sharp letter to Cornwallis and put an end to his entertainments. "I wish there was a Lady Huntingdon in every diocese in the kingdom!" said royal George. Her biographer tells us that she was often at Court, "and lost no opportunity of recommending religion to the attention of the great."

If Lady Huntingdon was autocratic, she had no thought

of continuous dominance in any affairs except in those of the Methodist Connexion which she herself had founded. In the matter of promoting religion she was unquestionably sincere. Her individual achievement was not of great magnitude, nor was it marked by audacity of conception or by the impulse of a strong intelligence; but it would be grossly unfair to say that she could have done nothing without her wealth and rank.

Nor would it be fair to judge her by the manner of her utterances. She was not a woman of literary habits or of sound education, and the expressions of which she made use are those of an artless, emotional nature, readily borrowing the worst conventions of a florid religious style. For example: "Glory! glory! be to our Dear Immanuel for the high favour shown to His poor Servants—chiefly raised by the students and Mr. Glascott!" Or again: "Dear Mr. Shirley is so blessed and owned of God at the Norwich Tabernacle, that I am constantly blessing and praising the Lord for the display of His Love and Favour to our poor unworthy Services for His Glory and the Salvation of precious souls. . . . All Glory to our divine Head for the success which attends our labours in the Lord's Vineyard!" This is not mere sanctimonious cant: it is an attempt to communicate the joy of a very excitable, a very zealous, and perhaps a rather fanatical woman. But remember, this woman had spent her life and her fortune with one single purpose. A little mad she may have been; never a hypocrite. It is, indeed, easier to defend her from the charge of hypocrisy than it is to defend her from the charge of fanaticism or of religious madness. Her failure to achieve anything commensurate with the intensity of her effort and the length of her life is not to be attributed to any mixture of motive or to any inconsistency of purpose, but to the instability of her disposition.

CHAPTER XIII

REVIVAL

JUST as the vulgar mind of to-day inconsequently applies the term Bolshevik to people who make it feel uncomfortable, so the vulgar mind of the middle eighteenth century inconsequently applied the terms Papist and Jacobite. The art of making these absurdities appear reasonable was then, as now, the special gift of the party journalist and the politician.

In 1745, the year of Prestonpans and the march to Derby, Wesley was often called a Jacobite. He was called, with equal sense, a Papist. Churchmen were alarmed by the astonishing growth of Methodism, and the ruling classes were alarmed by the spread of a democratic faith among the people. In June 1745, a Cornish lay preacher called Edward Greenfield was arrested on a warrant from Dr. Borlase. Wesley was in Cornwall at the time. He wrote: "I asked a little gentleman of St, Just, 'What objection there was to Edward Greenfield?' He said, 'Why, the man is well enough in other things; but his *impudence* the gentlemen cannot bear. Why, Sir, he says he knows his sins are forgiven!'"

So, with people making preposterous claims about forgiveness, and with something very much like a schism rapidly gaining ground, it was natural for the Church and the gentlemen to take up a more and more aggressive attitude.

Between 1745 and 1750 the attacks on Methodism were practically continuous. Rioting became more frequent, and took on a more serious character. Bishops were not ashamed to set their hands to monstrous libels against Wesley and his followers. Yet nothing could check the advance of the movement, and nothing could lessen the glowing energy of Wesley himself or the stubborn devotion of his men.

Wesley could never have built up the permanent structure of Methodism without the wonderful loyalty and courage of his lay preachers. He chose these men himself, and he rarely made a bad choice. There were fanatics like Bell and Maxfield, and there were lewd rogues like Wheatley; but the rarity of such examples among the immense number of preachers chosen between 1740 and 1790 is a proof of Wesley's knowledge of men, of his fine leadership, and the nature of his requirements.

The preachers were usually poor men. John Downe's widow was left with only sixpence in the world; and poor John Jane died in Ireland with one and fourpence in his pocket—"enough," said Wesley, "for any unmarried preacher of the Gospel to leave to his executors." They were sometimes the sons of tradesmen, like John Oliver and Alexander Mather; or soldiers, like Haime and Staniforth. There was not, among them, a man of birth or learning, or even a man who could have been described as genteel. Nelson, perhaps the most widely known of the preachers, was a stone-mason; Pawson was the son of a respectable farmer. Thomas Walsh, a converted Irish Catholic, and one of the noblest of this devoted band, may have had a rather better education than most of the others. The sufferings and performances of these men were little short of marvellous. Telford, quoting *Early Methodist Preachers*, says that Olivers, a Welshman, rode the same horse for a quarter of a century and a total distance of not less than a hundred thousand miles. If that is so, the performance of the horse is even more astonishing than that of the preacher. John Pritchard covered twelve hundred miles on foot in one winter and the following spring. In the matter of persecution, it is not easy to say who was the most savagely treated. Mitchell was thrown at night into a pond, and flung back repeatedly when he tried to get out of it. Nelson was beaten unconscious by some Yorkshire "gentlemen," and left for dead. Mather had a house pulled down over his head. Sticks and stones, filth and water, broken kettles and rusty pots, the bodies of small animals, and egg-shells filled with blood, were hurled at these good men in places where they were not welcome.

With such men working under his guidance, Wesley

organised the forces of revival. He himself was more active than any of them, and yet he found time for a large correspondence, for careful reading, and for the writing, editing or revision of an extraordinary number of books and pamphlets. He wanted to educate his people. He was not content to give them religious instruction only; he wanted to give them, in a simple and popular form, all sorts of curious and useful knowledge. All true knowledge, he saw, gave a fuller meaning to the praise of God. Nor was he concerned solely with the care of the mind and the spirit. Like every great missionary, he was anxious to promote general welfare, he gave particular attention to matters of health and cleanliness.

In 1746, Wesley founded a dispensary for poor people in London. He consulted "an apothecary and an experienced surgeon," and in the first three weeks he treated about three hundred cases. In the following year he published a work on the symptoms and treatment of ailments which he called *Primitive Physic, or an Easy and Natural Method of curing Most Diseases*. This curious book was one of the best known of his writings, and ran into many editions.

Primitive Physic, though rather a compilation than a piece of original research, is written in the clear, terse and fluent style of the author, and contains a great deal of really valuable knowledge. But some of the remedies (and some of the complaints) are certainly peculiar. To cure the quartan ague, for example, "apply to the suture of the head, when the fit is coming, Wall July Flowers, beating together leaves and flowers with a little salt." *Canine Appetite*, or the "insatiable desire of eating," is removed by dipping small pieces of bread in wine and applying them to the nostrils. For baldness, you are told to rub your scalp with honey and onions, and to "electrify daily." Bruises are to be treated with treacle spread on brown paper—a cure of which Wesley himself made frequent use. Another cure which he mentions more than once in his *Journal* is that for hoarseness: "Rub the soles of the feet before the fire with garlic and lard well beaten together." The most memorable of all the prescriptions is that relating to Old

Age: "Take tar-water every morning and evening . . .
or a decoction of nettles . . . or be electrified. . . . But
remember! the only radical cure is wrought by *death*."
And finally there is an excellent piece of advice: "I advise
all in or near London to buy their Medicines at the Apoth-
ecaries Hall. There they are sure to have them good."

To advocate electrical treatment in 1747 was not a little
remarkable. In 1756, Wesley procured a galvanic apparatus, and thousands of people were "electrified" in
Moorfileds, Southwark, and the Seven Dials.

It can hardly be said that Wesley, between 1745 and
1790, was more active at one period that he was at another.
His life was a noble monotony of preaching and travelling,
travelling and preaching; and wherever he came he gave
stability and inspiration to his societies. Those who are
anxious to follow him from week to week must turn to the
admirable pages of his *Journal*, and preferably to the Standard
Edition with its extracts from the smaller diaries and its
careful notes.

In trying to bring into our minds a living picture of
Wesley as he appeared to those who saw him and listened
to him, we have to think of a short, lean, muscular and
graceful man, gentle and restrained in movement, yet firm
and deliberate. He wore neat black clothes of extreme
propriety and plainness. His coat had a small upright
collar, over which fell the regulation white bands of the
clergyman. His breeches were simply fastened below the
knees, without buckles. The sleeves of a plain linen shirt
fitted closely round his wrists, and could just be seen below
the short cuffs of his coat. He never wore silk or velvet, or
anything which could be regarded as ornamental. Even
the fastenings of his shoes were of plain leather. When he
preached in the open air, he put on a black flowing cassock,
which reached to the ground behind him. Exact people
have inquired whether, at any time, he wore a wig: it does
not appear that he ever did so. All his life, or at any rate
from his Oxford days, he wore his own long, soft hair,
parted from the middle of the head, and falling in natural,
unstudied curls to the shoulders. His black hat, like the

rest of his dress, was severely plain, without braid or lace. On the road, he wore riding-boots, and in winter a heavy overcoat. At all times he was a pattern of neatness and cleanliness; and it is interesting to observe that what he most resented in his rough treatment by the mob was injury to his clothes. The danger of death never moved him, but he could not look without a sense of indignation upon a torn or muddy coat.

Absence of worry gave to his expression a peculiar serenity and confidence. His habitual aspect was that of good humour and temperate gaiety. No one ever saw Wesley in a temper. No one, until in old age he felt the sorrow of his brother's death, ever saw him give way to emotion. Winchester is right in saying that Wesley's countenance "betokened a singular union of firmness and benignity": those are the qualities which first of all impress themselves upon us when we look at any one of his portraits. His complexion was fresh and clear, weathered but not roughened by continual exposure to the open air.

He preached, on an average, about fourteen times every week. The first sermon was delivered at five in the morning, whenever possible, and between that and the second preaching of the day, Wesley might cover a distance of fifteen or twenty miles. His arrangements were always made beforehand, and nothing short of conditions which made travel impossible could prevent him from being in time. When he preached the Assize Sermon at Bedford in 1758, he could not stay to dine with the judge, because he had to be at Epworth, a hundred and twenty miles away, on the following night. He was not to be deterred by floods or snowstorms or darkness, and none but a very robust man could accompany him. But he would always turn aside to answer a call of real distress; he was always ready to go to the assistance of a persecuted or troubled society. His health was generally excellent, though at times he had touches of "fever," probably of an influenzic sort, or attacks of indigestion.

In the summer of 1745, Wesley was again in Cornwall.

At the time of this visit, the clans were rallying round the Young Pretender in Scotland, and it was easy enough to raise the Jacobite bogey in the south. To the credulous peasantry of Cornwall, or to some of them at least, Wesley was a Jacobite. Dr. Borlase, who, with all his learning and imagination, must have been in some respects an incredibly stupid man, raged furiously, and tried to press Wesley and his preachers for "His Majesty's land-service." At Tolcarn in Wendron, Wesley was told: "All the gentlemen of these parts say that you have been a long time in France and Spain, and are now sent hither by the Pretender; and that these Societies are to join him." This frothy nonsense, apparently unavoidable in times of national danger, had the effect of provoking a riot at Falmouth. In this riot, Wesley felt that his life "was not worth an hour's purchase." The story must be told later; it is enough to observe here that Wesley's calmness and courage in facing "beasts of the people" always had the effect, sooner or later, of bringing them to their senses.

On the 2nd of July, as Wesley was preaching at St. Just, there was a very peculiar scene. "Almost as soon as we had done singing, a kind of gentlewoman began. I have seldom seen a poor creature take so much pains. She screamed and scolded, and spit, and stamped, and wrung her hands, and distorted her face and body all manner of ways. I took no notice of her at all, good or bad; nor did almost anyone else. Afterwards I heard she was one that had been bred a Papist; and when she heard we were so, rejoiced greatly. No wonder she should be proportionably angry, when she was disappointed in her hope." And no wonder that mobs were hostile when they were foolish enough to believe that Wesley was a Catholic priest, raising forces for Prince Charlie.

As Wesley was finishing his sermon at St. Just, an important person called Mr. Eustick came riding into the crowd. He was armed with one of the many warrants which Dr. Borlase, in his perpetual fury, was so eagerly signing. "Sir," said Mr. Eustick, "I have a warrant from Dr. Borlase, and you must go with me." And then, turning

to an attendant preacher, he added: "Sir, are you not Mr.
Shepherd? If so, you are mentioned in the warrant too.
Be pleased, Sir, to come with me." Mr. Eustick was at
least civil: he may have known that the burly men of St.
Just were fond of Wesley, and were not deceived by crazy
rumours. Wesley and Shepherd walked with Mr. Eustick
to the inn where they were lodging. "Will you go with me
to the Doctor?" said Mr. Eustick. "At once, if you please,"
replied Wesley. "No! no!" said Mr. Eustick hastily,
". . . in the morning, if you will be so good as to go with
me, I will show you the way." The morning came, but Mr.
Eustick came not. They were told that he had been seen
coming towards the inn, but had turned abruptly into another
house. Wesley therefore went to this house and asked for
him. Mr. Eustick came down to the parlour with an
affectation of surprise, as of one suddenly reminded of his
business: "To be sure! I had almost forgot!—Sir, will you
be so good as to go with me to the Doctor's?" "Sir, I came
for that purpose." "Are you ready, Sir?" "Yes." "Oh,
well," said Mr. Eustick, "I am not quite ready myself. . . .
I will wait upon you in a quarter of an hour." Nearly an
hour later, Mr. Eustick came to the inn, and finding there
was no help for it, he called for his horse, and set out with
Wesley and Shepherd for the house of Dr. Borlase. But
Mr. Eustick was so artful in delaying, that he took an hour
and a quarter to cover between three and four miles, and
when he reached the house, Dr. Borlase had gone to church.
"Well, Sir," said Mr. Eustick to Wesley, "I have executed
my commission. I have done, Sir; I have nothing more to
say." And he trotted off down the lane.

Another curious encounter with a Cornish gentleman
took place in the afternoon. Wesley was preaching at
Gwennap. "I was reading my text," he says, "when a
man came, raging as if just broke out of the tombs; and
riding into the thickest of the people, seized three or four,
one after another. . . . A second gentleman (so-called)
soon came after, if possible more furious than he; and ordered
his men to seize on some others, Mr. Shepherd in particular." No one moved, and the fury of the poor gentleman

rose to a higher pitch: "Seize him, seize him!" he cried.
"I say, seize the preacher for His Majesty's service!" He
then rode up and struck several of his attendants, cursing
them bitterly for not doing as they were told. After that,
he sprang off his horse, ran up to Wesley, and caught hold
of his cassock. "I take you," roared the furious gentleman,
"I take you to serve His Majesty!" A servant took the
gentleman's horse, and the gentleman himself walked off,
arm-in-arm with Wesley. After they had gone for about
three quarters of a mile, the gentleman blustered himself
out of breath. Wesley observed that nothing could justify
him in thus seizing a clergyman by violence. "What!"
cried the other. "I seize you? And violently carry you
away? Oh no, no! Sir; nothing of the sort! You do me
wrong, Sir; indeed you do." And with a sudden happy
forgetfulness, he said: "I asked you to go with me to my
house, and you said you was willing; and if so, you are
welcome; and if not—why, you can go where you please."
He then got on his horse again, and escorted Wesley back
to his audience at Gwennap.

Such were the follies and humours of persecution, if
there is anything humorous in the silly escapades of country
bumpkins and the silly violence of crazy old bigots like
Borlase.

In the autumn of 1745, Wesley was in Newcastle, and
saw the town put in a state of defence against the rebels,
with guns on the walls and a blaspheming soldiery in the
streets. The poor people were in hourly fear of a Scotch
invasion. Men with horses, arms and servants came into
the town, and terrified citizens went out of it.

In 1746, Charles Wesley went to Cornwall. It was
rumoured that he had actually brought the Pretender with
him: Mr. Eustick came rampageously with a warrant to
apprehend him, and then faded away in his usual polite
futilities. Borlase could rant and stamp as he pleased, and
talk sententiously about spies and Romish dogs or sneaking
Jacobites; he could not check the advance of Methodism
in Cornwall; he would have done better, poor man, if he
had kept himself harmlessly amused and harmlessly deluded

with his Druid Seats of Judgment, his Rock Basons and his Altars.

By this time, Calvinistic Methodism was definitely associated with the revival in Wales, under the leadership of Howell Harris and the inspiration of Whitefield. Harris had the disposition of a peacemaker, and Wesley was more concerned with a general revival of religion than he was with doctrinal disputes. It was therefore understood that Harris and Wesley should work in concord, and that Wesley would not set up societies of his own in any town or village in Wales where the societies of Harris were already in existence. A joint conference at Bristol in January 1746 decided "that we [the Calvinists and the Wesleyans] should endeavour to strengthen and not to weaken each other's hands, and prevent any separation in the several societies; and that a brother from Wesley's society should go with Harris to Plymouth and the west, to heal the breach there made, and to insist on a spirit of love and its fruits among the people." In 1750, Howell Harris preached at the Foundry, and Wesley preached in Whitefield's Tabernacle.

Ireland had not yet been visited by Wesley. Methodism, in that land of Papistical dominance, had been first organised in Dublin in 1745 by a soldier whose name we do not know; he was followed in 1746 by Protean Cennick—first a Wesleyan, then a Calvinist, and finally a Moravian. Cennick was followed by Williams, a garrulous and indiscreet Welshman, who had been one of the causes of the trouble at Wednesbury.

But in Ireland the new revival had to face mobs of the most dangerous kind—religious mobs. Just as a quarrelling wife and husband will unite to repel an intruder, so the Catholics and Protestants united to repel a Methodist invasion. The Irish have a genius for agitation and a very striking manner of proving their independence. Nor were they inclined to regard any mission from England with particular favour. It is true that Whitefield had been well received in 1738 by Dr. Delany (afterwards the husband of

Wesley's Aspasia) and Bishop Burscough; but he was received as a visitor and not as a missionary.

John Wesley first landed in Ireland on the 10th of August 1747. He remained in Dublin for thirteen days. On the whole, he was pleased with what he found there. Rouquier, the curate of St. Mary's, was a cordial and honest man. Wesley preached to his "gay and senseless congregation," and Rouquier admired the sermon. But the Archbishop of Dublin would suffer no irregularities in his diocese; he would not tolerate lay preachers or religious meetings in the open air. Wesley met the Archbishop at Newbridge and had a long conversation with him: the Archbishop was not unfriendly, and Wesley was able to answer many of his objections.

The Marlborough Street society in Dublin was examined by Wesley, who found it full of zealous people, perhaps a little lacking in discipline. He did not make any attempt to extend the Irish mission at that time. His visit was in the nature of a reconnaissance. The great majority of the people were Catholics. He was not deterred by this, for he knew, as Dr. Simon observes with a rather surprising irony, "that it was possible to win the attention of Roman Catholics to the great doctrines of the gospel."

On the 9th of September 1747, Charles Wesley arrived in Dublin. Not long before, the mob had broken into the meeting-house in Marlborough Street, burnt the furniture, and looted a store-room on the floor above. On the evening of his arrival, Charles met a few sturdy people, who feared neither men nor devils nor a Catholic mob, in the ruins of the meeting-room.

Charles remained in Ireland for six months. He advanced the work of Methodism, but he had more than once to face a murderous rabble.

John Wesley returned to Ireland on the 8th of March 1748, and preached with particular success to the troops. He was nearly always popular with soldiers, who admired his pluck and his neat, manly bearing. But on this occasion he was tired, sometimes ill, and often discouraged by the indifference or hostility of the people. He went over again in April 1749, and in June he was in Cork. We shall have to refer later to the Cork riots of 1749-1750.

The educational experiment at Kingswood was greatly extended in the summer of 1748. The Kingswood school, as we have seen, was founded by Whitefield and was opened in 1740. It was originally intended for the instruction of colliers' children, but presently Methodists of all kinds began to send their children there. Wesley was therefore obliged to enlarge the original establishment. An "unknown lady" contributed eight hundred pounds towards the expense of a new building. This new building was added to the old one, and could accommodate fifty children, with a small staff of masters and servants. All the pupils were boarders. One room and a small study were reserved for Wesley himself. The children admitted to the school were to be within the ages of six and twelve, and they were taught reading, writing, arithmetic, English, French, Latin, Greek, Hebrew, history, geography, rhetoric, logic, ethics, geometry, algebra, physics and music. "The children of *tender* parents, so-called," said Wesley, "who are indeed offering up their sons and daughters unto devils, have no business here; for the rules will not be broken in favour of any person whatsoever."

No "tender parent" was likely to send a child to Kingswood, for the rules were extremely severe. With the excellent aim of bringing up the pupils in the fear of God and of giving them a remarkably sound education, Wesley drew up a system which, had it been drawn up by any other man, might have exposed him to the charge of unwarranted harshness.

The children had to rise at four and to attend service, after private prayers, at five every morning. Breakfast was at six, and lessons began at seven, continuing for four hours. There was a break at eleven for "working or walking." Dinner was at twelve, after which there was a short spell of work in the garden, or singing. From one to five, the lessons were continued. Between five and six was the time for "private devotions." From six to seven there was more working and walking, and more praying. After a supper of bread and butter, or bread and milk, the exhausted children were marched off to bed at eight.

There was no room in the Kingswood schedule for games; and, indeed, games were expressly forbidden. "He who plays when he is a child," said Wesley, "will play when he is a man." Instead of unprofitably hitting a ball or stupidly running races, the little boys were set to dig in the garden. At all times the pupils were under close supervision. No dangers were to be more strenuously repelled than those of "idleness and effeminacy."

It would be quite possible to argue in support of this method if it was not applied with such extraordinary rigour. It is bad to make little boys believe that playing with a ball is the most important thing in life, or that any lesson of a high moral value can really be learnt on a slippery pitch or a muddy field; but it is just as bad, or worse, to turn them out of bed at four in the morning, and to give them two shivering hours of religion. We are not surprised to learn that there was always trouble at Kingswood, that parties were formed among the masters, the maids and the boys, and that some of the rules were habitually broken. In 1748, there were six masters and twenty-eight pupils; in 1751, there were two masters and eleven pupils. Yet, with all its faults and failings, its little mutinies and scenes of hysterical fervour, Kingswood School did produce good results, and was the means of giving to many poor children an education that must otherwise have been for ever beyond their reach.

But if the wisdom of Wesley could sometimes be questioned, there could never be the least doubt as to the splendid honesty of his intention. Nor was any man more thorough in working out his own schemes. Wesley was not satisfied with the available books, and he therefore composed and printed for the use of his pupils an English Grammar, a Latin Grammar, French, Hebrew and Greek Grammars. He also edited and published many other books which he considered useful for the masters and the children. The special aim of Kingswood education was to fit the boys to become ministers—and ministers of the Church of England.

With a view to a wider scheme of advanced religious education, Wesley began the publication of the *Christian Library* in 1749, and continued to produce the volumes until 1755.

The idea of this was "to provide a complete library for those that fear God." The fifty volumes of the series contained "Extracts and Abridgements of the Choicest Pieces of Practical Divinity which have been published in the English Tongue." In matters of inclusion, exclusion or curtailment, Wesley naturally exercised an arbitrary choice, and was careful to give the whole series a tenor and teaching conformable to his own evangelical views. As a compendium of practical divinity or as a work of reference, the *Christian Library* has obvious limitations. But as an instrument of revival, there could be no question of its value. It is astonishing, and admirable, that a man with no place for regular study, no constantly available collection of books, and the most restricted opportunities for research, should have undertaken a task of such labour and magnitude. Wesley was a man travelling for God. We have to remember that, for more than one half of his waking life, he was actually in movement on the highway. The copy for the *Christian Library* was revised and prepared while the editor was on horseback, or in the parlours of the inns where he lodged for the night. Yet the work was not hurried or careless. These fifty duodecimo volumes, of a size convenient for pocket or saddle-bag, were for many years a source of religious knowledge or appropriate quotation for Methodists; they were reprinted, in thirty volumes, between 1819 and 1826.

In the meantime, the Calvinistic revival, led by Harris, Lady Huntingdon and Whitefield, was going forward in its own way. The chief original gain of the movement was confined to Wales; elsewhere it had an isolated or fortuitous character. It is, indeed, typical of the difference in leadership, that Wesley's revival showed always a parallel progress of impulse and organisation, while the Calvinists relied, in a considerable measure, on what their followers were prepared to do for themselves.

Fashionable Methodists were meeting in Lady Huntingdon's town house. Religious gatherings in a drawing-room had an air of singularity and of incongruity which was pleasing to those who wanted a new amusement. When Horace Walpole wrote to Sir Horace Mann in March 1749, he observed: "Methodism in the metropolis is more fashionable than anything but *Brag*; the women play very deep at both; as deep, it is much suspected, as the Matrons of Rome did at the mysteries of the *Bona Dea*." And he added, with his ordinary rancid humour: "Lady Frances Shirley has chosen this way of bestowing the dregs of her beauty; and Mr. Lyttleton is very near making the same sacrifice of the dregs of all those various characters he has worn. The *Methodists* love your big sinners, as proper subjects to work upon; and, indeed, they have a plentiful harvest."

John Wesley must have regarded this drawing-room evangelism with a shadow of mistrust. His own attitude towards fashionable people was interesting, and will have to be considered later in some detail. He was not unwilling to meet the polite religious assemblies of Lady Huntingdon, and never refused to take part in her services, but he seems to have doubted if he was really doing much good in the chapels or the salons of this excellent woman.

Yet Wesley and Lady Huntingdon had friends in common, besides Whitefield. Both of them, in 1748, had made the acquaintance of Grimshaw of Haworth, a sturdy independent revivalist. They both of them knew James Erskine, and the soldier convert, Colonel Gumley. And Lady Huntingdon, for the next twenty years, looked upon Wesley as one who was well disposed towards her own activities, and not likely to interfere with them.

Like Howell Harris, there was nothing that Lady Huntingdon desired more than peace between the Wesleys and Whitefield. To speak of reconciliation in such a case is perhaps to use too strong a term, but it is certainly correct to say that cordial relations between the leaders of the revival were restored by the end of 1749. In that year Whitefield preached in the Orphan House at Newcastle; in January 1750, John Wesley agreed to assist in Lady Huntingdon's chapel; and in the same month, Whitefield preached for Wesley, Howell Harris preached at the Foundry, and Wesley preached at the Moorfields Tabernacle. Harris, observes Wesley, was "a powerful orator; but he owed nothing to art or education." For a time, the forces of revival were united.

Early in 1750, the work of Methodism in London was not a little assisted by two earthquake shocks. Proof that the earth is not as solid as it appears to be very often has the effect of making flippant people abruptly serious. And even if the doom of Sodom is not to be apprehended in these latitudes, the lesson of a slight tremor need not be wholly disregarded.

The first of the shocks was felt on the 8th of February. Wesley was in London, and he thus records the event:

"It was about a quarter after twelve that the earthquake began at the skirts of the town. It began in the south-east, went through Southwark, under the river, and then from one end of London to the other. It was observed at Westminster and Grosvenor Square a quarter before one. There were three distinct shakes, or wavings to and fro, attended with a hoarse rumbling noise like thunder. How gently does God deal with this nation! O that our repentance may prevent heavier marks of His displeasure!"

A second shock, of much greater severity, occurred exactly a month later, on the 8th of March. It took place at the inconvenient hour of a quarter past five in the morning. Charles Wesley, at that moment, was preaching in the Foundry. "I was just repeating my text," he said, "when it shook the Foundry so violently that we all expected it to fall upon our heads. A great cry followed from the women and the children." John was in Bristol. He was evidently quoting from his brother's account when he said: "The earth moved westward, then east, then westward again, through all London and Westminster. It was a strong and jarring motion, attended with a rumbling noise, like that of distant thunder." But there was no serious damage. A few bricks were dislodged and a few chimneys collapsed, a few pictures were shaken off the walls, and the tea-cups rattled. Still, it was sufficiently alarming. People ran out into the streets and hurried quickly to the open spaces of Moorfields or Hyde Park. Bad consciences made many cowards, and the populace, uncomforted by geological knowledge and ignorant of the firm Devonian platform far below them, anticipated a more drastic visitation of divine wrath.

The clergy were not slow in taking a proper advantage of the situation. Romaine published *An Alarm to a Careless World*. Dr. Doddridge drew a gloomy moral from *The Guilt and Doom of Capernaum:* "You have now, Sirs," he cried, "had repeated and surprising demonstrations of the Almighty Power. . . . His hand hath once again, within these five weeks, lifted up your mighty City from its Basis, and shook its million of inhabitants in their dwellings. The palaces of the great, nay, even of the greatest, have not been exempted." Sherlock, the Bishop of London, issued a *Letter to the Clergy and People of London on the Occasion of the Late Earthquakes*, in which he thundered, like a faithful minister, about the judgments which might be expected to fall upon a wicked people. In the twelve pages of his pamphlet, Sherlock gave an appalling description of popular morals, not seeing, perhaps, that the failure of his own clergy might be held partly accountable for the state of affairs. George Whitefield, who was then in London, wrote a description of the earthquake in a letter to Lady Selina: "God has been terribly shaking the Metropolis," he said. And he pointed to the universality of judgment: "Winds may blow, rains may and *will* descend, *even upon persons of the most exalted stations.*" Had not the royal dishes been rudely shaken in the very palace of St. James's?

It only needed the prophecy of a crazy soldier to throw the whole town into a panic. The soldier prophesied the partial destruction of London and Westminster on the 4th of April. He was very properly clapped into Bedlam, but the prophecy had done its work. What with the exploitation of terror by Doddridge, Sherlock and Romaine, a certain heaviness in the air, and a prophecy of disaster, nothing could check the popular madness.

On the 4th of April, or before, timid people packed their coaches and drove out into the country. Those who could not afford coaches ran away on foot with packs on their backs. Others considered that it was only necessary to get out of the way of falling buildings, and they drove or walked to the hills and open spaces.

As the night came on, fears rose to a more dreadful pitch. Churches were filled with dark masses of groaning penitents. Crowds pressed upon the doors of every Methodist chapel. At the Foundry, people came all night long, begging admittance for the love of God. The sky was cloudy and still, the night fell with thick darkness. At midnight, the praying, weeping and distracted multitudes listened for the sudden clangour of the last trump.

In this wonderful scene of darkness and dismay, Whitefield preached the most effective of all his powerful sermons. He went to Hyde Park. He found the Park filled with an innumerable crowd of people: ladies in their *earthquake gowns*, ready to sit up all night, gentlemen shivering under their riding-cloaks, huddled clusters of the undistinguished vulgar. Some were on foot, some were sitting inside their coaches; others were warming themselves at braziers.

Out of the black night of doom came the solemn and tremendous voice of Whitefield, calling to repentance the sinners of London. Even in Hyde Park, there never had been, and there never will be, a more prodigious effect of oratory.

John Wesley "improved the occasion" as best he could; but he had not the advantage of being on the spot. He gave a discourse on *The Cause and Cure of Earthquakes*, and he issued a collection of *Hymns Occasioned by the Earthquake, March* 8, 1750.

Perhaps, as the people came back rather foolishly to their forsaken homes, and saw London standing firm with its cold chimneys, there were some whose faith came to an end with their fears. Perhaps the pale mockery of those daring or desperate fellows who had stayed in their town houses turned many waverers from the way of salvation. But the combined influence of the earthquakes and the oratory, and even of the unfulfilled prophecy of disaster, was certainly to promote the general cause of religion, and particularly the cause of Methodistic religion.

CHAPTER XIV

GRACE MURRAY

THE story of Grace Murray and her second marriage is usually related with a more or less evident degree of confusion by Wesley's biographers. It is a story which seems to interfere with, or even to unsettle, the regular features of idealised character; a coarse dab of raw colour on the otherwise immaculate picture of a saint.

But such a view is altogether mistaken. In the first place, we should be little moved by the example of a man in whom the natural human impulses were absent; in the second, there is nothing in the episode which can lower Wesley's reputation. To exaggerate the importance of this episode would certainly be a grave error: on the other hand, to leave Grace Murray with a casual reference would be to leave in needless obscurity an essential aspect of John Wesley as a man.

It has already been said that Wesley had no time to fall in love in the desperate sense of the term. He was here to-day and gone to-morrow. His hours of merely social relaxation were exceedingly few. His ordinary contact with those he met was that of a preacher, a teacher or an organiser. The work was everything. He was not likely to form an attachment for any woman who was not closely associated with him in that work, with opportunities for being continually with him. Grace Murray had both these advantages. She became the housekeeper of the Orphan House at Newcastle; she was, in her own way, a teacher and a preacher; and Wesley chose her to be one of his travelling companions.

Grace Murray was born in 1716 at Newcastle. Her parents were Robert and Grace Norman, and her station in life appears to have been that of humble respectability. Up to the age of eight she was of a serious disposition, read her Bible, and gave away her pennies. But between eight and nine she went to a dancing class, and according to prosy Tyerman, "became an admired companion of the gay and frivolous." Presently she was flirting with boys. At the age of eighteen she came to London, where she had a sister, and entered domestic service. In 1736 she married Alexander Murray, at one time a sailor before the mast, but a man with some pretensions to Scotch gentility.

The death of her first child had the effect of making Grace Murray turn to religion. She attended the preaching of the Methodists, probably at the Foundry, and was particularly touched by a sermon of John Wesley's in which he said, "Is there anyone here with a true desire to be saved?" She also listened to Whitefield and Charles Wesley. In 1740 she wrote a letter to Charles Wesley; a letter which is somewhat remarkable, and illustrates very well the religious emotions of a convert and her own peculiar religious temperament:

> "My Rev. Father in Christ,
> "My heart being now open before God. I write as in His presence.—The first gift of Faith I received after I had seen myself a lost Sinner, bound with a thousand Chains and dropping into Hell. Then I heard His voice, Be of good Cheer. . . . I went on in great Joy for four months. Then Pride crept in, and I thought the work was finished, when it was but just begun. There I rested, and in a little time fell into doubts and fears whether my Sins were really forgiven me, till I plunged into the depth of Misery. . . . My Soul was like the troubled Sea. Then did I see my own evil Heart, my cursed, devilish Nature. . . . My love was turned to Hatred, Passion, Envy. . . . In my last Extremity, I saw my Saviour full of Grace and Truth. . . . Now my Joy is calm and solid; my Heart drawn out to the Lord continually. He is my Strength and my Rock. . . ."

When Mr. Murray came back from one of his voyages, and found that his wife had turned Methodist, he fell into a dreadful rage. He stamped and cursed, and swore that he would go "as far as ships could sail." Actually, he went farther. He went on board a ship bound for Virginia in 1741, and was drowned at sea. It is fair to add that he is supposed to have regretted his nasty temper and his rash words before he left England.

Mrs. Murray returned to her mother's house in Newcastle, and may have been there on the occasion of Wesley's first visit in 1742. Her name appears as one of the leaders of the Foundry bands in April of that year; so we can assume that Wesley had already recognised her capacity for Methodist work. She became a leading Newcastle Methodist, led the classes, visited the neighbouring villages, spoke to the people and assisted in the prayers.

There is no doubt that she was an exceedingly attractive woman. We do not know if John Wesley met her on his arrival in Newcastle, but it was not long before he gave her an appointment at the Orphan House. It was supposed that Grace Murray would marry a man called Brydon, but she threw him over. She was fitfully occupied at the Orphan House, but grew peevish and quarrelsome, and when she heard that Brydon had married someone else, fell into a state of dangerous melancholia. Her "joy" had not been as solid as she imagined it to be. Brydon became indifferent to religious affairs, and Grace Murray feared that "his blood would be upon her head."

Again she saw herself dropping into hell. She was tempted to dash her brains out. For two years she was a sad example of what is known to religious psychology as counter-conversion. She knew better than all the preachers; nay, better than the Bible. She was lost in horrid alternations of pride and despair. Then she recovered her former peace (or so it seemed) and went back to her service at the Orphan House.

This comely widow was not only a capable housekeeper; she was an excellent nurse. When the preachers were ill at Newcastle, they were sent to the Orphan House to be cared for by Mrs. Murray. And it is observable that the preachers seemed to be more frequently ill at Newcastle than anywhere else. One in particular, John Bennet, was seized by a fever which kept him for twenty-six weeks in the Orphan House. John Bennet fell in love with Grace, and from this time (1746) they wrote letters to each other.

In August 1748, Wesley was at Newcastle, and found himself indisposed. If we take the evidence of his *Journal*, the indisposition was a very slight one. It did not interfere seriously with his preaching. Only on one day, the 6th of August, was he obliged to lie down. Ten grains of ipecacuanha cured him. But he thought it necessary to rest at the Orphan House and to be attended by the skill and the sweet cares of Grace Murray.

Wesley had a very high opinion of his Newcastle house-keeper. He said: "She has every qualification that I desire. She understands all I want to have done. She is remarkably neat in person, in clothes, in all things. She is nicely frugal, yet not sordid. She has much common sense: contrives everything for the best; makes everything go as far as it can go; foresees what is wanting and provides it in time; does all things quick, and yet without hurry. She is a good work-woman; able to do the finest, ready to do the coarsest work: observes my rules . . . and takes care that those about her observe them." He admired her success among the bands or classes, the exemplary method of her public praying, the neatness and piety of her discourse, her obvious talents for religious administration. She was a brave, brisk and healthy woman, a Christian not lacking in zeal or experience: such, at any rate, was the opinion of Wesley.

Dr. Simon, writing of the episode of 1748, says, "For some time he had been thinking about her as a wife." There does not appear to be any authority for this state-ment, although it is in keeping with what we know of Wesley's habitual methods of cool deliberation. But if he had been thinking for some time about marriage with Grace Murray, he had not given her the least inkling of what was in his mind, and she was completely taken by surprise when he made his proposal.

"This is too great a blessing for me," she cried; "I can't tell how to believe it. This is all I could have wished for under heaven."

Now, there can be no question of Grace Murray being a very good woman or a very bad woman; there can be no doubt that she was a poor, silly creature who could not make up her mind. The most singular thing about her is that she was, in many ways, so ordinary. Her religious history, with its glooms and raptures, shows a disposition to violent mental disturbance. But her exclamation on hear-- ing Wesley's proposal was that of a person whom no excite- ment could scare from a position of defensive ambiguity: instead of a plain yes or no or an appeal for time, she could only gasp "it was too great a blessing" and "she couldn't tell how to believe it." The truth of the matter is that she was thinking about marrying John Bennet, the Bolton preacher. She had not said yes or no to John Bennet either; and now, here was Mr. Wesley making his astonish- ing proposal.

It is difficult to explain what followed; and in all prob- ability, neither Grace Murray, nor John Wesley nor John Bennet, if they were raised from the dead, could give us much assistance. It is significant that a gap occurs in the published *Journal* between the dates of the 12th and the 16th of August 1748.

Nothing could long detain Wesley from his work. He had decided to leave Newcastle on the 16th. On the night before his departure, evidently without coming to a definite understanding with Grace Murray, he told her that "he was convinced God had called her to be his fellow labourer in the Gospel." He promised to take her with him to Ireland in the spring. Grace replied, that she could not bear the thought of separation for a moment, and begged that she might accompany him on the morrow.

Tyerman has suggested that Mrs. Murray had not for- gotten that Wesley, in his journey south, would call upon John Bennet. Indeed, he goes much further: he says, "Is it unfair to suspect some dishonourable collusion here?" No such thing as dishonourable collusion need be sus- pected, nor, in the circumstances, would collusion of any sort have been possible; but it is certainly likely enough that Grace wanted to review the position with her other suitor. It is not unfair to suspect that Mrs. Murray, though immensely flattered, had certain misgivings. Whatever her ambitions may have been, she had never considered that she might become the wife of John Wesley. She had never discouraged Bennet, and she must have thought of him as a very suitable husband: a man of some eminence as a lay preacher, with an important circuit of his own, and with no overwhelming superiority of taste or education.

However that may be, Wesley agreed to take her with him. They were presumably accompanied by one of the lay preachers, Mackford. Wesley merely notes: "We left Newcastle. In riding to Leeds, I read Dr. Hodge's *Account of the Plague in London*."

On the 24th of August they met Grimshaw at Haworth; and on the following day, Wesley, Grimshaw, Mackford and Colbeck encountered a furious mob at Barrowford, near Roughlee. On the 27th they met John Bennet at Miller's Bar in Rossendale. Four days later they arrived at Bennet's home in Chinley. Here, Grace Murray, to whom the idea of separation from Wesley had been so distressing only a fortnight before, was left to the care of Bennet, and Wesley set out on the road to London. Mackford returned to his work at Newcastle, and Grace Murray and Bennet were left alone.

Here was a thorny situation. We do not know if Bennet, at this time, knew anything about the relations between Mrs. Murray and John Wesley, nor do we know if Mrs. Murray had given Wesley a formal promise of marriage. There is no doubt that Wesley regarded Grace as his future wife, and that he had not felt the slightest hesitation in leaving her with Bennet. There is no room in a saintly character for ordinary suspicions.

Grace Murray and John Bennet set forth on a missionary tour among the Derbyshire hills. On the face of it, this was hardly a prudent excursion, but we may remember that they were associated for professional purposes, and neither Bennet nor Mrs. Murray can be accused of a lack of zeal.

During this excursion, Bennet urged Grace Murray to become his wife. If he knew that she was informally engaged to Wesley, his importunity might well be given a harsher name; but presumably he did not know of this engagement. It is possible to excuse Bennet; indeed, there is good reason to believe him blameless; it is not so easy to find an excuse for Grace Murray, who listened amiably to these new proposals. "I told him," she said, "that I could not give him my answer, for if I were to marry, it would take away my usefulness to God's cause, I feared, and then I would rather die. He said that it would never do so, as I should go about with him, and that there was as much need of usefulness in his circuit as in any other. Still I objected, and said *I could not marry without Mr. Wesley's consent;* yet he argued with me until I was brought to reason upon the matter. . . . I said, 'If Mr. Wesley will give his consent, I will yield.' He said, 'I will write him this night, and let him know.' So on this *I partly gave my promise.*"

The same hesitation, the same ambiguity. The most we can assume in her favour is that she did not really consider herself bound to Wesley. Yet we can hardly suppose her ignorant of Wesley's own conviction in the matter. She appears to be lightly poising between ambition on the one hand, and a growing affection on the other.

Some time in September, probably before he left London on the 12th, Wesley received a letter from Bennet, asking his permission to marry Grace Murray; and a letter from Grace Murray herself, saying that she believed God intended her for John Bennet. "I was utterly amazed," said Wesley; "but wrote a mild answer to both, supposing they were married already."

But Grace Murray had returned to Newcastle, where she carried on an affectionate correspondence with Bennet and Wesley at the same time, still piously wavering, and still unwilling to commit herself. In February 1749, she informed Bennet that Wesley had asked her to go with him to Ireland; Bennet, if he loved her, was to meet her at Sheffield; otherwise, she could not answer for the consequences.

Bennet arranged to go to Sheffield, but was prevented at the last moment, and Mrs. Murray went on to Bristol without seeing him. She had a little boy in the school at Kingswood. At Bristol she met Wesley.

Grace was now convinced that her pledge to Bennet

was not indissoluble. On the other hand, she saw that her pledge to Wesley was of a different kind altogether, and she agreed to accompany him. Wesley must have been convinced, for his part, that she was not, and never had been, affianced to John Bennet. Without such a conviction he could not have invited her to go with him to Ireland, and thus to be openly associated with him on terms of peculiar intimacy and confidence.

On the 3rd of April, Wesley says, "I set out for Ireland." He travelled through Wales, and on the 8th of April he married his brother Charles and Sarah Gwynne at Garth: we may assume that Grace Murray was present at this wedding, though we have no direct evidence. Wesley proceeded to Holyhead by slow stages, and sailed for Dublin, with Grace Murray and William Tucker, on the 15th of April.

Wesley and Grace Murray remained in Ireland from the 15th of April to the 20th of July 1749. They reached Bristol Quay on the morning of the 24th of July.

During the whole period of the Irish campaign, the conduct of Mrs. Murray was extremely edifying. "She examined all the women in the smaller societies, and the believers in every place. She settled all the women bands, visited the sick, prayed with the mourners." Wesley regarded her "both as a servant and a friend." She looked after him carefully, saw that he was properly supplied with necessary things, and "told him with all faithfulness and freedom if she thought anything amiss in his behaviour." At Dublin, they entered upon a provisional contract of marriage, *de præsenti*. And all the time, Grace neither wrote to John Bennet, nor did she receive any letters from him. We know of nothing which can explain this peculiar silence of Bennet, unless we are to suppose that he regarded any further pursuit as hopeless. But he had no reason to take such a view of the case.

Before she had been long in Bristol, after her return from Ireland, Grace Murray heard some idle talk about Wesley and a woman called Molly Francis. Immediately she wrote an affectionate letter to Bennet, and he agreed to meet her on her journey back to Newcastle. She accompanied Wesley to London in August.

We learn, from entries in the *Journal* of Charles Wesley, that his brother, with T. Butts, Captain James and Grace Murray, overtook Charles and his wife at the Passage, on their way to Ludlow. This was on the 7th of August. On the 10th, Charles notes: "My brother . . . set out at four [from Ludlow] with Grace Murray and James Jones. T. Butts and I took horse at six. . . . I preached at Evesham . . . the next evening met my brother and G. M., who came through Birmingham to Oxford; and on Saturday, August 12th, I attended him to London."

In London, undecided as ever, Grace Murray consulted a friend on the subject of marriage with Wesley. "Sister Murray," said the friend, "never think of it. . . . It will never do. The people here would never suffer you. And your proud spirit would not bear their behaviour; you have not humility enough, or meekness, or patience; you would be miserable all your life. . . . If you love yourself, or if you love him, never think of it more."

On the 28th of August, Wesley and his companion left London on their way to the north. They reached Epworth on the 3rd of September, and here they met John Bennet.

From this point, the affair becomes more tenebrous than ever. In the course of a dreadful interview, Bennet announced that Mrs. Murray had sent him all the letters that John Wesley had written to her. When Dr. Simon says that "Wesley was surprised . . . and saw that he had made a mistake," he is surely erring on the side of mildness. Wesley wrote to Grace on the following morning, observing that he thought it was not proper they should converse any more together. After reading this letter, the wretched woman ran to Wesley "in an agony of tears," and begged him not to talk in such a way, unless he wanted to kill her. But while this was going on, Bennet came into the room and "claimed her as his right." Wesley, for the second time, perplexed and troubled beyond measure, gave her up to Bennet. In a little while, he was told that "Sister Murray was exceedingly ill." He could not refuse to visit her.

"How can you think I love anyone better than I love you!" she cried pathetically. "I love you a thousand times better than I ever loved John Bennet in my life. But I'm afraid that if I don't marry him, he'll go stark, staring mad." Bennet, accompanied by a friend, visited her in the evening. After a great deal of argument, she said: "Very well; I *will* marry John Bennet." Next morning, she told Wesley of this, and he, says Tyerman, "was more perplexed than ever." So he very well may have been: his candour and simplicity were baffled by the weakness or caprice of this wavering widow.

Leaving Bennet at Epworth, Wesley and Mrs. Murray proceeded on their way to Newcastle. Perhaps it was the turn of Bennet to be perplexed. As for Wesley, he could not resolve upon a line of action; and the widow had lapsed into her chronic state of piteous ambiguity. On the 6th of September, when they reached Newcastle, he said brusquely, "Which will you choose?" She declared, "I am determined, by conscience as well as by inclination, to live and die with you." He therefore wrote a long and reproachful letter to Bennet, which was dispatched by hand, and was never delivered. A copy of this letter was forwarded to Charles at Bristol.

Wesley and his brother had agreed that neither would marry without the consent of the other. John, like a man of honour, felt himself bound by this agreement, and he therefore wrote to Charles, telling him of his intentions. He also desired to come to an understanding with Bennet, and to send his reasons for marrying to all his preachers and the affiliated societies.

Towards the end of September, he went with Grace Murray to Hindley Hill, near Allandale. Grace had requested that the Dublin contract might be renewed in the presence of suitable witnesses, and this was now done. The chief witness was Christopher Hopper, a lay preacher of some repute.

As the solemn contract *per verba de præsenti* was being read over, Hopper observed that Grace Murray was trembling. He asked her if she felt any scruples, and Wesley also put the same question. She replied firmly, "I have none at all." Soon after the contract had been duly attested, Wesley got on his horse and started for Whitehaven. Grace Murray remained at Allandale, and Hopper was dispatched to Chinley in order to break the news to Bennet.

It might have been supposed that Wesley and Grace Murray would be married before many weeks had passed; but now an angry, impetuous, hurrying little man suddenly rushed upon the scene and drastically put an end to all ambiguities and hesitations and delays.

Charles Wesley probably received his brother's letter, enclosing a copy of the one sent to John Bennet, towards the end of September.

At once this quiet man, happy in the newness of his married life, became resolute, pugnacious and assertive. Nay; he fairly bounded with anger. The battling boy of Westminster had never been extinguished: in a flash he was up in arms. This ridiculous marriage! Marriage? It was not to be thought of for a moment. John must be mad, bewitched, robbed of every trace of reason or propriety or self-esteem.

Without setting pen to paper, or pausing longer than was necessary to collect a few clean shirts and handkerchiefs, Charles ran off to the posting-station, and travelled with incredible velocity to Newcastle. When he got there, he was told by a woman called Jeannie Keith (no friend of Grace Murray's, we imagine) that the town was in an uproar over John's intended marriage, and all the societies ready to fall in pieces. This was precisely what Charles had expected.

The angry little man, hurrying and fuming, went on to Whitehaven, burst in upon his brother, and told him bluntly and forcibly that if he married so mean a woman as Grace Murray, the whole Methodist organisation would collapse in miserable disorder. John, unprepared as he was for this raging little person and these whirlwind arguments, mildly put forward his reasons for marrying and gently defended the character of Mrs. Murray: he said that she was "indefatigably patient and inexpressibly tender; quick, cleanly and skilful; of an engaging behaviour, and of a mild, sprightly, cheerful and yet serious temper; while her gifts for usefulness were such as he had not seen equalled." Birth did not matter in such a case, and, since he had decided to marry, he "knew no person so proper as this."

Charles could not move his brother, but he was not defeated; on the contrary, he was the more resolute; he determined that no obstacle and no consideration should stand in his way. He meant to put a stop to this marriage, and nothing could prevent him from doing so. On the day after this meeting, he galloped back to Hindley Hill, and there he met Grace Murray. He kissed her. "Grace Murray!" he cried in his sudden dramatic way, "you have broke my heart!" Then, impetuous and plausible, he persuaded her to go back with him to Newcastle. Mrs. Murray got up behind Charles on his horse, and away they went.

John Bennet had been sent for in the meantime, and when Charles and Grace arrived at Newcastle he was waiting for them.

On the 27th of September, John came from Whitehaven to Hindley Hill, and there he learnt that Mrs. Murray had been carried off by Charles. One of his preachers burst into tears when he saw him, and vowed that he would fetch her back. Poor John let him go, but he resigned himself to the will of God. He guessed what was happening. On the following day he wrote: "I was calm though sad. . . . If I had had more regard for her I loved than for the work of God I should now have gone straight to Newcastle, and not back to Whitehaven. I knew this was giving up all."

At that time, Whitefield was travelling in the north. Charles had met him, and had told him of the tangled affair of Grace Murray and her two suitors. Whitefield had taken the part of John Wesley and had advised delay. But Charles would hear of no such thing; he was in no mood for delays. He, at least, knew how to deal with irresolute widows. He frightened Grace Murray into believing that she was obliged to marry Bennet. As for the contract *de præsenti*—"Tush, tush!" cried Charles, with a quick,

destructive gesture; "it is nothing at all; it is a mere foolery."
He ran with the faintly protesting woman to the place
where Bennet was lodging, and there Mrs. Murray fell at
her lover's feet and begged his forgiveness. Masterful
Charles had won the day. And now, he said, he would not
leave Newcastle until they were married. Accordingly, on
the 3rd of October, at St. Andrew's Church, and in the
presence of Charles Wesley and George Whitefield, Grace
Murray became Mrs. John Bennet.

Whitefield, knowing that John Wesley was on his way
to Leeds, arranged to meet him there. When they met,
Whitefield gently told the other what had happened at
Newcastle. On the following day, Charles arrived with
Mr. and Mrs. Bennet.

Instead of being appeased by victory, Charles was in a
furious rage with his brother. "I renounce all intercourse
with you!" he exclaimed savagely. "I renounce all intercourse
with you, but what I would have with a heathen man or a
publican." And he walked, muttering peevishly, to the
other end of the room.

An extremely painful scene was changed to one of peace
and thanksgiving by the tearful prayers of Whitefield and of
John Nelson. Volatile, affectionate Charles was quickly
melted; he ran to his brother, and the two Wesleys embraced
each other in silence. Bennet, perhaps a little apologetic,
was brought into the room, and Wesley kissed him. After
that, the brothers had a private interview: Charles, not
believing for a moment that he had acted ungenerously,
and sure that he had been the saviour of Methodism, put
all the blame on Grace; and John, with his wonderful
resignation, again bowed meekly to the will of God.

The entries in Wesley's published *Journal* at this period
give no indication of these deplorable events. On the contrary, they present an unbroken record of preaching and
travelling.

On the 5th of October, Wesley attended the preaching
of Whitefield at Birstall; on the 6th he himself preached at
Birstall, then returned to Leeds, and preached twice to "a
crowded audience." In the afternoon of the following day,

he rode to Bromley, and preached to a large and quiet congregation: "Great attention appeared in every face, but no shaking among the dry bones yet." Nothing was allowed to interfere with the work; but it would be wrong to suppose that Wesley was not profoundly unsettled by what had taken place. On the very day of the Bromley preaching, he sent a letter to his friend Thomas Bigg at Newcastle:

"My dear Brother,

"A loving husband is a very amiable character: A fond one, I think, is not so. But if I had a wife, I believe I should be the latter; and perhaps you may lean to the same extreme. To you, therefore, I can freely speak my mind.

"Since I was six years old, I never met with such a severe trial as for some days past. For ten years God has been preparing a fellow labourer for me, by a wonderful train of providence. Last year I was convinced of it; therefore, I delayed not, but, as I thought, made all sure beyond a danger of disappointment. But we were soon afterwards torn asunder by a whirlwind. In a few months, the storm was over: I then used more precaution than before, and fondly told myself that the day of evil would return no more. But it too soon returned. The waves arose again since I came out of London. I fasted and prayed, and strove all I could; but the sons of Zeruiah were too hard for me. The whole world fought against me; but above all, my own familiar friend. Then was the word fulfilled, 'Son of man, behold! I take from thee the desire of thine eyes at a stroke; yet shalt thou not lament, neither shall thy tears run down.'

"The fatal, irrevocable stroke was struck on Tuesday last. Yesterday I saw my friend (that was), and him to whom she is sacrificed. I believe you never saw such a scene. But 'why should a living man complain? a man for the punishment of his sins?'"

For a short time, Bennet and Wesley remained on good terms with each other, and it is to be observed that Wesley visited Rochdale within a fortnight of the scene at Leeds, at Bennet's invitation. Bennet, however, appears to have been a treacherous, unfriendly man: he left the Wesleyan societies with a following of some hundreds, denounced Wesley as a teacher of Popish doctrines, and became the pastor of a Calvinistic church near Warrington. He died in 1759 at the age of forty-five.

Mrs. Bennet was left with five boys. She conducted prayer-meetings, and became once more a faithful Methodist worker. After their parting at Leeds, Wesley did not meet Mrs. Bennet again until 1788, three years before his death. Mrs. Bennet died in 1803, aged eighty-five.

Among the surprising and distressing features of this episode, none is more strange than the violent interference of Charles Wesley. Natural impetuosity may explain his quick words and headstrong actions; but the most impetuous man does not travel for nearly three hundred miles in post carriages, keeping up a blazing temper all the way, without some adequate reason.

Charles, no doubt, had a reason; and probably he had more than one. He had seen Grace Murray, and formed his own impressions. He believed that if his brother married her, he would not only suffer personally from the effects of an entirely unsuitable alliance, but would bring disruption of the most miserable kind upon the religious societies of which he was the head.

Unless we assume that Charles knew a great deal more about Grace Murray than we know at present, there seems to be something a little exaggerated in this attitude. It looks as though Charles was perilously near being a snob, if not something even worse. Wesley rightly drew attention to the usefulness of Mrs. Murray, and we have observed her taking over, and successfully performing, the duties of supervision. Wesley was never more successful than he was during his travels with this excellent helper. A lady, such as the irreproachable Sarah Wesley, would not have done half as well. Ah yes! Charles might have answered; the position could be tolerated (though it was far from desirable) as long as Mrs. Murray was the attendant, the servant of John: if she became his wife, that was another matter.

But this was not the only objection. Grace Murray, said Charles, had promised to marry John Bennet—that was clear—and she had then engaged herself to another, and that other was John Wesley. How could his brother exempt himself from the charge of having seduced the affections of a woman who was already betrothed? If John married her in these circumstances "his doing so dishonest an action would destroy both himself, and me, and the whole work of God." Here, rather than in the question of social disparity, was the serious objection. John Wesley, the most saintly of men, was in danger of being pointed at as a vile seducer. It was this dreadful possibility which sent Charles fuming to the north, and left such a long gap in his *Journal.* It was a view of Bennet as a grossly injured man that made Charles wickedly splutter at poor John the words of publican and heathen. John, if he had been an ordinary man, might have called Charles an interfering booby, meddling in matters of which he knew nothing at all. Indeed, he might have been infinitely more severe.

And what is to be said for Grace Murray herself? The fatuous gentleman (Aaron Hobart Seymour) who wrote the *Life of Lady Huntingdon,* thus describes Grace Murray: "She possessed superior personal accomplishments, united to a mind cultivated by education, and an imagination brilliant and lively in the highest degree." Mr. Seymour does not say from what source he obtained this pretty portrait: we can only suppose that it came out of the liveliness of his own genteel fancy. Dictatorial Tyerman, on the other hand, is too ruthless by far when he disposes of her in a single sentence: "Grace Murray was a flirt."

It is not necessary that we should trouble ourselves very much about the character, the virtues, or the failings of Mrs. Murray. Only an imagination "brilliant and lively in the highest degree" can make her remarkable. She was a cheerful, zealous, handsome woman, with a weak and vacillating mind. She appears to have been an excellent servant, as long as she was merely carrying out orders. No one can doubt that she was perfectly virtuous and rather stupid. In view of the evidence, we cannot see her as a pious coquette, but only as an amiable, hesitant creature who could not for the life of her make a decision. All her virtues were those of a subordinate. She had never anticipated Wesley's proposal, and we cannot blame her for being flattered and flustered by the idea of marrying a man so good, so famous and so exalted. She allowed herself to dangle, in her silly way, between Wesley and Bennet; and so she might have gone on dangling, if it had not been for the hustling vehemence of Charles.

Nothing is to be gained by speculating on what might have happened if Wesley, and not John Bennet, had married Grace Murray. Whatever the results of such a marriage might have been, they would probably have been far happier than the results of Wesley's most unfortunate success in his second courtship.

CHAPTER XV

MARRIAGE

WESLEY often showed how little he understood the ordinary woman. He knew nothing of passion, and hated nothing more than sensuality. He despised vehemently the mere shadow of affectation. The charm of women was transformed by the spiritual action of his mind into the evidence of piety or grace. The simplicity, the chivalry and candour of his approach to women, noble and beautiful in themselves, disposed him to idealisation.

At the same time, however susceptible he may have been, he was a practical man, who regulated his life by a method of inflexible discipline. He could account, without dishonour, for every moment of his busy existence. Either he was preaching, or he was travelling to preach, or he was dealing with a point of religious administration, or he was reading for improvement, or writing, editing or compiling some book or pamphlet. His life was consecrated to the great work of his mission. Even supposing that he ought to marry, the ordinary woman is not the proper wife for such a man.

In 1751, Wesley married because he thought it was right for him to do so. He wrote in his *Journal*, under the date of the 2nd of February 1751: "Having received a full answer from Mr. P[erronet], I was clearly convinced that I ought to marry. For many years I remained single, because I believed that I could be more useful in a single than in a married state. And I praise God, who enabled me to do so. I now as fully believed, that in my present circumstances I might be *more useful* in a married state; into which, upon this clear conviction, and by the advice of my friends, I entered a few days after." Four days after making this entry, he wrote: "I met the single men, and showed them on how many accounts it was good for those who had received that gift from God, to remain single for the kingdom of heaven's sake, unless where a particular case might be an exception to the general rule." He evidently regarded himself as a particular case.

Mr. Vincent Perronet, whose advice settled the question, was the vicar of Shoreham in Kent. He was one of the first of the clergymen who associated themselves with the Wesleyan revival, and his two sons, Charles and Edward, became itinerant preachers. Perronet was devoted to John Wesley, and the Wesley brothers used to call him the Archbishop or the Umpire of Methodism. He was ten years older than Wesley, and had no hesitation in giving him counsel.

At the time of John Wesley's decision, he was at the Foundry in London. Charles Wesley was also in London, staying, with his wife, at the West Street chapel-house. On the 2nd of February, the very day on which John recorded his decision, Charles made the following entry in his own *Journal*:

"My brother, returned from Oxford, sent for and told me *he was resolved to marry*! I was thunderstruck, and could only answer, he had given me the first blow, and his marriage would come like the *coup de grâce*. Trusty Ned Perronet followed, and told me, the person was Mrs. Vazeille!—one of whom I had never had the least suspicion. I refused his company to the Chapel, and retired to mourn with my faithful Sally. I groaned all the day and several following ones, under my own and the people's burden. I could eat no pleasant food, nor preach, nor rest, either by night or by day."

Mrs. Vazeille appeared to Charles, and to nearly every one else, as the last person in the world who ought to become the wife of John Wesley. She was the widow of Anthony Noah Vazeille, a Huguenot merchant, who lived in Threadneedle Street and had a country house at Wandsworth. Before her marriage, her name was Goldhawk; but Goldhawk was only the English form of some other name. She had four children, and a fortune of ten thousand pounds invested in three-per-cent stock.

The widow Vazeille had made the acquaintance of the

Wesleys through the Perronet family at Shoreham. It seems likely that she was also known to the banker, Ebenezer Blackwell, an early Methodist and a close personal friend of John Wesley. Blackwell was a City man, and he may have known Vazeille, and the Perronets, like the deceased merchant, were Huguenots. Charles Wesley first mentions Mrs. Vazeille under the date of the 20th of July 1749—"At Ned Perronet's I met Mrs. Vazeille, a woman of a sorrowful spirit." This immediate impression may be ambiguous, but is not alarming. From what follows, it is clear that Charles and his wife were soon upon friendly terms with Mrs. Vazeille. In May 1750, the widow accompanied Charles on a visit to the Gwynnes at Ludlow, where "they showed her all the civility and love that they could show: and she seemed equally pleased with them." On the 26th of May, Mrs. Vazeille and Mrs. Wesley travelled together in a chaise to Evesham, while Charles and Mr. Waller accompanied them on horseback. On the 28th the party visited Blenheim, and on the following day Charles took Waller and Mrs. Vazeille to see the gardens and colleges of Oxford. Three days later, Charles and his wife "took up their quarters at Mrs. V's [in Threadneedle Street]" for rather more than a week.

Up to the summer of 1750, therefore, Charles Wesley did not look upon Mrs. Vazeille with disapproval; he treated her with obvious consideration, introduced her to his wife's family, and was hospitably entertained at her own house.

John Wesley, when he announced to his brother his intention of getting married, did not give the name of his proposed wife. That name was blurted out by "trusty Ned Perronet," and it was no sooner heard by Charles and his wife than both of them "retired to mourn." And yet, not many months before, they had been the guests of Mrs. Vazeille. Why did they regard the choice of John with such overwhelming despair?

Mrs. Vazeille was a friend of the Perronets, who were intimate personal friends of the Wesleys; she had a "sorrowful spirit" and was interested in the doctrines of Methodism; she was forty-one years old, an excellent mother and apparently a woman of some charm. If John had obstinately resolved to marry, why should Mrs. Vazeille have been so particularly unsuitable?

Without being prejudiced by a knowledge of what actually followed, it is not at all easy to answer this question, unless we suppose Charles to have been a penetrating judge of character. Moore, speaking of the widow Vazeille in 1751, says: "She appeared to be truly pious, and was very agreeable in her person and manners." On the other hand, Jackson says: "Neither in understanding nor in education was she worthy of the eminent man [Wesley] to whom she was united; and her temper was intolerably bad." A modern biographer does not hesitate to call her "an essentially vulgar woman with a tendency to hysteria." Tyerman believes that she was insane.

Nothing is known of Wesley's courtship, or of the circumstances in which he first met Mrs. Vazeille; nor is it known when he made his proposal, or even, with certainty, when he was married.

The few facts that are known concerning this marriage are very singular. On the 2nd of February, Wesley made up his mind; and on the same day, Edward Perronet was told that he had chosen Mrs. Vazeille. But Wesley had arranged to leave for the North of England on the 11th. Apparently he did not contemplate getting married for some little time. On the 10th, however, he fell on the frozen road in the middle of London Bridge and seriously injured his foot. Instead of setting out for the north, he was carried in a chair to the house of Mrs. Vazeille in Threadneedle Street. Here, he says, "I spent the remainder of the week, partly in prayer, reading and conversation, partly in writing an *Hebrew Grammar*, and *Lessons for Children*." If this was the time of Wesley's courtship, it must have been a courtship of the oddest kind. Perhaps the "conversation" was mainly on business matters. Wesley would not touch Mrs. Vazeille's money, and insisted on the capital being secured on herself and her children.

Now, it must have been soon after his accident on the Bridge (a most unhappy slip) that Wesley decided to post-

pone his journey until the 18th. In his *Journal*, he says:
"Mon. 18, was the second day I had appointed for my
journey. But I was disappointed again, not being yet able
to set my foot to the ground. However, I preached (kneeling) on Tuesday evening and Wednesday morning." What
did he do on Monday? On Monday, if the *Gentleman's
Magazine* is to be trusted, he married Mrs. Vazeille.

The entry in the *Gentleman's Magazine* reads thus:
"February 18.—Rev. Mr. John Wesley, Methodist
Preacher, to a Merchant's widow, with a Jointure of £300
per annum." But the *London Magazine* alters the date:
"February 19.—Rev. Mr. John Wesley to Mrs. Vazel of
Threadneedle Street, a widow lady of large fortune." And
we turn, with pardonable perplexity, to the note in the
Journal: "Mon. 18, was the second day I had appointed for
my journey. *But I was disappointed again.* . . ."

One might have supposed that a man who kept his *Journal*
with such care would have recorded, however briefly, the
fact of his marriage. He may have refrained from setting
this down out of deference to the wishes of Mrs. Vazeille,
who knew that parts of the *Journal* were published. That
may be an adequate explanation of silence; but how can we
explain the deliberate statement that he was "disappointed"
on the 18th because he could not start on his journey? Did
he intend to take his wife with him? Or was he really
married on the 18th? It seems more probable that the
London Magazine is correct, and that he was married on
the 19th: the *Journal* has no entry under this date; indeed,
there is none until five days later, the 24th. After this, there
is no entry until the 4th of March, when he says, "Being
tolerably able to ride, though not to walk, I set out for
Bristol."

So far as we know, there is no entry in a church register
which determines the place and the date of Wesley's marriage.
It has been suggested that Wesley was married by his friend
Charles Manning of Hayes, though Dr. Simon tells us of
a local tradition about the marriage of Wesley in Wandsworth Parish Church.

In the *Journal* of Charles Wesley there are several curious entries relating to this period. On Sunday, the 17th of February, he says: "At the Foundry I heard *my brother's lamentable apology*, which made us all hide our faces. Several days afterwards I was one of the last that heard of his unhappy marriage." The entry for the same date in John Wesley's *Journal* is: "I was carried to the Foundry, and preached kneeling (as I could not stand), on part of the Twenty-third Psalm."

On the 27th of February, Charles wrote: "My brother came to the Chapel-House with his wife. I was glad to see him; saluted her; stayed to hear him preach; but ran away when he began his apology." In March, while John Wesley was away in Bristol, the following entries were made by Charles:

"March 15th. I called on my sister; kissed and assured her I was perfectly reconciled to her, and to my brother.

"March 18th. I finished Marcus Antoninus, having learnt from him, I hope, some useful lessons, particularly not to resent, not to revenge myself, not to let my peace lie at the mercy of every injurious person.

"March 19th. I brought my wife and sister together, and took all opportunities of showing the latter my sincere respect and love."

These entries are extremely interesting. Charles and John were both present at the Foundry on the 17th of February; but John, who was married either on the following day or on the 19th, said nothing whatever about this to Charles, who was actually "one of the last" to hear the news. John's "lamentable apology" was undoubtedly a general public declaration of his reasons for marrying. There seems to be evidence here, either of precipitancy or of deliberate concealment on the part of John. And yet John was the most candid and the most honourable of men. He can hardly have been unaware, on the Sunday, that he was going to be married on the Monday or Tuesday morning. But Charles was kept in the dark. Indeed, we do not know of any friend of Wesley's who was invited to the ceremony; every record of that ceremony has mysteriously vanished.

However sharp the disagreement between the brothers, it is certainly very strange that Charles was not even given a chance of being present at John's wedding. Perhaps the turbulent final scenes of the Grace Murray episode were too fresh in the mind of John; but even that hardly accounts for the appearance of unseemly haste, of secrecy and obscurity in this unfortunate marriage.

Mercurial Charles had some reason to feel injured. A happy choice, or happy chance, directed him to the *Golden Book* of Marcus Aurelius: excellent reading for an injured or an angry man. When he called on Mrs. John Wesley, he was able to assure her of a perfect reconciliation. Four days later, he persuaded his wife to meet her new "sister," and by that time he had so far changed his attitude that he could speak of "sincere respect and love" for Mrs. John. All this is in keeping with a brusque and explosive character, actually based upon real affection and a love of peace. But it shows, at the same time, that Mrs. John Wesley did not then appear to Charles as a woman unworthy of his friendship and respect. He was ready to welcome her in his own house and to see her drinking tea with his dear Sally.

Mrs. Vazeille before her marriage with Wesley cannot have been a cross, unpleasant, unmannerly woman. No such person could have been the friend of good Perronet, or well received by the Gwynnes at Ludlow. No such person would have been allowed by Charles to travel with dear Sally in a post-chaise. Nor is it conceivable that Charles and his wife could have stayed in the house of any one who seemed undesirable as an acquaintance. And there is every reason to believe that Perronet and Blackwell, both of whom were consulted by John Wesley on the subject of marriage, knew perfectly well that he intended to marry Mrs. Vazeille, and advised him to follow his inclination.

An unhappy change in the manners and disposition of poor Mrs. Wesley appears to have taken place not long after her marriage. She was a very ordinary woman—we are not unwilling to admit that she may have been vulgar and hysterical—but she had certainly made a most unfortunate choice.

After his return from Bristol, Wesley observed, "I cannot understand how a Methodist Preacher can answer it to God, to preach one sermon or travel one day less, in a married than in a single state." He told Henry Moore that he had come to an understanding with his wife, before their marriage, on this essential condition: he was not to preach one sermon or travel one mile the less because he had a wife. Here was the source of the trouble.

In June 1751, about four months after the wedding, Charles Wesley found his sister-in-law in tears. She complained bitterly of her husband's inattention, and Charles did his best to soothe her. After this, she tried to keep up with John Wesley on his travels. But Mrs. Wesley liked to be comfortable; she was even used to a moderate degree of luxury. It did not please her to be on the road for hours together, with the chance of a handful of pebbles or a few clods of earth being flung in through the coach window. Wesley observed cheerfully, "The more she travels, the better she bears it"; but his optimism was not justified.

Mrs. Wesley could not endure the rudeness of the people, the hardness of the beds, the agony of the jolting vehicles, the bad food, the hot or cold or muggy or boisterous weather. In the summer of 1752, she accompanied Wesley to Ireland, taking with her Miss Jenny Vazeille, her daughter: they had a rough passage and were extremely sick—"particularly when we had a rolling sea." She must have regretted vehemently the comforts of Threadneedle Street. In November, Vincent Perronet wrote to Charles Wesley: "I am truly concerned that matters are in so melancholy a situation. *I think the unhappy lady is most to be pitied*, though the gentleman's case is mournful enough." Still the wretched woman travelled up and down the country, with an occasional rest in Bristol and London.

This went on until 1755. Mrs. Wesley had now become intolerably jealous. During the absence of Wesley in Cornwall she opened a packet of his letters, and found among them a few lines addressed to a Mrs. Lefevre. After this, she behaved with most exasperating alternations of tears, malevolence and fury. Charles Wesley, in a letter to his wife written in 1756, says: "I hope Mrs. W. keeps her distance. If malice is stronger than her pride, she will pay you a mischievous visit. Poor Mr. Lefevre laments that he cannot love her. Blessed be God, I can, and desire to love her more." But Charles and Sally, with the best will in the world, could not remain on friendly terms with such a sad, outrageous creature.

John Wesley, by his own imprudence or simplicity, made matters infinitely worse. He had appointed as housekeeper of the Kingswood school a woman called Sarah Ryan. This woman had been converted from a somewhat irregular life, and we will charitably suppose that she was a good and respectable housekeeper. But she had married three husbands in succession, without waiting for the usual formalities of death or divorce. It should be said, in her defence, that each of the three husbands treated her abominably. If Wesley was unwise in giving her a position of responsibility at Kingswood, he was a thousand times more unwise in choosing her for his confidential correspondent. In 1757, the year of her removal to Kingswood, she was thirty-three. Before her appointment, she had been in domestic service, and had afterwards joined a group of Methodist women at Christopher Alley in Moorfields.

It is reasonable that Wesley should have corresponded with his Bristol housekeeper, but hardly reasonable that he should have written to her with peculiar intimacy. "Surely," he said to her in one of his letters, "God will never suffer me to be ashamed of my confidence in you. I have been censured for it by some of your nearest friends; but I cannot repent of it." He believed that she was a good and pious woman, exceptionally well fitted for her work. In his letters, he pressed her to give him an account of her spiritual experiences, and he questioned her anxiously in regard to weakness, pride, unprofitable images, disorders of the body, the vanity and folly of dreams, the imminence of temptation. If he was misled, he was misled by his own candour and innocence; but we know of nothing in the conduct of Sarah Ryan, after her appointment to Kingswood, which is not entirely in her favour. She died in 1768.

The installation of this housekeeper, and the fact of her correspondence with Wesley, had the natural effect of adding fuel to the blazing jealousy of Mrs. John. In January 1758, she found in Wesley's pocket a letter addressed to Mrs. Ryan. At the end of the month, Wesley sent the following letter to Sarah Ryan at Kingswood:

"My dear Sister,
    "Last Friday, after many severe words, my wife left me, vowing she would see me no more. As I had wrote to you the same morning, I began to reason with myself, till I almost doubted whether I had done well in writing, or whether I ought to write to you at all. After prayer that doubt was taken away. Yet I was almost sorry that I had written that morning. In the evening, while I was preaching at the Chapel, she came into the chamber where I had left my clothes, searched my pockets, and found the letter there, which I had finished, but had not sealed. While she read it, God broke her heart; and I afterwards found her in such a temper as I have not seen her in for several years. She has continued in the same ever since."

In the following month, he again wrote to Mrs. Ryan in the most unguarded manner:

"Your last letter was seasonable indeed. I was growing faint in my mind. The being continually watched over for evil, the having every word I spoke, every action I did, small and great, watched over with no friendly eye; the hearing a thousand little, tart, unkind reflections, in return for the kindest words I could devise—

Like drops of eating water on the marble,
At length have worn my sinking spirits down.

Yet I could not say *Take Thy plague away from me*; but only, *Let me be purified, not consumed*."

From the correspondence of Wesley himself, and from other sources, we learn the sad and sordid particulars of his life with this increasingly demented woman. After 1756 they do not seem to have been together for long periods. As you read Wesley's account of his amazingly active existence, you hardly notice that he was married for thirty years.

The chief cause of Mrs. Wesley's atrocious behaviour was a violent, insane jealousy. "On one occasion she seized his letters and other papers, and put them into the hands of such as she knew to be his enemies, that they might be printed, as presumptive proof of illicit connections." In order that the proof might be as plain as possible, she interpolated passages of her own crazy devising, or even forged entire letters. She would travel a hundred miles, much as she disliked travelling, in order to see who was in the carriage with her husband. She declared that Charles Wesley's wife had been for years the mistress of John. When John was in the house with her, she watched his chamber door continually, and allowed no one to visit him without her leave. If he left his study for any length of time, she would open his desk and go through his papers, taking away any of which she disapproved. She railed and swore at the servants, using the coarse, virulent language of a fishwife. Her lies, if anyone had believed them, might have caused irremediable mischief. She said that Wesley "had laid a plot to serve her as Susannah was served by the two elders." There was no limit to the folly, indecency and extravagance of her accusations. That she was actually violent in deed, and assaulted her husband, is doubtful, though most of Wesley's early biographers record this with assurance.

In any case, the authentic episodes are ugly enough and pitiful enough in all conscience. All that we can be thankful for is, that in the thirty years between their marriage and her death Wesley saw so little of his wife. Mrs Wesley left her husband on several occasions, and for periods of some years, though she did not finally desert him until 1776.

Wesley's attitude towards his wife is marked by persevering affection and by inexhaustible patience. He reproved her firmly, but never with bitterness. Yet his words, at times, had a peculiar, though not intentional, sting: "Do not any longer contend for mastery, for power, money, or praise. Be content to be a private insignificant person, known and loved by God and me. . . . Then shall I govern you with gentle sway, and show that I do indeed love you." Wesley held the apostolic view, that wives ought to submit to the rule of their husbands. But he could never be accused of lacking in consideration. In the summer of 1768, he received the news that his wife was ill. He had just reached Bristol after a tiring journey from South Wales. Immediately he took a chaise and posted to London, reaching the Foundry before one o'clock in the morning. He discovered that "the fever had turned and the danger was over." At two o'clock he started from London, and was in Bristol again before the evening of the same day. He had thus travelled a total distance of about two hundred and fifty miles in order to be assured of his wife's condition, and to see that she was receiving proper care.

Under the date of the 23rd of January 1771 there occurs a famous passage in Wesley's *Journal*: "For what cause I know not to this day, my wife set out for Newcastle, purposing 'never to return.' *Non eam reliqui; non dimisi; non revocabo*."

Jenny Vazeille, Mrs. Wesley's daughter, had married William Smith, a Newcastle Methodist. It may therefore be assumed that Mrs. Wesley stayed with her son-in-law at Newcastle. But although Wesley was firm in the matter of *non revocabo*, his wife returned with him to Bristol in 1772. In 1774 she was still in correspondence with him: Tyerman has printed a silly, querulous letter of hers, belonging to this year. By 1776, they appear to have finally separated.

Mrs. Wesley died on the 8th of October 1781. John Wesley, at that time, was travelling and preaching in the West of England, and did not hear of his wife's death until his return to London on the 11th of October. He records the fact in his *Journal* with extreme brevity: "I came to London, and was informed that my wife died on Monday. This evening she was buried, *though I was not informed of it* till a day or two after."

The tombstone of Mrs. John Wesley commemorated her

as "a woman of exemplary piety, a tender parent, and a sincere friend." It would be most ungenerous to suppose that the person who devised this epitaph was entirely in the wrong; but perhaps we should make some allowance for the polite manners of the century, and for the general elegance of funeral inscriptions at that period.

It is possible to exaggerate the importance of Wesley's marriage, or to linger with a too protracted sorrow over its miserable details. Wesley could never have sunk to the level of domesticity. His energies alone would have driven him to the change and adventure of a roving life: we cannot imagine such a man returning each day to the same familiar fireside. But his energies were devoted to a single purpose, his rovings had a single aim.

If we examine the lives of great men, we shall find them always methodical; we shall find them uniting, like Wesley, copious vitality with consistent effort. Wesley placed his work before everything else. His idea in marrying was to find a helper, an associate, a companion; but above all a helper. His wife, he thought, would be of invaluable assistance as a worker among the women in every town where he had founded a Methodist society. A suitable marriage could have doubled the effectiveness of his mission. And he would have had constantly with him a trusted friend, able to give him advice, or to confer with him on matters of discipline or administration.

That he should have chosen Mrs. Vazeille is certainly incomprehensible. Something might have been said in favour of his marriage with Grace Murray; but nothing could have been said in favour of his marriage with this poor, vulgar, disastrous widow.

The marriage of Wesley was a blunder, but not a blunder which had tremendous consequences. Mrs. John Wesley could not endure the hardship of travelling for at least nine months out of the twelve; she was left behind. Mrs. John Wesley had fits of violent jealousy; but Mrs. Ryan went on cutting the joints and airing the linen at Kingswood. And if Mrs. John Wesley stole papers and told lies, if she screamed or ranted, or ran to the neighbours with many inventions of scandal—John Wesley groaned in his tribulation, but he did not travel one mile or preach one sermon the less.

In his effective aspect, therefore, Wesley cannot be said to have been injured by his marriage. His blunder was a source of private misery and of intense disappointment, but not of continued suffering; nor was it the cause of any loss in authority or prestige. There is so great a gulf between the holy stature of John Wesley and the poor insignificance of Mrs. Vazeille, that we are shocked, not so much by the unhappiness of the marriage as by its dreadful images of incongruity.

Perhaps the widow Vazeille had few amiable qualities and many bad ones; but she had her grievances too. Her second marriage was just as unfortunate for her as it was for Wesley. She might have been happy and harmless with some retired merchant or City drudge: it is difficult to imagine what she was thinking about when she accepted Wesley, a leader of evangelistic religion. From her point of view, he could never have been a satisfactory husband; indeed, her desertions are less surprising than her returns. Whatever her failings, it is proper to feel at least a little pity for a woman whose life was made wretched by her own fatal miscalculation.

CHAPTER XVI

BEASTS OF THE PEOPLE

DURING the first twenty years of his mission (1740-1760) Wesley was often called on to face the ugly violence of mobs. He was frequently exposed, not only to the risk of savage treatment, but to the risk of death. And not Wesley alone, but Charles Wesley and Whitefield, and indeed most of the early Methodist preachers, faced the same peril. Seward, after being blinded by a mob at Caerleon, was beaten or stoned to death by another mob at Hay. Whitefield, covered with blood and on the point of falling, was rescued in the nick of time from the brutal fury of an Irish crowd at Dublin. Charles Wesley narrowly escaped with his life at Devizes. Preachers were dragged out of their houses at night and driven half naked over the cold moors. They were trampled upon, or flung into water, or worried by dogs. Methodist women, even those who were pregnant, were treated with unspeakable barbarity. Fatal injuries were frequent. The houses of Methodists were burnt or pulled down, and their goods were stolen or wantonly destroyed. In many cases, the mob was organised by clergymen or local squires; and in nearly every case the magistrates were in sympathy with the rioters, and would neither intervene nor administer justice.

The most formidable anti-Methodist riots occurred between 1742 and 1751, chiefly in Staffordshire, Cornwall, and the South of Ireland. After 1751, although mob interference had by no means come to an end, disturbances were of a more effervescent and local character, and were less frequently encouraged or promoted by deliberate agitators.

Much depended upon the attitude of the magistrates; and it is greatly to the credit of the mayor of Bristol in 1740 and to the chairman of the Middlesex Bench in 1741, that even in those early days both of them took stern measures against the rabble who tried to break up Wesley's meetings.

It would, of course, be entirely wrong to look for the sinister connivance of the squire, the clergyman and the justice in every case of prolonged rioting. There are born rioters, just as there are born fighters, if the two are not the same; and it is generally easy to find people who like the excitement of a row. But it was unquestionably the attitude of the clergy and of the landed classes which gave the mob its privilege and excuse, even when it was not led in person by gentlemen or curates.

It is a proof of the irresistible vitality of the Methodist movement, that neither danger, violence, nor intimidation had the slightest effect upon its advance. The number of people who were frightened away from Methodism was exceedingly small; the number of those who were gained by the Methodist example of courage and manliness, and above all by the superb coolness of Wesley himself, was exceedingly great.

We have to distinguish between mere rowdiness, such as might occur at a political meeting, and the appearance of a really murderous or violent intention. There is a difference between the fiercely playful beating of drums, howling of ballads, rasping of fiddles or ringing of bells, and the desire to rush the platform and kill the speaker.

For example, the village crowd at Pensford near Bristol tried to drive a baited bull among Wesley's congregation. It was an ugly scene. The bull, torn by dogs and men and weak from loss of blood, could only stagger blindly among the people; it was dragged and thrust—a mere bleeding mass—towards the table on which Wesley had been preaching. Wesley pushed aside the head of the bull, so that the blood might not drop on his clothes. At last the table fell down, and the preacher was forcibly carried away by his friends; and then, at a little distance, he "finished his discourse without any noise or interruption." This was in 1742. Here, the baiting of the preacher was only a secondary consequence of baiting the bull, and although Wesley says the mob was "hired," it was all part of an afternoon's frolic, mere British playfulness. A more serious disorder took place in the same year at Great Gardens, between Whitechapel and Coverlet's Fields, where an attempt was made to break up the meeting with a herd of cows, and Wesley was struck in the face by a stone.

But the first actual rioting occurred in South Staffordshire in 1743. In this year, the tide of violence was rising in several places, and Charles Wesley had met raging mobs at Sheffield in May and at St. Ives in July. The Staffordshire riots began in October.

On the afternoon of the 29th of October, Wesley was quietly writing in the house of Francis Ward at Wednesbury, when he was told that a mob had surrounded them. In a little time, and as Wesley believed in answer to his prayer, the people dispersed. At five o'clock the house was again surrounded by a roaring crowd, all shouting, "Bring out the Minister! Give us the Minister!" The captain of the mob was brought into the house, and after a few words with John Wesley he became as mild as a lamb. He went out, and brought back with him two angry fellows who were "ready to swallow the ground with rage." But even these were overawed by the peace and composure of Wesley.

After this, Wesley asked them to make way for him, and he left the house and stood up on a chair in the middle of the crowd. "What do you want with me?" he said. They answered, "We want you to go with us to the Justice." He replied, "I will go with all my heart." And after he had spoken a little, the temper of the mob changed: they cried out, "He is an honest gentleman, and we will spill our blood in his defence!" Wesley then asked, "Shall we go to the Justice to-night, or in the morning?" Most of the people were in favour of going at once, so they set out— Wesley at the head of the mob, talking to the leaders, and followed by two or three hundred. An advance party ran on to the house of Mr. Justice Lane, about two miles from Wednesbury. Mr. Lane received the party. "What have I to do with Mr. Wesley?" he said. "Go and carry him back again." And he turned out the deputation and bolted his door. When the main body came up, they were told that Mr. Lane was in bed. His son came downstairs and advised the people to go home and be quiet. There was a pause, and then it was decided to go to Mr. Justice Persehouse at Walsall.

It was a dark night, and raining hard. But they all trudged on to Walsall, only to find that Mr. Justice Persehouse was also in bed. At the second check, they decided o go back, and a party of about fifty men undertook to escort Wesley. But they had not gone a hundred yards before a new mob came plunging out of the darkness, scattered the Wednesbury men and laid hold of their prisoner.

In the hands of the Walsall men, Wesley was now in danger of a bloody death. He could not make himself heard, for the noise on every side was "like the roaring of the sea." He was dragged back by the hair when he attempted to enter a house, and was carried bodily away by the moving mass of the rioters. So he was taken from one end of the town of Walsall to the other. Once he stood in a doorway and asked if they would hear him speak. Most of them shouted in reply, "No, no! Beat his brains out! kill him at once!" According to Charles Wesley: "Some cried 'Drown him! throw him into a pit!' Some, 'Hang him up upon the next tree!' Others, 'Away with him!' . . . and some did him the infinite honour to cry in express terms, 'Crucify him!' One and all said, 'Kill him!' but they were not agreed what death to put him to. In Walsall several said, 'Carry him out of the town: don't kill him here: don't bring his blood upon us!' To some who cried, 'Strip him; tear off his clothes!' he mildly replied, 'That you need not do: I will give you my clothes, if you want them.'"

Wesley observed, that although many people tried to get hold of his collar or coat to pull him down, none of them succeeded. He tells us how a man struck at him from behind with an oaken stick, and how the blows were miraculously turned aside; and how another, forcing his way through the press, raised his arm to strike, and then let it fall gently on Wesley's head, remarking somewhat foolishly, "What soft hair he has!" Others, who thrust savagely towards him with sticks or stones in their hands, found themselves powerless in the immediate presence of Wesley, although in the darkness of the stormy night they could not clearly see his face. Wesley, remember, was a little man, and in any circumstances he must have been invisible to the greater part of the mob. As they hustled him down a steep hill, he knew that if he fell he would be trampled to death: "But," said Charles, with one of his delightful touches of affectionate admiration, "his feet never once slipped; for in their hands the angels bore him up. . . . The spirit of glory rested on him. As many as he spoke to, or but laid his hand on, he turned into friends." And in all this howling tumult, the Preacher was not deserted by his followers, four of whom kept as near to him as possible: William Sitch, Edward Slater, John Griffiths, and a brave girl named Joan Parks.

As the mob poured out of Walsall, still howling for the death of the prisoner, a sudden change of mood took place among the leaders. A great hulking fellow turned to Wesley and said abruptly: "Sir, I will spend my life for you: follow me, and not one soul here shall touch a hair of your head."

In a few moments, those who were near Wesley had become his bodyguard. They hurried him out of the town and down to the bridge. At this point there seemed every likelihood of a scuffle, if not of a final attempt at murder. The bodyguard therefore took Wesley to one side and got him across the mill dam below the bridge. His brother, in giving the story of John Wesley's escape, which he had from those who were present, says: "The instrument of his deliverance at last was the ringleader of the mob, the greatest profligate in the country: he carried him through the river upon his shoulders." This crossing of the river gave John a moment of uneasiness: "It came into my mind," he says, "that if they should throw me into the river, it would spoil the papers that were in my pocket; for myself, I did not doubt but I should swim across, having but a thin coat and a light pair of boots." At last he was brought safely across the fields to Francis Ward's house at Wednesbury.

A few days later, the Justices Lane and Persehouse saw fit to issue a proclamation, in which they declared that "several disorderly persons, styling themselves Methodist Preachers, go about *raising routs and riots*, to the great damage of His Majesty's liege people, and against the Peace of our Sovereign Lord the King." These were the very Justices who had refused to intervene when John Wesley, in peril of his life, was dragged to their houses by the mob.

Early in the following year (1744) a systematic and atrocious persecution of the Methodists was organised by the "gentlemen" in the neighbourhood of Wednesbury and Walsall. Houses were totally wrecked, sick women were pulled out of their beds, children were driven into the streets (no one daring to take them in), goods and stores were destroyed or carried away, furniture was hacked to pieces, cattle were maimed, linen was torn up and papers stolen, men were beaten with clubs, and their wives and daughters horribly abused. The "gentlemen" who were responsible for this appalling state of affairs had threatened to dismiss every collier or servant in their pay who did not take a hand in the looting and rioting; and they drew up a paper to be signed by those who would engage themselves "neither to invite nor receive any Methodist Preacher." In this villainy, a clergyman, whose infamous name is not preserved, took a leading part. Such was *Modern Christianity, Exemplified at Wednesbury, and Other Adjacent Places in Staffordshire.*

The Cornish riots of 1745, though neither so extensive nor so horrible as those in Staffordshire, were not without their fearful scenes of terrorism and brutality. Dr. Borlase and the Cornish gentlemen were still raging against the Methodists. In the previous year, poor James Dale appealed to Borlase for justice against a rioter who had broken into his house and stolen his goods. He might as well have appealed to some Druidical rock. "Thou *conceited* fellow!" roared the Doctor: "What! art thou too turned religious? They may burn thy house if they will: it is no concern of mine!"

We have to recall that in 1745 many of the Cornish people seriously believed that Charles and John Wesley were agents of the Pretender, raising forces and inciting men to overthrow the lawful king. This extraordinary idea had much to do with the Falmouth riot of the 4th of July.

Wesley had just escaped from furious Borlase and futile Eustick. He rode from Gwennap to Falmouth, and at three in the afternoon he was in the house of "a gentlewoman who had long been indisposed." He had not been in the house for many minutes before it was "beset on all sides by an innumerable multitude of people." The sound of this mob exceeded, in mere loudness and confusion, anything that Wesley had previously heard. The lady and her daughter tried to quiet them: they might as well have whispered to a hurricane or argued with the rising sea. Wesley and the servant-girl, Kitty, soon found themselves alone in the house, to shift for themselves as best they could.

The mob now raised their voices in a single cry: "Canorum! Canorum! Bring out the Canorum! Where is the old Canorum?" The word had no meaning; it was an invention of the Cornish rabble, and was applied to every Methodist. As the Canorum did not show himself, the people forced the outer door and flowed roaring into the passage. There was only a thin partition between the rioters and the two people in the house. Wesley took down a large mirror that was hanging on the partition so that it might not be damaged. On the other side there was a strenuous heaving and pushing and battering and cursing.

"Oh, Sir!" cried poor Kitty; "what must we do?" "We must pray," said Wesley; and he observed afterwards, "At that time, to all appearances, our lives were not worth an hour's purchase." "But, Sir," said Kitty, "is it not better for you to hide yourself? to get into the closet?" "No," answered Wesley; "it is best for me to stand just where I am." Some privateersman, who saw that a little discipline was needed, pushed away the others impatiently, and with loud shouts of "Avast lads! avast there!" set their shoulders against the partition.

Down came the door, hinges and all; and Wesley coolly stepped out into the midst of the rabble, as though he was only walking out of his own front door to take an airing.

"Ah!" said he, looking them in the face; "which of you has anything to say to me? Here I am, you see. Why all this turbulence? To which of you have I done any wrong? To you?—or you?—or you?" Speaking and smiling, he passed out of the house and walked to the middle of the street. "Do you desire to hear me speak?" "Yes! yes!" cried the rabble: "he shall speak: let him speak; nobody shall hinder him." Wesley had purposely left his hat in the house, so that they might clearly see his face. But he stood on a level road, and he could only be seen by those who were in the front of the crowd. The privateersmen and the "captains" of the mob made a little space for him, and swore bloodily that he should have a hearing.

In no other known instance has a mob so effectively been subdued by the influence of a single man, or by the power of the spoken word. Mr. Thomas, a clergyman, came up and asked the people if they were not ashamed of themselves. He was backed, we are glad to notice, by two or three "gentlemen of the town," and Wesley was escorted, "speaking all the time," to Mrs. Maddern's house. Here, the gentlemen proposed to have Wesley's horse brought to the door, but on second thoughts they considered it advisable not to face the crowd again. The horse was sent on to Penryn, and Wesley was taken out of the back of the house and put into a boat. The mob, or a part of it, was still in an ugly temper. As the boat pulled along by the edge of the creek towards Penryn, a number of angry men ran to meet Wesley at the landing-place. When he came up the steep narrow passage from the sea, he found a group of men waiting for him. He looked at the first man, and wished him a good night. The man said nothing until Wesley had quietly mounted his horse; then he observed, "I wish you was in hell," and turned back to his companions. In the church accounts of Falmouth there appeared, later, a charge of nine shillings for "driving the Methodists out of the Parish."

Wesley believed that he was never in greater danger of being killed than he was at Falmouth. He never saw more plainly the hand of God. At Walsall, he was not deserted by friends, who might have put up a desperate resistance if matters had come to the worst. At Falmouth, he was alone; for poor Kitty could have done nothing, and she was hustled away as soon as the door was broken in. Here, he observes, "although the hands of perhaps some hundreds of people were lifted up to strike or throw, yet they were one and all stopped in the mid-way, so that not a man touched me with one of his fingers; neither was anything thrown from first to last; so that I had not even a speck of dirt on my clothes."

It is extremely interesting to note the second entry in Wesley's *Journal* relating to Falmouth. It was made on the 18th of August 1789, less than two years before his death, and forty years after the riot:

"In the afternoon, as we could not pass by the common road, we procured leave to drive round by some fields, and got to Falmouth in good time. The last time I was here, above forty years ago, I was taken prisoner by an immense mob, gaping and roaring like lions. But how is the tide turned!—high and low now lined the street from one end of the town to the other, out of stark love and kindness, gaping and staring as if the King were going by. In the evening I preached on the smooth top of the hill . . . to the largest congregation I have ever seen in Cornwall, except in or near Redruth. . . . God moved wonderfully on the hearts of the people, who all seem to know the day of their visitation."

And forty years before, Falmouth had tried to murder the preacher, and had gone to the length of paying nine shillings to have a horse led and a boat rowed in order "to drive the Methodists out of the Parish."

Neither John nor Charles was in Exeter at the time of the hideous though brief riot on the 6th of May 1745; but in 1747, at Devizes, Charles had to face a mob as fierce as any of those which had threatened his brother.

For two or three years after the Falmouth riot, there were few occasions on which Wesley himself was threatened with violence. Noisy rabbles with bells, drums and horns, met him in some places; unruly drunkards blustered and swore and kicked the doors and the furniture; but there was not much organised rioting until the affair at Barrowford, near Colne, in 1748.

Wesley's method in dealing with mere rowdyism is nowhere better exemplified than at Plymouth, on the 27th of May 1747. The episode is best related in his own words:

" About six in the evening I went to the place where I preached the last year. A little before we had ended the hymn came the Lieutenant, a famous man, with his retinue of soldiers, drummers and mob. When the drums ceased, a gentleman-barber began to speak; but his voice was quickly drowned in the shouts of the multitude, who grew fiercer and fiercer as their numbers increased. After waiting about a half of an hour, perceiving the violence of the rabble still increasing, I walked down into the thickest of them, and took the captain of the mob by the hand. He immediately said, 'Sir, no man shall touch you. Gentlemen, stand off; give back. I will knock the first man down that touches him.' We walked on in great peace; my conductor every now and then stretching out his neck (he was a very tall man) and looking round to see if any behaved rudely, till we came to Mr Hyde's door. We then parted in much love. I stayed in the street near half an hour after he was gone, talking with the people, who had now forgot their anger, and went away in high good humour."

Of all the mobs that John Wesley encountered, the most efficiently organised was that of Colne, in Lancashire. This mob had a Commander-in-Chief, who issued orders and proclamations, as well as pints of ale: this Commander-in-Chief was the Reverend George White, the curate of Colne.

On the 16th of August 1748, Wesley, accompanied by Grace Murray and one of his preachers (Mackford), left Newcastle. On the 24th they were at Haworth. The rector of Haworth was the famous Methodist, William Grimshaw. It is probable that Wesley received from Grimshaw a disquieting account of what was going on at Roughlee and

Barrowford, in the Colne district on the other side of the hills. At any rate, on the day following their arrival at Haworth, Wesley and Grace Murray, accompanied by Grimshaw and Mackford, rode over the high country towards Barrowford. They were to meet Thomas Colbeck, a young preacher, at Roughlee. As they came down into the valley, friendly people met them and advised them to go no farther. The forces of Commander White had been fully mobilised, and were moving out in order of battle. Roughlee, so far, was quiet. Wesley and his companions pushed on to Roughlee, and here they met Colbeck. It was now decided that Wesley should begin his preaching at once, but first of all, Grace Murray, on the advice of Grimshaw, was taken to a place of safety. "At half an hour after twelve," said Wesley, "I began to preach: I had about half finished my discourse, when the mob came pouring down the hill like a torrent."

The Reverend George White, whose behaviour leads us to suppose that he had mistaken his calling, had issued the following proclamation:

"NOTICE is hereby given, that if any Men be mindful to enlist into His Majesty's Service, under the Command of the Revd. George White, Commander-in-Chief, and John Bannister, Lieutenant-General of His Majesty's Forces for the Defence of the *Church of England* and the Support of the *Manufactory* in and about Colne, both of which are now in Danger, etc., etc., let them now repair to the Drumhead at the Cross, when each Man shall have a Pint of Ale in Advance, and other Proper Encouragements."

No proclamation could have been drawn up in more effective terms. George White had no business in the Church, but he would certainly have been useful in the regular army. He used to walk about carrying "a large pistol." He knew how to give his men "proper encouragements," and he knew how to make them believe they were fine fellows, serving the king, and saving at one stroke the Church of England and the "manufactories" of Lancashire. His use of military jargon gave a plausible appearance to his manœuvres, and gave his people a gratifying sense of being nobly united in the performance of a great duty. These are the gifts of the born commander. And it is to be observed that Wesley himself, in speaking of the Colne mob, makes use, for the first time, of military expressions : "The whole army," he says, "drew up in battle array." It is to be deplored that George White drank himself to death four years later.

As the forces of Mr. White poured down the hill towards Barrowford, Mr. White, like a real commander, posted himself in a house at some distance to the rear. His leaders were instructed to bring Wesley to the house.

But at this point it would be unfair to regard the behaviour of the Colne mob as that of an army. No mob ever treated Wesley with such outrageous violence, even if he was in greater danger of death at Walsall and Falmouth. He was requested to go with the leaders; but before he had walked many yards, a man struck him in the face, and another threw a stick at his head. In the house at Barrowford, Wesley, Grimshaw, Colbeck and Mackford were confronted by George White and his friends. After more than two hours of rambling discourse (for several pints of ale had probably been taken "in advance") Wesley agreed that he would not, at that time, preach again at Roughlee. He had tried to leave the house in the midst of the general confusion, but had been struck to the ground, and forced back again. At last, it was agreed that he might go. He was taken by Mr. White out of one door, while Grimshaw, Colbeck and Mackford went out by another.

The mob was waiting for them. Grimshaw was thrown down and covered with mud; Colbeck was treated in the same fashion; Mackford was dragged about by his hair, and received permanent injuries. The Methodists who had come from Roughlee and Barrowford, to see what was going on, were forced to run for their lives. They were beaten with clubs, trampled under foot, and furiously pelted with clods and stones: one was compelled to jump from a high rock into the stream, and as he crawled out, wet and bruised, he was threatened with a second ducking. "All this time," said Wesley, addressing Mr. White, "you sat well pleased . . . not attempting in the least to hinder them."

A few days later, Wesley preached at the Cross in Bolton.

"There was a vast number of people, but many of them utterly wild. As soon as I began speaking, they began thrusting to and fro, endeavouring to throw me down from the steps on which I stood. They did so once or twice; but I went up again, and continued my discourse. They then began to throw stones. . . . One man was bawling just at my ear, when a stone struck him on the cheek, and he was still. A second was forcing his way down to me, till another stone hit him on the forehead . . . the blood ran down, and he came no farther. The third, being got close to me, stretched out his hand, and in the instant a sharp stone came upon the joints of his fingers. He shook his hand, and was very quiet till I concluded my discourse and went away."

Wesley himself was not in Cork at the worst period of the rioting of 1749 and 1750. It has been said: "For duration and intensity, it may be doubted whether the annals of Methodism supply anything like a parallel to these infamous riots."

The Cork mob was led by a person called Nicholas Butler: he was a singer of ballads, a vagabond by profession. In sheer brutality and indecency it would certainly be hard to find a parallel to Nicholas Butler even in the black history of Irish mobs. The doings of this brute and his followers were tacitly encouraged by the mayor of Cork and the Roman clergy.

Butler used to go about in the dress of a clergyman. Sometimes he had a Bible in one hand and a packet of ballads in the other. He kicked and assaulted Methodist women, and slashed them with a sword. He led his mob to Methodist houses, broke into them, and stole or destroyed what they contained. Assaults upon women, with the seizure or destruction of their property, were among the ordinary procedures of the Butler mob. Neither the mayor nor the aldermen of Cork would listen to complaints; no jury would find a true bill against Butler's men or the anti-Swaddlers, as they were called; and this state of things went on for more than a year, until a higher authority was forced to intervene in order to prevent a national scandal of the first magnitude.

John Wesley saw enough of the beastliness of the mob at Cork when he was there in May 1750. The mayor gave instructions to the town drummers and the serjeants, ostensibly to keep the people in order, but actually to interfere with the preaching of Wesley and to let the rabble have their own way. As Wesley came out of the meeting-house and saw a tumultuous crowd before him, he called on one of the serjeants to keep the King's peace; the serjeant replied, "Sir, I have no orders to do that." Wesley therefore walked through the rabble, looking them in the face and forcing them out of his path. Even a large party at Dant's Bridge, who were shouting "Hey for the Romans!" let him go by without molestation. But the furniture in the meeting-house was wrecked, burnt, or carried away.

"It was my rule," said Wesley, "confirmed by long experience, always to look a mob in the face." That was the obvious rule for a brave man; but something more than mere bravery saved Wesley from the worst effects of violence. If he had been a soldier on active service, people would have said that his life was charmed. Stones, aimed at him, missed their mark or hit the enemy instead. Cudgels were thrust aside, or knocked out of murderous hands, by some invisible force. It was not courage alone that saved Wesley. He was preserved by tranquil dignity, by cool, steady and courteous behaviour, by the entire absence of malice or anger, but above all by those peculiar graces and powers which accompany the man of God.

CHAPTER XVII

THE GREAT VULGAR

IF there is a middle place between good and evil, in that place you will surely find the great company of the foolish, those misty souls, made to inhabit the huge vacuity of Limbo. The state of a hearty sinner is never hopeless; but the fool, impervious to light or wisdom, has always been a source of despair; there is no vestige of responsibility, no faculty of apprehension, within the empty darkness of his poor mind.

In common with every other Christian teacher, Wesley found that he could make no headway against the foolish. He could beat down the more vigorous and palpable forces of evil, he could come to grips with intelligent opposition; but levity and folly brought him to a dead stop. He was a man of exquisite breeding, to whom, with all his wide tolerance, rudeness was always offensive; he was a scholar, to whom ignorance appeared always deplorable.

The eighteenth century was the last great period of the English gentleman. In that century, a surprisingly large number of people really did succeed in doing exactly as they pleased. An imperfect knowledge of social history, or a confusion of romantic ideas, might lead us to think of the eighteenth century as a period of extreme politeness, of culture, good taste and prevailing elegance; and a casual acquaintance with the best of its literature might certainly confirm that impression. Some of us are inclined to regret, in our own slipshod times, what we imagine to have been the quiet amplitude of eighteenth-century conversation, and the grace or wit of eighteenth-century letters. In actual fact, there was probably never a time in which the ordinary talk of fashionable people was coarser, duller, or more insipid.

Men who can do as they please usually think first of amusing themselves. Before the age of mechanised industry, almost the only people who were able to do nothing but amuse themselves were the people described by John and

Charles Wesley as the "so-called gentlemen" or "the great vulgar."

The country was full of clowns upon horseback, whooping and hallooing and blowing their absurd little hunting-horns among the fields and lanes of a happy and admiring land. The town was full of preposterous dandies, more stupid, more vain, more over-dressed than the heartier bucks and blades of the Restoration. Instead of being able to talk and write with elegance, few men of fashion could speak or spell without continual blunders. Stupid indecency was more acceptable than wit, and more certain of being understood. Slang was never more prevalent. The standard of education expected in a man of birth was never lower. But the general characteristic of high society was not so much a vigorous indulgence as mere silliness. If you doubt this, you have only to look at the pictures of Hogarth or the satires of Swift.

It is appropriate to quote here a letter from Wesley to a woman of rank, written in 1760. After warning her of the danger of indifference, he says:

"Is your taste now for heavenly things? Are you not a lover of pleasure, more than a lover of God? And O what pleasure! What is the pleasure of visiting? of modern conversation? Is there any more reason than religion in it? Setting religion quite out of the question, I cannot conceive how a woman of sense can—relish, should I say? no, but suffer, so insipid an entertainment."

So much for the element of politeness. The sons of Belial, the rowdies and roysterers, belong to another group. Gentlemen, we have observed, associated themselves with curates and colliers in stirring up the mobs against the Methodists. Such an association was the obvious consequence of being idle and stupid rather than the consequence of being depraved or bloodthirsty. Stupid people, if they want to assert themselves, can only do so by means of noise and violence. Besides, a riot was a pleasing alternative to hunting the fox or baiting the bull or indulging in the more ordinary forms of manly exercise.

But, before we examine Wesley's attitude towards the great vulgar, it is necessary to examine the attitude of the great vulgar towards Wesley. It has to be remembered that Wesley, from a society point of view, was a man of no importance. Whitefield's ministry was divided between England and America, but he worked in England for a total period of something like twenty-two years, and White-field, not Wesley, was always the fashionable Methodist preacher. Wesley confined his ministry to the common people, and particularly to the new industrial classes. He rarely entered the houses of great people, and it would be correct to say that the never did so willingly. He could never have become one of Lady Selina's tame chaplains. He was therefore personally unknown to people of high rank; his occasional appearance in the Bath chapel or at Lady Hunt-ingdon's Chelsea house had little effect upon those who saw him. Up to the very last year of his long life he remained, in this sense, an obscure man, with no change in his views concerning the great, and no change in their views con-cerning him. In most of the fashionable memoirs of the period, there is no mention of Wesley at all. In 1739, at the very beginning of his mission, he was already speaking with a shade of contempt about the "fine gay things" who strolled up to hear him at Bath: in 1790, a year before he died, he recorded a meeting at Shrewsbury in these words: "In the evening I preached to a crowded audience. . . . But I was much ashamed for them. The moment I had done speaking, I suppose fifty of them were talking at once; *and no wonder*, they had neither sense nor good manners, for they were gentlefolks."

Conventional society always assumed that Methodism was exclusively the affair of the common people, and had nothing to do with their betters. To suggest that well-bred people had "sinful hearts" was to be "highly offensive and insulting." Well-bred people had bishops and chaplains who knew their places, and were careful to observe the deference due to rank.

The general position of Wesley in regard to the gentle-folk of his period is of extraordinary significance, not only with reference to his own character, but with reference to the social and religious history of the times. There is something in this position which implies a great deal more than the obvious difference in view between a field-preacher and the idle great. It is interesting to see how Wesley himself explains, and justifies, his attitude. In a letter written in 1764 to a nobleman who was not unfriendly, he says:

"I have neither personal hopes nor fears from you. I want nothing which you can give me; and I am not afraid of your doing me any hurt; though you may hurt yourself and the cause of God. But I cannot answer your envy, jealousy, pride or credulity. As long as these remain objections, however cut off, will spring up again like Hydra's heads. . . . Have they not set your lordship farther and farther off, ever since I waited upon you at——? Why do I ask? Indeed, not upon my own account. *Quid mea? Ego in portu navigo.* I can truly say, I neither fear nor desire anything from your lordship; to speak a rough truth, I do not desire any intercourse with any persons of quality in England. I mean, for my own sake. They do me no good, and I fear I can do none to them. If it be desired, I will readily leave all these to the care of my fellow labourers. I will article with them to do so, rather than this shall be any bone of contention."

And in other places he observed: "In most genteel religious people there is so strange a mixture, that I have seldom much confidence in them. . . ." "How unspeakable is the advantage in point of common sense which middling people have over the rich! There is so much paint and affectation, so many unmeaning words and senseless customs among people of rank, as fully to justify the remark made seventeen hundred years ago, *Sensus communis in illa fortuna rarus.*"

Wesley was therefore convinced that his work lay among the poor and "middling" people. He could do no good to the others, and they could offer him no real assistance. It would have been a waste of time if he had gone out of his way to preach to lords and ladies, and he was ready enough to leave them to the Calvinistic efforts of Lady Huntingdon and her staff of chaplains. The very fact of Calvinism being well received by fashionable listeners may have helped to confirm his own attitude.

At the same time, it would be unfair not to mention three Scottish widows who gave Wesley a great deal of encouragement—Lady Frances Gardiner, Lady Maxwell, and Lady Glenorchy. In 1770 Lady Maxwell, an avowed Methodist, opened a school for poor children in Edinburgh, which she maintained for forty years, and left fully endowed. At the time of her meeting with Wesley she was about twenty-two years old, and had been widowed some three years previously. Lady Gardiner never got beyond the stage of a sympathetic interest; but Lady Glenorchy turned a Popish church into a Methodist chapel.

Another reason for the attitude of Wesley is to be found in that part of the drama and literature of the period which may be taken as representing polite opinion. Allusions to Methodists in plays and books intended for a polite audience were almost invariably hostile and often outrageously indecent. The great majority of these allusions were charges of hypocrisy and lewdness. Nor is there much to choose, for sheer profanity and malice, between the comedies of Foote and the scurrilous diatribes of the Bishops Lavington and Warburton. Of the poets, Cowper alone could praise the new revival, and praise in noble lines the character of Wesley. The magazines and reviews, at least until the last three decades of the century, were generally hostile and abusive.

An author in the *Monthly Review* for August 1749, spoke of the Methodist preachers as "the most wild and extravagant, the most ridiculous, strolling, fanatical, delirious and mischievous of all the Saints in the Romish communion." That may be taken as a fair example of the frenzied vituperation which can be found in scores of instances. But it should be noted that the *Gentleman's Magazine*, however viciously it may have attacked his followers, never attacked Wesley in person, and ultimately (when it was respectable to do so) regarded him not only seriously, but with a lively approval.

Fielding attacked the Methodists with heedless flippancy. Smollett denounced them in his *History of England*, but changed his tune when, in the last year of his life, he wrote *Humphrey Clinker*. Richardson, who could never have been violent about anything, treated Methodism with a stern reserve.

Wesley's particular view of high society is well shown in one of the most vigorous of his appeals:

"You eat and drink, and sleep and dress and dance and sit down to play. You are carried abroad. You are at the masquerade, the theatre, the opera-house, the park, the levee, the drawing-room. What do you do there? Why, sometimes you talk; sometimes you look at one another. And what are you to do to-morrow? The next day? The next year? You are to eat and drink, and sleep and dance, and dress and play again. And you are to be carried abroad again, that you may look at one another! And is this all? Alas, how little more happiness have you in this, than the Indian in looking at the sky or water. Ah, poor dull round! I do not wonder that Colonel M—— (or any man of reflection), should prefer death . . . to such a life as this."

Both John and Charles Wesley referred often to "the great vulgar and the small"—meaning by the first, those who were of gentle birth, and by the second, those who were shabbily genteel, or, in the purely social sense of the term, common. We find Charles using these terms in 1741, and John employed them from 1745 onwards.

In order to study more closely Wesley's relations with the upper classes (a study of real importance in the estimate of his character), we have to turn more particularly to his *Journals*. Here, writing under the influence of immediate impressions, he shows what he thought and felt when he came into contact with the gentlefolk and nobility of his day; and here we have, not only an essential aspect of Wesley himself, but a vivid though flickering series of little social pictures. It will be interesting to look at some of these pictures, taken, as far as possible, in chronological order. You will find in some of them a touch of irritation; in others, a touch of neat humour; and in all of them a consistency of outlook and experience.

When, after the encounter with Nash in 1739, some Bath ladies wanted to see Wesley, he observed: "I do not expect that the rich and the great should want either to speak with me, or to hear me; for I speak the plain truth; a thing you hear little of, and do not desire to hear." Wesley was then thirty-six years old, at the beginning of his active ministry. There may seem to be a certain arrogance and even a lack of charity in his remark, but it shows an attitude from which he never departed, and one which repeated experiences only tended to confirm.

Yet Wesley was of all men the most charitable, and until he was definitely repelled he did not regard the salvation of the great vulgar as altogether beyond his ability. Only a few days after talking to the ladies at Bath, he was preaching to Whitefield's congregation at Blackheath. "I was greatly moved," he said, "with compassion for the rich that were there, to whom I made a particular application. Some of them *seemed* to attend, while others drove away their coaches from so *uncouth* a preacher."

He was always astonished by a voluntary religious movement on the part of these people. In 1742, after his first visit to Newcastle, he stopped at Boroughbridge. "Here," he stated, "to my great surprise, the mistress of the house, though much of a gentlewoman, desired she and her family might join with us in prayer. . . . Perhaps even this seed may bring forth fruit."

On the occasion of his second visit to Newcastle, he said: "I could not but observe that the very best people, so-called, were as deeply convinced as open sinners. Several of these were now constrained to roar aloud . . . and these generally not young (as in most other places), but either middle-aged, or well stricken in years."

Again, at Bath in 1744, he notes: "Many of the audience appeared to be deeply convinced; and one, though a gentlewoman, could not conceal the emotion of her mind, but broke out into strong cries and tears."

And again, at Cardiff: "The word seemed to sink deep into the hearers, though many of them were of the genteeler sort."

There was an excellent scene at Bath in January 1743: "Some of the rich and great were present; to whom, as to the rest, I declared with all plainness of speech, 1. That, by nature, they were all children of wrath; 2. That all their natural tempers were corrupt and abominable; and 3. All their words and works—which could never be any better but by faith; and 4. A natural man has no more faith than a Devil, if so much. One of them, my Lord——, stayed very patiently until I came to the middle of my fourth head; then, starting up, he said *'Tis hot! 'Tis very hot!* and got downstairs as fast as he could."

Some of the most fashionable crowds who listened to Wesley came to hear him in places where we should hardly have expected to find them; for example, in Ireland, in Scotland, and in parts of Wales. He noted, in April 1748: "I preached at Clara (in King's County) to a vast number of well-behaved people; although some of them came in their coaches, and were (I was informed) of the best quality in the country. How few of these would have returned empty, if they had heard the word of God, not out of curiosity merely, but from a real desire to know and do His will?"

He observed elsewhere: "The poor in Ireland, in general, are well-behaved; all the ill-breeding is among well-dressed people." And he reflected that the manners of the provincial gentry in his own country were greatly inferior to those of the colliers and keelmen. Preaching to the Hampshire Militia, he said, was like "music to a horse."

At Holyhead, in 1750, when on his way to Ireland, there was a curious invasion:

"In the evening I was surprised to see, instead of some poor, plain people, a room full of men daubed with gold and silver. That I might not go out of their depth I began expounding the story of Dives and Lazarus. It was more applicable than I was aware; several of them (as I afterwards learned) being eminently wicked men. I delivered my soul, but they could in no wise bear it. One and another walked away, murmuring sorely. Four stayed till I drew to a close; they then put on their hats, and began talking to one another. I mildly reproved them, on which they rose up and went away, railing and blaspheming. I had then a comfortable hour with a company of plain, honest Welshmen."

At Brecon he once preached on "the bulwarks": "A multitude of people attended, and even the gentry seemed, for the present, almost persuaded to be Christians." At Monkton, near Pembroke, he preached in the church to a crowded congregation: "many of them were gay, genteel people. So I spake on the first elements of the Gospel; but I was still out of their depth. *O how hard it is to be shallow enough for a polite audience!*" When he was at Glasgow, he found a serious assembly, and chose a theme fit for "experienced Christians." But soon "a heap of fine gay people came in." And he goes on: "I could not decently break off what I was about, though they gaped and stared abundantly. I could only give a short exhortation in the close, *more suited to their capacity.*" Again, on the occasion of a later visit to Wales:

"At Pembroke, in the evening, we had the most elegant congregation I have ever seen since we came into Wales. Some of them came in dancing and laughing, as into a theatre; but their mood was quickly changed, and in a few minutes they were as serious as my subject, Death. I believe, if they do not take great care, they will remember it—for a week!"

It is not so much the rudeness or roughness of the great vulgar that Wesley deplores, as their invincible stupidity. He can deal with colliers, or with "honest Welshmen," who try to understand; but he cannot plumb the emptiness of these gay triflers. Again and again you have this note of humorous despair, or of real sorrow. It is hard to get a rich man to heaven, hard to get a fool there; and as for a rich fool, there seems to be no hope for him. The difficulty is to be shallow enough, to keep within genteel capacity. At Portarlington in 1769, Wesley was not a little embarrassed, he says, by a large company of *quality*. He knew that his discourse was "heathen Greek" to them; he had to "dilute it as much as he could, that it might not be quite too strong for their digestion." What is plain to the Christian of experience, let him be the most humble of labouring men, goes clean over the head of the squire or the gay lady. Strike upon these heads with your strong words, and you do but perceive an ominous resonance.

So, when Wesley (like Voltaire, but in what a different style!) wrote his *Thoughts on the Earthquake at Lisbon*, he directed it "not as he designed at first, to the small vulgar, but to the great; to the learned, rich and honourable heathens, commonly called Christians."

In 1759, he cried from his heart: "It is well a few of the rich and noble are called. O that God would increase their number! But I should rejoice (were it the will of God) if it were done by the ministry of others."

He did not wish to meet the rich and the noble; on the contrary, he tried to avoid them. He was not happy in their society. When he was a very old man, in 1785, he found himself in a house "full of genteel company" at Killchrist: "I was out of my element," he says, "there being no room to talk upon the only subject which deserves the attention of a rational creature." In April 1758, when he was in Dublin, he wrote: "I dined at Lady ——. We need great grace to converse with great people! From which, therefore (unless in some rare instances), I am glad to be excused. *Horae fugiunt et imputantur!* Of these two hours I can give no good account."

And we must not forget that the "so-called gentlefolk" were not only among the chief organisers of mobs, but were also the most frequent of casual interrupters at Wesley's meetings. Whether those interrupters were "pretty butterflies" or bawling bumpkins, there could never be a doubt of their gentility. At Epworth, in 1763, "A kind of gentle-man got a little party together, and took huge pains to disturb the congregation. He hired a company of boys to shout, and made a poor man exceedingly drunk, who bawled out much ribaldry and nonsense, while he himself played the French horn." At North Taunton, in 1765, there was a similar occurrence:

> "I had hardly ended the psalm, when a Clergyman came, with two or three by the courtesy of England called gentlemen. After I had named my text, I said, 'There may be some truths which concern some men only; but this concerns all mankind.' The minister cried out, 'That is false doctrine; that is predestination!' Then the roar began, to second which they had brought a huntsman with his hounds; but the dogs were wiser than the men, for they could not bring them to make any noise at all. One of the gentlemen supplied their place. He assured us he was such, or none would have suspected it; for his language was as base, foul and porterly, as ever was heard at Billingsgate: dog, rascal, puppy, and the like terms, adorned almost every sentence."

Even when the interruptions of the great vulgar were less obstreperous and less violent, they were sufficiently irritating. And Wesley noted the most trivial of these interruptions, sometimes indulgently and sometimes with sorrow and reproach.

For instance, at Liverpool in July 1764, he observed that he found there "more courtesy and humanity . . . than at most sea-ports in England." In Liverpool, he said, "the rich behaved as seriously as the poor." But the following passage occurs in his note of a Liverpool meeting: "Only one young gentlewoman (I heard) laughed much. Poor thing! Doubtless she thought, *I laugh prettily!*"

There are many such references in the *Journal* to "fluttering things," "gay things," "butterflies," and so forth. Indeed, the interruptions of tittering misses, who fancied they "laughed prettily" were often the only interruptions at meetings where many superior people were present. At Bridgewater, in 1769, Wesley recorded: "The very gentry (all but two or three young women) behaved with good sense and decency."

John Wesley never lost his temper or his coolness. He could be stern, immovable as a rock; but never fretful, never excited or angry. It is only with reference to gentle-folks that he almost invariably shows a touch of impatience, and allows himself to bring into play the keen edge of sarcasm.

There are, no doubt, many reasons for this. Idiocy and ignorance are things too dull and massive to be moved by serious appeal, and flippancy is a thing too light to hold the meaning of a serious message. It is flimsy folly, rather than active wickedness, which opposes or escapes from the preaching of truth. It is the muddled mind which remains for ever impervious. The devil, as Wesley knew, is the patron of blockheads, the prime apologist of the fool and the jester. Wesley was therefore bitterly grieved by an obstacle which he could never penetrate and never remove. He found in the poor people qualities of good sense and of c'ear thinking which he rarely discovered in the rich. He saw too often in birth and elegance something which appeared to be in fundamental opposition to wisdom, truth and light. He was aware of this opposition, not only in the great vulgar, but in those who aped gentility—in the rising masses of the small vulgar, who were beginning to spend their money on finery and to waste their minds in idleness. As a man of true breeding, he was vexed by rudeness or by uncouth manners. As a scholar, he was appalled by ignorance and by silly improprieties of speech. But chiefly as an evangelist, he was disheartened by the attitude of those who should have been bright examples of real nobility and faith. He was too charitable to suppose that no religion existed in the upper classes. He called upon those classes with a fine, plain sincerity, as in the words of his eloquent *Appeal*:

"Now cannot *you* join in all this? Is it not the very language of your heart? Oh when will you take know-ledge, that our whole concern, our constant labour is, to bring all the world to the religion which you feel—to solid inward, vital religion! What *power* is it, then, that keeps us asunder? . . . If we differ in small things, we agree in that which is greatest of all. How is it possible, then, that you should be induced to think or speak evil of us? How could it ever come into your mind to oppose us or to weaken our hands?"

The opposition was clearly strengthened by the attitude of the clergy. It has to be admitted that the English Church of the eighteenth century was not disposed to assist a revival of religion. We have already examined the state of the Church, and we have seen how fatally its temporal interests were involved in the interests of patronage. At that time, indeed, men of all callings were shamefully dependent upon their ability to please their patrons. Clergymen were less concerned with their vocation than with the pursuit of benefice or sinecure. And an institution is never more careful to insist on form and prerogative than when it has lost sight of its original purpose and sunk to the level of aggressive futility.

To the High Churchmen, Wesley appeared as a dangerous fanatic, not merely irregular in his practice, but tending to disturb the settled order of society. The order of castles and cottages was the order of God, and it had a spiritual as well as a temporal significance. Men were not equal in the sight of heaven, and it was extremely undesirable to stir up any kind of religious sentiment based upon the equality and accessibility of spiritual values. It was this belief which caused the tremendous outcry when Dr. Dodd, a clergyman of the Church of England, was executed for forgery, or when Earl Ferrars was hung for the murder of his steward. Those sentences were in keeping with the formality of the law, but by no means in keeping with the conventional privileges of the Church and the aristocracy. Human law, like divine wrath, was considered as operating chiefly upon the undistinguished masses. There was assumed to be a very great difference between the gentleman sinner and the common wretch. This assumption has a direct bearing upon the preaching of Wesley; for he preached to the common wretches, abandoned by the Church; while the clergy protected the privileged gentlemen upon whose favour their preferment depended. Hence, the clergy represented Wesley to their patrons as a mischievous, revolutionary fellow who was trying to overset the ecclesiastical power and the social balance. He was cheapening the right of admission to heaven (a tariff in which he had no right to meddle), and practically telling poor men they were as good as their betters.

It only needed the consciousness of failure on the part of the Church and of insecurity on the part of the ruling classes to give a special character of obstinacy and malice to the opposition. Yet, before the end of his life, Wesley had gone a long way towards winning the esteem of the broader Churchmen. Men of true piety (and the Church was not altogether without them) had to admit the extent and splendour of his achievement, even while they deplored his occasional departure from strict ecclesiastical forms. But the great vulgar remained obdurate: at best they could only show a sneering toleration. Consequently, there was no change in the attitude of Wesley towards the rich and the great. To him, they were still the great vulgar; people for ever beyond the reach of his effort and for ever deaf to his message.

Charles Wesley, who was more frequently in social contact with persons of quality, shared his brother's general opinion, but perhaps with a greater readiness to be tolerant. In his Marylebone house he entertained noblemen at his musical parties, and he did not find them insufferable. Yet Charles Wesley, four years before his death, composed a lively portrait of the man about town:

> "What is a modern Man of Fashion?
> A man of taste and dissipation.
> In sleep, and dress, and sport and play
> He throws his worthless life away;
> Has no opinion of his own,
> But takes from leading Beaux the *ton*;

With a disdainful smile or frown
He on the riff-raff crowd looks down:
The world polite—his friends and he;—
And all the rest are—Nobody!
Custom pursues, his only rule,
And lives an Ape, and dies a Fool!"

Both Charles and John Wesley were baffled by the great of this world. The illustrious vulgar were too proud to be saved and too foolish to understand: if they occasionally condescended to listen, they would never submit to be taught; and always they turned back, like a sick dog, to matters of immediate interest. Nor could Whitefield and all My Lady's Preachers do more than make salvation an occasional theme for polite curiosity.

CHAPTER XVIII

THESE DRY BONES

ALCOHOL, as a factor in the social history of England, has to be reckoned with after 1723 or 1724.

Up to the introduction of cheap gin and whisky in 1723, drunkenness may be considered one of the privileges of the aristocratic and the wealthy. The duller inebriations of beer and cider had been within the reach of poor men from a much earlier date, but the satisfaction of complete insensibility was only procurable by the masses after the coming of gin.

It was quickly perceived by men of business (on whom the greatness of our land has always so happily depended) that large fortunes could be made out of selling liquor. The success of these enterprising men is best revealed by a few plain figures. In 1727, the consumption of spirits in England was 3,500,000 gallons. By 1742, the figure had risen to 7,162,000; and in 1751 it was 11,000,000. *Crescentem sequitur cura pecuniam majorumque fames*, and the prosperity of our drink trade was assured.

In 1751, there were 17,000 gin-shops within the Bills of Mortality. Men were made drunk for a penny, and dead drunk for twopence. They were provided by the liquor-shop with clean straw, on which they could lie until they were sufficiently conscious, either to stagger home or to buy some more gin. The cheerfully bloated form of the jolly beer-drinker was chased away by the sallow, emaciated wretch who lived upon drams. Pawnbrokers, and those who made coffins or blew bottles, were exceedingly prosperous. Women filled their babies with gin, and with gin they sank themselves in mournful decay.

A more naked, a more careless degradation was never seen in the great towns of England. The efforts of Jekyll, under the Walpole ministry in 1736, had failed to check the appalling increase of unlicensed retailers; nor were the new measures introduced by the Pelham ministry in 1751 able to effect more than a very slight reduction in the annual consumption of spirits. Misery, violence and disease, crime and immorality of every description, were poisoning the national life. A melancholy, tattered procession was always moving towards the jail or the hospital, the madhouse or the graveyard. It was unsafe to walk in the streets of London, even in the daytime. Horace Walpole, writing in 1751, observed: "One is forced to travel, even at noon, as if one were going to battle." The harlot's cry was not weaving the winding-sheet of old England more swiftly than it was being woven by the new grog-shops and the new distilleries. Beer Street may not have been as jovial, as wholesome and sunny, as Hogarth would show us; it was the highest level of human felicity and worthiness compared with the squalid horrors of Gin Lane.

Drink, by the middle of the century, had therefore become what we now call a social problem. The growing industries of the country were seriously threatened by this rampant evil; a great burden of idleness, poverty and sickness fell upon the tax-payer; the fighting services, at a time of national danger, were only maintaining with difficulty a normal standard of discipline. Economist and moralist joined in deploring this new menace, a thousand times more deadly than Frenchman or Jacobite, and tried to find a cure.

Wesley, who represented more signally than any other man the protest of religion, addressed himself to the drunkard with peculiar directness and energy. "Are you a man?" he cried. "God made you a man, but you make yourself a beast. Wherein does a man differ from a beast? Is it not chiefly in reason and understanding? But you throw away what reason you have; you strip yourself of understanding. You do all you can to make yourself a mere beast; not a fool, not a madman only, but a swine, a poor filthy swine." And with even greater vehemence in another appeal, he wrote: "Friend, stop! you have the form of a man still. And perhaps some remains of understanding. O may the merciful God lay hold of that!" Drink, he said, was "fashionable poison." The sale of it could not be defended on any pretence. "It is amazing that the preparing or selling of this poison should be permitted, I will not say in any Christian country, but in any civilised state. 'Oh, it brings a considerable sum of money to the government.' True; but is it wise to barter men's lives for money? Surely that gold is bought too dear, if it is the price of blood."

A man of strong common sense, like Wesley, would certainly have advocated prohibition. He lived to see a considerable improvement in the state of England; but in 1750, with every sixth shop in London a grog-shop, a thoughtful patriot had small reason to be cheerful. And Wesley had suffered, again and again, from the unruliness of drunken mobs.

But the more rowdy or dangerous forms of opposition were now disappearing. From 1750 onwards, Methodism began to win the respect or affection of the people. The lions, in Wesley's phrase, became lambs; the dry bones were coming to life.

On the other hand, the attacks of the Church party and of the Press were almost continuous.

Lavington, the Bishop of Exeter, who, with turbulent Warburton, may be taken as representing the violence of episcopal reaction against the new revival, published in 1749 the first part of his obnoxious treatise on *The Enthusiasm of the Methodists and Papists compared*. He denounced the Methodists as people with "sanctified singularities, low fooleries and high pretensions." The windmill, he said, was in their heads; they were carried away by intoxicating vapours and fumes of the imagination, by the phantoms of a crazy brain or the uncouth effects of a distempered mind and body. Much more he said that was equally abusive, nonsensical and vulgar. Indeed, the Bishop's treatise may be properly regarded as the uncouth effect of a distempered mind. Yet, before his death, twelve years later, Lavington had changed his opinion of Wesley and had seen his own errors.

It was not the policy of Wesley to answer printed attacks, except when they might have caused real injury to Methodism, or when they were written by a person of eminence. He treated a merely personal attack as a thing of no consequence. He answered Lavington, briefly reminding him that "Any scribbler, with a middling share of low wit, not encumbered with good nature or modesty, may raise a laugh on those whom he cannot refute, and run them down when he dares not look them in the face." Yet he concluded by signing himself "Your friend and well wisher."

The Bishop returned to the assault, indecently foaming with rage, and pouring out a torrent of nasty abuse. Of Whitefield he says, "No man ever so bedaubed himself with his own spittle." Wesley and his preachers are accused of "the ostentation of sanctified looks . . . swelling words of vanity and loud boastings . . . a strain of Jesuitical sophistry, artifice and craft, evasion, reserve, equivocation and prevarication."

To this wild spluttering Wesley again replied, more sternly, even harshly, but still over the signature of a "friend and well wisher."

It would be most unprofitable to quote or to follow the worse than rude attacks of the Bishops of Exeter, Gloucester and London. The tone of the prevailing ecclesiastical abuse is trenchantly exhibited by Lavington, and the example given above will be sufficient. Those who wish to examine more closely the printed writings against Wesley must go to the solemn and swollen volumes of Tyerman, the most grimly industrious of biographers.

Wesley had to attend to matters of greater importance than repartee with bishops. His disciplined organisation was rapidly growing. It was large enough to provide continual anxieties and episodes.

But the increase was mainly confined to England. Wales, under the preaching of Harris and Whitefield, had accepted the Calvinistic theology, in name if not in substance. Scotland, first visited by Wesley in 1751, was only coldly attentive; it was full of "dead, unfeeling multitudes." In Ireland, Methodism had always a rather colonial, isolated character.

In 1751 there was trouble at Kingswood School, and graver trouble was caused by James Wheatley, a Methodist preacher, who had behaved in a manner so highly scandalous as to call for the immediate intervention of Wesley. After investigation of his case, Wheatley was expelled from the Methodist Connexion. This extraordinary person then proceeded to Norwich, where he gained in a short time about two thousand converts. The people of Norwich set up a wooden tabernacle for Wheatley, and he became a most popular evangelist. But the members of a cheerful society called the Hell Fire Club, allying themselves incongruously with the churchmen of Norwich, ran out of the house of the Blue Bell, smashed the tabernacle, stripped the preacher, flung squibs and crackers among the saved souls, threw stones and mud and rioted in every street of the town. Blasphemous pantomimes followed, with almost incredible mockery of sacred things, a pregnant woman was kicked to death, and another was violated in circumstances of peculiar horror. It would hardly be correct to describe the Norwich riots as anti-Methodist demonstrations, for Wheatley was not, at that time, a member of the United Societies, and was bitterly incensed against John and Charles Wesley, who had expelled him. An advertisement, signed by the two Wesleys and disclaiming their connexion with Wheatley, had been circulated in the town. The riots were a demonstration against Wheatley himself, known to be a lewd fellow, and against his followers, assumed to be idle people enticed from their proper occupations.

But we are justified in calling Wheatley an extraordinary person. Not only did he live down his reputation in Norwich, but he stood his ground, continued his preaching, and eventually had a fine chapel built for his people in the veryheart of the city. In 1754, he was again charged with indecent behaviour; he was tried before an ecclesiastical court in 1756, and was obliged to leave the country. After a period of exile, he came back to Norwich, and preached for several years to his "dear lambs."

The scandal of Wheatley, almost the only one of its kind in the earlier history of Methodism, induced Wesley to examine more closely the doctrine, behaviour and reputation of his preachers. In 1752, both the Wesleys and the leading preachers put their hands to a statement of policy in which they agreed that, if they heard any ill report of one of their number, they would communicate it at once to the person concerned, and would say nothing of it to any one else. In 1753, the Leeds Conference issued the famous *Rules of a Helper*. These *Rules* contain the whole substance of the Methodist policy for preachers, and, indeed, the Methodist policy of social conduct. They are of the first importance to those who would understand the spirit of Wesley's organisation, and his own attitude towards society. The following maxims may be regarded as the essential points of the *Rules*:

"Be diligent. Never be unemployed a moment. . . .

"Converse sparingly and cautiously with women; particularly with young women in private.

"Take no step towards marriage without acquainting us with your design. . . .

"Believe evil of no one. . . .

"Speak evil of no one. . . .

"Do not affect the gentleman. You have no more to do with this character than with that of a dancing-master. A Preacher of the Gospel is the servant of all.

"Be ashamed of nothing but sin: not of fetching wood (if time permit), or drawing water; not of cleaning your own shoes, or your neighbours'.

"Be punctual. Do everything exactly at the time. And, in general, do not mend our rules, but keep them. . . .

"You have nothing to do but to save souls. Therefore, spend and be spent in the work. . . .

"Observe. It is not your business to preach so many times . . . but to save as many souls as you can. . . . Therefore, you will need all the sense you have, and to have your wits about you."

The last paragraph is an addition made in 1780. These excellent rules, the standing orders of the Methodist army, mark at once the aim and character of Wesley and the qualities which he desired to find, or to cultivate, in his men.

In 1753, England was divided by Wesley into twelve circuits, and the leading preacher in each circuit was called the "assistant." All the preachers were chosen by Wesley. Before he could be an "itinerant," a man had to prove his capacity as a "local preacher." There was no ambiguity about the discipline or rules of procedure. Most of the men were young; Wesley himself described them as "a handful of raw young men . . . without name, learning or eminent sense." But he added proudly, "That which God has wrought by these despised instruments has continued increasing for fifteen years together." This was written in 1753.

The duties of the preachers were clearly defined. They were to get up at four in the morning, but they were not to preach more than twice a day, except on Sunday. They were on no account to introduce hymns of their own composing. They were to do their utmost to put down the habit of dram drinking, and to oppose the lesser but flagrant evils of smuggling and bribery. If they could make nothing of a paragraph of Plato, and were not even able to hobble through the Latin of Cicero's letters, they were not unskilled in their own business, the calling of men to a knowledge of God. Wesley, knowing the delights of classic scholarship, deplored the fact that his young men had so little learning between them; but he knew that they were extremely well fitted for their appropriate place in the Methodist revival.

Methodism had now (1750) acquired a definite institutional character; it had also acquired, in actual fact, though certainly not in intention, the character of a separate religious body outside the Church of England.

Separation from the Church was a thing always dreaded by Wesley, and he opposed vehemently every tendency to emphasise the differences between the Methodist societies and the Establishment. To him, there was nothing more distressing than the appearance of Dissent, and no words more detestable than those of schism, reform, independence or exclusion. Yet it must have been evident, from the very beginning, that the new congregations could never be included, either within the walls of churches or within the boundaries of the ecclesiastical province. The discipline which united the Methodist societies and so effectively

controlled their development could only result in the for-
mation of an independent body. Any formal alliance with
the clergy had been made impossible by the attitude of the
clergy themselves. Within the ranks of Methodism there
was, unquestionably, a feeling of growing resentment
against the Church. Too often the Methodists were shamefully repelled from the Communion or shamefully passed by
at the very Table.

On the other hand, the Church could point with disapproval to the irregular practices of the Methodist leaders,
and to the almost imperceptible line which, in some places,
divided the Methodists from the recognised forms of
Dissent. Nor can it be doubted that the less intelligent and
more pugnacious followers of Wesley often treated the
parochial clergy with defiance or disrespect. Again, the
question of caste was involved; for by far the greater number
of the Wesleyans were labouring men, industrials or small
traders; while the Church represented the special religion
of the opulent classes, the rich and the aristocratic: it is
extremely important to remember this fact, with all its implications. A separate organisation, though not necessarily a
separate code of doctrine, was therefore unavoidable.

From time to time the question of separation was argued
warmly at the Conferences. Wesley, greatly as he deplored
the fact of such a question being raised at all, was bound to
admit that it was possible to argue about the *expediency* of
separation. The advance of Methodism, the continued
preaching of the Gospel and the fullest possible effort
towards a revival of true religion had to be set before any
other consideration whatsoever. Perhaps there were points
in the liturgy and decretals of the Church which, as his
preachers affirmed, were repugnant to reason, or even "anti-
Christian, Popish and diabolical." Writing to Samuel
Walker of Truro, he admitted "that he could not answer
these arguments to his own satisfaction." In 1755, the
matter was discussed at the Leeds Conference, but without
a definite result.

By 1758, Wesley had become more convinced that
separation was not even expedient, and was undesirable on

many grounds. It would, he said, lead to bitterness, controversy and confusion. It would prejudice those who loved God. It would be a stumbling-block to the godless multitudes, and would prevent them from listening to the new preachers. It would lead to frightful divisions in the ranks of the Methodists themselves. In his mind, the Church, however fallen her state, was a vital part of England and still preserved the best religious traditions of the nation. His affection for the Church was an aspect of his affection for England, and rested upon a real sentiment of patriotism. He looked upon the clergy as his brethren, and the prayers of the Church as "substantial food for any who are alive to God." In the most unequivocal style, he urged his people to attend the Church services on every possible occasion, and to remember that they were united to her, just as they were united to their own societies, in common opposition to the devil and all his works.

In the meantime, the vital statistics of Methodism showed a steady increase. Wesley had concentrated on the towns, he had wisely decided to preach most where most could hear him, and in practically every large town there were flourishing societies. And since the preaching of Wesley was mostly directed towards the new industrial classes, it had a great and increasing influence upon the economic history of England.

Methodism taught people to be industrious, clean, efficient and trustworthy; Wesley, eminently practical as he was, always laid stress upon the importance of order, regularity and cheerfulness in the normal occupations of life. He taught a code of inflexible honesty. He denounced in the most emphatic manner the crimes of defrauding the revenue and receiving bribes; although people of the highest respectability bought smuggled silks or tea, and freely extended their respectable hands for election money.

Already the influence of Wesley had spread beyond the limits of his own societies. Dry bones were shaking hopefully in quarters where Methodism itself could not be admitted. The people were being led back to religion.

And still, while setting religion above all besides, Wesley

had constantly in mind the educational needs of his people. Not only the *Christian Library* and various abridgements, grammars and school-books were produced in the spare time of this tireless man; in 1753 he printed a *Complete English Dictionary*. The purpose of this undertaking is quaintly expressed in the title: "*The Complete English Dictionary, Explaining most of those Hard Words which are found in the Best English Writers. By a Lover of Good English and Common Sense. N.B.—The Authour assures you he thinks this is the best English Dictionary in the World.*" In the Preface, a piece of sly jesting almost worthy of Swift, he explains his procedure:

"I have often observed, the only way, according to the modern taste, for any Authour to procure commendation of his Book, is vehemently to commend it himself. For want of this deference to the Publick, several excellent Tracts lately printed . . . are utterly unknown or forgotten. Whereas, if a writer of tolerable Sense will but bestow a few violent Encomiums on his own Work . . . it will pass through six editions in a trice; the World being too complaisant to give the Gentleman the lie, and taking it for granted he understands his own Performance best . . . Many are the Mistakes in all the other English Dictionaries which I have yet seen. Whereas I can truly say I know of none in this; and I conceive the Reader will believe me; for if I had, I should not have left it there."

Wesley not only did all that he could for the instruction of others; he let slip no occasion for instructing himself. He was anxious to follow new discoveries, and took special interest in Franklin's investigations concerning electricity. He saw the vast possibilities which would come into view as the result of a more complete knowledge of the "electrical fire." "What an amazing scene," he said, "is here opened, for after ages to improve upon!"

It is typical of the immense energy of Wesley, that he wrote more, read more and thought more, in the time set apart from his main vocation, than most men read, write or think in the whole course of their lives. Yet, though he had a good physique, he was not a man of an exceptionally strong constitution. He was not seldom troubled by fevers, coughs and pains in the breast. In the winter of 1753 and the spring of 1754 he was definitely ill. At the end of November 1753, he retired to the friendly and comfortable house of Blackwell at Lewisham. Here he was nursed for about five weeks, and though he broke the doctor's orders in regard to writing, he was obliged to refrain from active work. On the evening of his arrival at Blackwell's house he composed his famous and most characteristic epitaph:

> "Here lieth the Body of
> JOHN WESLEY
> A Brand plucked out of the Burning;
> Who died of a Consumption in the Fifty-first
> Year of his Age,
> Not leaving, after his Debts are paid,
> Ten pounds behind him:
> Praying,
> God be merciful to me, an unprofitable Servant!

He ordered that this, if any Inscription, should be placed on his Tombstone."

On New Year's Day 1754, he was able to return to London, and on the 4th of January he was at Bristol Hotwells, for a course of the waters. Here he began his *Notes on the New Testament*—"a work which I should scarce ever have attempted, had I not been so ill as not to be able to travel or preach, and yet so well as to be able to read and write." We do not know if he was accompanied by Mrs. Wesley. On the 26th of March, he preached again, after an interval of four months.

At the end of 1755, Wesley was in correspondence with John Fletcher, then a tutor to the sons of Thomas Hill of Tern Hall in Shropshire.

Fletcher, when vicar of Madeley, became one of the closest of the friends of Wesley and one of the most saintly of Christian ministers. He had been "converted" about this time, mainly by the preaching of the Methodists.

Wesley did not meet Fletcher until after his ordination in March 1757.

The dark year of 1756, with England gloomily arming herself for a war with France, found many of Wesley's men serving with the colours. The Methodists had proved themselves good soldiers at Fontenoy, eleven years before, when they went into action singing the noble hymns of Charles Wesley. In March, Wesley dined with the Colonel of a foot regiment at Canterbury, who told him, "No men fight like those who fear God; I had rather command five hundred such men, than any regiment in His Majesty's Army." Wesley, who had the makings of a first-rate general, always loved soldiers, and he must have listened to the Colonel with glowing satisfaction. As he looked at the troops in Canterbury, he felt that "the fear and the love of God would prepare them either for death or victory." He remembered how eagerly the Irish garrisons had followed his preaching; indeed, only a few months later he wrote: "Still, in Ireland, the first call is to the soldiery."

In 1758 the work in Ireland suffered a grievous loss by the death of Thomas Walsh, one of the most brilliant and most devoted of Wesley's young preachers. He could preach both in Erse and English, and Wesley said that no one "in so few years as he remained upon earth, was an instrument of converting so many sinners from the error of their ways." Wesley met him in June at Limerick, "alive, and but just alive." Walsh had worn himself out at the age of twenty-eight. He had abjured Catholicism in his youth, and had become a zealous Methodist. No preacher had been more successful, and none more brutally persecuted. He had accompanied Wesley during his visits to Ireland, and had come over to England and preached to the London Irish, and with Wesley at Beaconsfield and High Wycombe. Walsh was more intellectual than the majority of the itinerant preachers, and Wesley bitterly lamented his loss: "Surely," he cried, "Thy judgments are a great deep!"

The gloom of the opening of the Seven Years' War was lifted in 1759 by a succession of victories; Minden in September, Quebec in October, and Quiberon in November.

The genius of Pitt was saving England, and frightened men were no longer mumbling of invasion or looking timidly across the Channel for the topsails of a French fleet. Britannia, making good resolutions about tea and gin, found her nerves more steady, and herself in a better posture for the ruling of the waves.

CHAPTER XIX

BERRIDGE OF EVERTON

THAT peculiar man, John Berridge, is a figure of very considerable importance in the history of Methodism. The strangeness of his colloquial manner, his odd personal habits, and the daring irregularity of his preaching may indicate nothing more than eccentricity; but the extraordinary results of his ministry were due to powers of no common kind.

The work of Berridge at Everton, and in its neighbourhood, led to an independent revival. This revival, marked by scenes which recalled those of the earlier days at Bristol and Kingswood, attracted the notice and stimulated the effort of the entire Methodist movement.

Wesley visited Everton, and took his usual pains to collect the fullest possible evidence. He looked on Berridge as a man signally favoured by God. Nor did the palpable drift of Berridge towards Calvinism, in his later years, affect Wesley's admiration for his powers and character. As bright signs of the wider revival, the scenes at Everton and the work of Berridge claimed the earnest attention of Wesley, and had a definite influence upon his thoughts.

Perhaps it is never easy to determine where mere eccentricity comes to an end and where actual insanity begins. You will find the same man described by those who like him as an amusing, whimsical fellow, and by those who do not like him as a raving lunatic. Southey describes Berridge as "the insane vicar," and speaks of the Everton revival as a case of "spiritual influenza," with ugly symptoms of "indecency and extravagance." But Wesley had written, "In May (1759), the work of God exceedingly increased at and near Everton," and he was in no doubt as to the divine commission of Berridge. We shall be in a better position to form our own opinions when we have examined some of the evidence relating to this very singular man.

John Berridge was the son of a prosperous Nottingham

farmer. He was born in 1716, and took the degree of B.A. at Clare Hall, Cambridge, in 1738, and the degree of M.A. in 1742. "John," his father had said, "I find you are unable to form any practical idea of the price of cattle, and therefore I shall send you to college, to be a light to the Gentiles." For some years, he was a resident Fellow of his college, a Moderator of the classes, and a most industrious scholar. It is asserted that he studied for fifteen hours a day. In 1749 he accepted the curacy of Stapleford near Cambridge, and in 1755 he was presented by his college with the living of Everton, on the eastern borders of Bedfordshire.

The spiritual history of Berridge, like that of nearly all the revival leaders, was metamorphic. As a young man, he said, "he went to Jesus as a coxcomb, and gave himself fine airs." He had first of all believed in salvation through good works and the due observance of pious exercises, and it was not until after he had become a vicar that he saw the need for an inward realisation of faith. He then "fled to Jesus alone for refuge." Yet, while he preached the new birth and the necessity for winning salvation by personal effort, he floundered into the ungainly Calvinism of Lady Huntingdon's group and accepted their vague predestinarian views.

Up to 1756, Berridge had presumably conducted himself like any other inconspicuous clergyman in matters of church procedure, though he must always have been extremely odd in speech, manners and writing. After his change of doctrine, which appears to have taken place in 1756, he became a fervent evangelist, preaching in barns and meeting-houses, and visiting other parishes.

He did not describe himself as a Methodist, nor did his converts necessarily join the Methodist societies, but he both met and corresponded with Wesley and Whitefield, and, in spite of doctrinal differences, always regarded Wesley as a close personal friend. His circuit was a small one, and his work was chiefly confined to a few villages in the eastern part of Bedfordshire and the southern part of Cambridge. Hicks, the vicar of Wrestlingworth, near Potton, assisted him very considerably.

Berridge was a tall man with a deep voice. His face was rugged and whimsical, with a square, low forehead, a jutting nose, a long upper lip and a heavy chin. He spoke in a broad, familiar style, and often with a startling audacity of expression. No one could have been less concerned with elegance, but no man had a more original style in devotional composition. His pious flippancy has the tone of extravagance which is often a feature of religious revivals, but the peculiar force and colour, the roughness and richness of his oratory were distinctly individual. Of later preachers, Spurgeon, perhaps, most closely resembled him. For twenty-four years he rode about a hundred miles and preached ten or twelve sermons every week. Each year he spent part of his time in London, preaching in Whitefield's Tabernacle, and in other places. After his friendship with Lady Selina, he became a private chaplain to the Earl of Buchan. He kept open house at the vicarage for those who came to visit him; he rented houses and barns, raised a number of lay preachers, and devoted the whole of his income (which was not a small one) to his work. When he thought of marriage, he consulted the Scriptures as to the desirability of "taking a Jezebel," and the Scriptures convinced him that he had better remain single.

"Soon after I began to preach the Gospel at Everton," wrote Berridge, "the churches in the neighbourhood were deserted, and mine so overcrowded that the Squire, who did not like strangers . . . joined with the offended parsons, and soon after . . . I was summoned before the Bishop. 'Well, Berridge,' said His Lordship, 'did I institute you to Eaton or Potton? Why do you go preaching out of your own parish?' 'My Lord,' says I, 'I make no claims to the livings of those parishes: 'tis true I was once at Eaton, and, finding a few poor people assembled, I admonished them. . . . At that very moment, My Lord, there were five or six clergymen out of their own parishes, and enjoying themselves on Eaton bowling-green.' 'I tell you,' retorted His Lordship, 'that if you continue preaching where you have no

right, you will very likely be sent to Huntingdon jail.'
'I have no more regard for a jail than other folks, but I
had rather go there with a good conscience than be at
liberty without one.' His Lordship looked very hard at
me: 'Poor fellow,' said he, 'you are beside yourself, and
in a few months you will be either better or worse. . . .'
His Lordship then pathetically entreated me . . . not
to embitter the remaining portion of his days by any
squabbles with my brother clergymen, but to go home
to my parish, and so long as I kept within it, I should be
at liberty to do as I liked there. 'As to your conscience,'
said His Lordship, 'you know that preaching out of
your parish is contrary to the canons of the Church.'
'There is one canon, My Lord,' said I, 'which I dare
not disobey, and that says *Go preach the Gospel to every
creature.*'"

Still, things might have gone hardly with Berridge, if it
had not been for the protection of noble patrons. An old
Cambridge friend used his influence with Pitt, and Lady
Huntingdon procured the support of Chancellor Henley.
So "the old devil," as the squires called him, continued his
most irregular and most sensational preaching.

Wesley first met Berridge on the 9th of November 1758,
at Everton. This was before the climax of the Everton
revival, but Wesley noted that there had already been "the
same violent outward symptoms" which had occurred under
his own preaching nearly twenty years before.

Berridge and Wesley at once set out for Wrestlingworth,
about five miles away, where they lodged with Mr. Hicks.
Wesley preached in the church at Wrestlingworth on the
same evening, and again on the following morning. "In
the middle of the sermon," he wrote, "a woman before me
dropped down as dead, as one had done the night before."
After that, he preached at Everton, "and some were *struck*
just as at Wrestlingworth." On the 18th of December, he
was again at Everton, and preached in the church soon after
six in the evening. "God gave me great liberty of speech,
and applied his word to the hearts of the hearers; many of

whom were not able to contain themselves, but cried aloud for mercy." In March 1759, Wesley visited Everton on his way to Norwich. He was not a witness of the extraordinary scenes which took place at Everton during the summer.

The "great increase in the work of God" began about the middle of May 1759.

Inside the church at Everton, while Berridge was preaching or conducting his service, some of the people fainted and fell quietly on the floor, others roared and screamed, sinking down in horrible contortions; at one moment they felt themselves dropping into the blazing cavity of hell, and at the next, they were rising in ecstasies of joy and gratitude. Those who were less affected stood on the seats of the pews in order to see the disturbed congregation. The noise was incredible. Rustic boots hammered against the boards, broke the benches and split the sides of the pews. Children set up a shrill wailing. Women shrieked horribly, clapped their hands, or fell upon each other's necks. Some uttered short ejaculations of praise, and others shouted in wild triumph. Below the louder sounds there was all the while a noise of hard breathing, as of men half strangled and gasping for life. And above all the appalling din could be heard the powerful voice of Berridge, praying and preaching and calling on sinners, louder and more unmelodious, and louder still, until no voice, no human head or heart, could bear the strain any longer, and he walked out through the stricken multitude.

Berridge walked from the church to the vicarage, and there the work was continued. People were carried into the house like casualties from the scene of some hideous disaster. Children raved and struggled in the passages. It was observed by a witness that "almost all on whom God laid His hand turned either very red or almost black." Some laughed foolishly "with extreme joy," tears of inexpressible emotion running down their pale, radiant faces.

In some instances, the process of conversion was rapid, in others it was most painfully prolonged. While some were singing praises in the vicarage parlour, others were lying with closed eyes, with chattering teeth, and heels drumming on the floor-boards. Strangers, after looking on placidly, all at once staggered down on their knees, or ran against the wall, roaring for mercy. Careless young women, cool and curious at first, broke out all together in "a loud and bitter cry." Some of the congregation, tottering from the church towards the house, fell on the side of the road, or under the shrubs in the vicarage garden, where they were found lying like dead bodies. Some, unmoved by the service, had gone away stolidly enough, and were overcome and stricken down before they could reach their own cottages. A stranger coming to Everton, and knowing nothing about the "spiritual influenza," would have thought he had come to a place where every other man was a lunatic or a drunkard.

The same thing, but with rather less violence, was going on at Wrestlingworth. The "arrows of the Lord" flew among the congregation of Mr. Hicks. "While he was preaching, fifteen or sixteen persons dropped down. A few of these cried out with the utmost violence, and little intermission, for some hours; while the rest made no great noise, but continued struggling, as in the pangs of death." Here, as at Everton, the more desperate cases were carried, or made their way, to the parsonage. "Their cries increased beyond measure, so that the loudest singing could scarce be heard."

It is remarkable that such things were brought about by Mr. Hicks, who, only a short time previously, had not only scoffed at the doings of Berridge, but had actually refused the Communion to those of his parishioners who went to hear the Everton preaching. Perhaps he was disturbed by the fate of others who opposed Berridge; for three farmers who tried to prevent people from going to Everton were all dead within a month. He had been "convinced of sin" in August 1758, and had "first preached the Gospel" on the 17th of September.

Berridge proceeded to extend his operations, and to carry the spiritual contagion over a wider area. He went to Meldred or Meldreth, a village in South Cambridgeshire, about fifteen miles from Everton, and there he preached for the first time in the open air. He was accompanied by Hicks, and they preached to several thousands of people; but it is to be observed that preaching in the open air very rarely, if ever, produced the extraordinary scenes which occurred in churches and chapels.

He went on to Shelford, about four miles south of Cambridge: a table was set up on the common, and about ten thousand people came to hear the preaching. "The audience," he said, "behaved with great decency." We hear nothing of loud outcries or sudden conversions.

After this, Hicks and Berridge toured in various parts of the counties of Cambridge and Hertford, "preaching in the fields, wherever a door was opened, three or four days in every week."

During the months of June and July 1759, many astonishing scenes took place at or near Everton, and among the villages to the south of Cambridge. Jane Thorn and Patty Jenkins of Potton had trances and saw visions of ineffable glory. Redeemed souls walked together in the lanes or through the fields, chanting hymns of praise. Still, the more notable conversions took place among men, and it was the men who fell into ugly fits, with dreadful sweating and awful heavings, groanings and violent bodily disturbances. Symptoms of this kind were rare among the women.

Crowds gathered in the early hours of the morning to hear Berridge, or even to hear his man-servant, Caleb Price. Nor did Mr. Price unworthily represent his master, for he caused more than twenty persons to fall down beneath the arrows of conviction. At Grantchester, seventeen people were "broken down" more or less spontaneously by the mere singing of hymns, and an innocent child of seven saw many visions. At Everton, powerful men were seized by the hand of the Lord, shaken like clothes drying in the wind, or flung to the ground as though by the blow of a giant, or they stood gaping and staring, full of a huge dismay. In the churchyard, women fell among the graves, plucking at the turf and grass with convulsed fingers. Others burst into peals of hideous laughter.

The preachers of Berridge moved about in twos and threes, singing hymns on the Cambridge moors, and bringing repentance to the lonely shepherdess. "Justified" children were no more afraid of the dark. Gypsies and hawkers, wandering into the zone of the new influence, or breathing, as Southey might have said, the new contagion, felt themselves transformed into creatures of light. Even good clothes and fine manners were not always a sufficient protection. The most burly and boisterous profligates were hustled into agonies of dreadful remorse. No sinner could listen with impunity to the warning, threatening voice of Berridge.

At Stapleford, where Berridge had been a curate ten years before, he preached to about fifteen hundred people. Many were disposed to mock, and some talked loudly about horsewhips.

But a terrible example of mockery punished was provided by Thomas Skinner. He was the chief of the scoffers, and all at once he became "the most horrible human figure ever seen." His large black wig fell awry on his purple, distorted face; he roared incessantly, "throwing and clapping his hands together with all his force." He fell down, his body heaving and swelling as though it would burst. Mr. Berridge retired to refresh himself, and when he came back to the preaching-ground, the wretched Skinner had not yet risen; there he lay, howling and tormented, a most profitable sight to those who lacked conviction. "All the people," said an eye-witness, "were now deeply serious."

In the meantime, Mr. John Dennis, aged twenty years, was stretched out on a table, his neck as rigid as iron: in this posture he "unfolded the whole Christian system" in a melodious voice, his eyes fixed in a glassy upward stare. He had had fits before, but never one so illuminating. When he recovered, he had no idea, or so he said, of what he had been talking about. Southey speaks cruelly of Mr. Dennis as an "impostor" who gave "exhibitions."

So the work went on. If there were not a few "impostors" and "exhibitors," there were many to whom the experience of conversion was an overpowering reality.

At Thriplow or Triplow, in Cambridgeshire, there was a meeting of about two thousand people. They dropped down singly or in bunches, and those who were still standing formed rings round the prostrate. Some were in the red visions of hell, and others in radiant views of paradise. At last, even some of the chosen began to wonder if all this was really the work of God, or the work of the devil. Mr. Keeling of Potton, an early convert, grew dark, sullen and reserved. But Skinner, Dennis, and the sorrowful shepherdess of Shelford Moor were lively examples of redeemed sinners.

On Sunday, the 5th of August, John Wesley came back to Everton, anxious to hear about the revival and to collect evidence. He preached both at Everton and at Wrestlingworth, in the churches, but there were few scenes of emotion. On Monday he talked to Ann Thorn, and two others, who had been in trances. About five in the afternoon, while the people were singing hymns, Berridge told him that a girl of fifteen called Alice Miller had fallen into a trance. Wesley at once went to see her, and afterwards wrote the following extraordinary account in his *Journal*:

'I found her sitting on a stool and leaning against the wall, with her eyes open and fixed upward. I made a motion as if going to strike; but they continued immovable. Her face showed an unspeakable mixture of reverence and love, while silent tears stole down her cheeks. . . . Her pulse was quite regular. In about half an hour I observed her countenance change into the form of fear, pity and distress. Then she burst into a flood of tears, and cried out, 'Dear Lord, they will go to hell! the world will go to hell!' Soon after she said, 'Cry aloud! Spare not!' And in a few moments her look was composed again, and spoke a mixture of reverence, joy and love. Then she said aloud, 'Give God the glory.' About seven her senses returned. I asked her, 'Where have you been?' 'I have been with my Saviour.' 'In heaven or on earth?' 'I cannot tell; but I was in glory!''

If this account is a proof of Wesley's readiness to accept

281

the religious nature of such an experience, it is also a proof of his readiness to guard against deception and of his care in observing. He tested the reflexes of the eyes, and cautiously examined the pulse. He noticed minutely every change of expression. When the girl had recovered, he questioned her at once in regard to the nature of her ideas and sensations while in the trance. He noted, speaking of the outward symptoms, that, "they attend the beginning of a general work of God. . . . But after a time they gradually decrease, and the work goes on more quietly and silently."

He continued to watch closely the proceedings at Everton, which interested him profoundly, and he came back there at the end of the month. He preached in the church, and many people sank down "in agony of prayer." A young man and a young woman were conveyed with difficulty to the parsonage, "in violent agonies both of body and soul."

But the climax of the Everton revival was now past. Wesley again visited Everton at the end of November, and found that Berridge had gone to preach before the University of Cambridge. "I observed," he says, "a remarkable difference since I was here before, as to the manner of the work. None now were in trances, none cried out; none fell down or were convulsed. Only some trembled exceedingly; a low murmur was heard, and many were refreshed with 'the multitude of peace.'"

Wesley now reviewed his attitude towards what we have previously called the phenomena of conversion. He was ready to believe that there was, in some cases, a mixture of dissimulation, and that some of the people at Everton had pretended to see what they did not actually see, and had imitated the cries and convulsive motions of those who had been really overpowered by the Spirit of God. But the presence of dissimulation, he contended, and rightly, should not lead to the denial or the underestimation of the whole work. The shadow was no disparagement of the substance, nor the counterfeit of the real diamond. He preached for Hicks at Wrestlingworth, and here again he found that the people were deeply attentive, but not so affected as they had been when he previously visited them. Berridge, returned from Cambridge, told him that only one person had cried out, and that only for a very short time, during the University sermon; a few others had dropped down, without making any sound.

It was about this time that Everton was visited by Lady Selina and her chaplains. The godly Fletcher, not yet appointed to the living of Madeley, had volunteered to assist Berridge, and this notable concourse of evangelistic clergy, under noble patronage, drew to Everton a crowd of ten thousand people. Berridge accompanied Lady Huntingdon, with Venn and Fletcher, to London, where, says the biographer of the Countess, "her Ladyship was anxious to introduce him to the religious circles of the metropolis, with a view to his spiritual improvement." Lady Huntingdon was a woman of excellent intentions.

In January 1762, less than three years after the revival, Wesley paid two visits to Everton. He found the people not only "more settled," but in danger of running to another extreme—that of disparaging the least appearance of religious enthusiasm. On Sunday, the 10th of January, he took the morning and afternoon services in the church, observing before him a grave, seemly and pious congregation, attentive, though not openly moved. There were no more fits, visions or trances.

The work of Berridge was accomplished: he had a parish full of quiet, godly people, and he had stirred to a sense of religion many hundreds in other parishes. The vicar of Everton had nearly twenty years of evangelical preaching before him, but he did not any more lead his listeners in the dangerous ways of fervour and frenzy.

Wesley and Berridge, if they did not meet or correspond frequently, were always friends. Wesley, probably realising that Berridge might be left to work in his own field, did not continue to visit Everton, or to travel in the area covered by the ministry of Berridge and his preachers. He met Berridge when the latter was in London, nor does the great Calvinist controversy of 1771 appear to have led to any bitterness between them.

As he grew older, Berridge became more and more outrageously eccentric. His letters, especially those written to his patroness, Lady Huntingdon, are often full of a jocular sanctimonious extravagance, a shocking warmth and vulgarity of metaphor which are probably without a parallel in any other correspondence. In one of his letters to the elect lady he said, "My instructions must come from the Lamb, not from the Lamb's wife, though she is a tight woman." The following extraordinary epistle was sent to Lady Huntingdon not long after the loss of her daughter:

"My Lady,
"My poor clay ever wants to teach God how to be a good potter; and may not your Dresden have something in it which resembles my Delf? You would not, like Uzziah, lay your hand on the Ark of God; but may you not be too solicitous about a driver of the cart? and a blinder Hobgoblin than myself you need not desire. Indeed I am so dissatisfied with my own carting, that, if I durst, I should throw the whip out of my hands. Every hour I lose my way; every day forget what I learnt the day before; neither instruction nor corruption mends me. Yea, verily, though I know myself to be a most stupid ass, yet at times I am a most conceited one. Though not fit to drive a dung-cart, yet at some certain seasons I can fancy myself qualified to be the King's coachman. . . . Oh! I am sick, sick, mighty sick of this self. How can you but rejoice for that unhappy creature who was delivered from this self, almost as soon as she felt the curse of it!

"J. B."

In 1792, the year of his death (if the date given in the *Whole Works* is correct), there appeared a series of five letters by Berridge under the title of *Cheerful Piety, or Religion without Gloom*. Our conclusion after reading these letters is, that Berridge, however pious and cheerful he may have been, was certainly mad, though perhaps religiously mad, if he sanctioned the publication of such amazing essays. The fifth and last letter is addressed to the Countess of Huntingdon. It shows the typical utterance of Berridge in its most exaggerated form. The letter is not dated, but internal evidence shows that it must have been written during the period of his itinerant preaching—that is, not later than 778. From this letter we select the following passages, leaving the reader to form his own judgment:

"I am one of those strange folks who set up for Journeymen without knowing their business, and offer many precious wares to sale without understanding their full value. I have got a Master too, a most extraordinary person, whom I am supposed to be well acquainted with, because He employs me as a riding Pedlar to serve near forty shops in the country, besides my own parish; yet I know much less of my Master than I do of His wares. . . . When my Master first hired me into His service, He kept a brave table, and was wondrous free of His liquor; scarce a meal passed without roast meat and claret; then my heart said *I love Jesus*, and was ready to boast of it too; but at length He ordered his table to be spread with meat from above and water out of the rock. This my saucy stomach could not brook; my heart thought it pernicious fare, and my tongue said it was light food. Now my love for Jesus disappeared, and I yet followed Him only for the loaves and fishes, and, like a true worldling, I loved His larder much better than His person. Presently my Master detected me in a very dirty trick, which discovered the huge pride and amazing impudence of my heart. Hitherto I had been a stranger to the livery my Master gives His servants, only I knew He had many rarities, such as pearls and diamonds, and plenty to dispose of. Accordingly I had begged a bracelet of Him, a necklace, ear-rings, a nose-bob, and other pretty things, which He readily parted with, being of a most exceeding generous nature. And it will not amaze you to hear I had the vanity to fix these odd ornaments about my old face, intending to make a birthday suit to appear in at Court.

"Well, to be sure, while I was thus busy about mending my old rags, and putting on my pearls, etc., in comes my

Master, and gives me a sudden grip which went to the very heart of me, and said in an angry tone *Varlet, follow me!* I arose and followed Him trembling whilst He led me to the house of correction, where He first set my feet in the stocks, and stripped me of my ornaments; He then took his afflictive rod, and laid upon me very stoutly, till I cried for mercy, but He declared He would not lay aside the rod till He had scourged away every rag from my back, and indeed He was as good as His Word . . . at length being almost choked with the dust and stench that came out of my rags in the beating, I fell down at my Master's feet. Immediately the rod dropped from His hand, His countenance softened, and with a small still voice He bid me look up. I did; and then I got the first sight of His robe, the Garment of Salvation.—Truly, Madam, it was a lovely sight! A charming robe reaching from the shoulders down to the feet, well adapted for covering and defence. . . . *There, prodigal Jack*, He said, *put this on thy back, and then thou mayest shame even an angel.* . . . I thanked Him, and bowed."

Such passages are not infrequent among the published writings and the correspondence of Berridge, and they provide an indication of the state of his mind and the nature of his "cheerful piety." Yet he could impress Wesley, and most of those who met him, with what appeared to be a deep and true sense of religion. Whittingham, who knew him intimately, said, "I can scarce recollect a man so conscientious, so uniformly, yet so pleasantly spiritual."

In practical matters, Berridge had a great deal of humorous wisdom. He advised a country parson to keep a barrel of ale in the house, so that, when a man came to see him on business, "his ears may be more open to your religious instructions." To his young curate he said, "Lift up your voice and frighten the jackdaws in the steeple; for if you don't cry aloud when you are young, you'll never do it when you are old." He had engravings of the great reformers hung on the walls of his study, and a framed looking-glass over the fireplace. "There," he would say to a visitor, "is

Calvin; there is Luther; and there," pointing to the glass, "is the devil."

His descriptions of men were often delightfully pointed: of Glascott, one of Lady Huntingdon's preachers, he said, "He has not a dozing face, with a hoarse doctrinal throat; but a right sharp countenance, with a clear Gospel pipe."

He was born, he said, with a foolscap on his head, and all his life he was free, jovial, and sometimes coarse or careless in his jesting. No one can doubt his zeal. In 1767, when Lady Huntingdon was writing "scorpion letters" to him, and urging him to come to her chapel at Bath, he reminded her that it would not be easy to find some one to take his place at Everton:

> "I fear my weekly circuits would not suit a London or a Bath divine, nor any tender evangelist that is environed with prunello. Long rides and miry roads in sharp weather! Cold houses to sit in with a very moderate fuel, and three or four children roaring or rocking about you! . . . Rise at five in the morning to preach; at seven breakfast, and tea that smells very sickly; at eight mount a horse with boots never cleaned, and then ride home, praising God for all mercies."

We have already seen that he refrained from marrying, partly because he was warned by his Bible, but chiefly because he thought marriage would impair his usefulness as a preacher. "No trap so mischievous to the field-preacher as wedlock," he said, "and it is laid for him at every hedge corner. Matrimony has quite maimed poor Charles (Wesley) and might have spoiled John (Wesley) and George (Whitefield) if a wise Master had not graciously sent them a brace of ferrets."

John Berridge died on the 22nd of January 1793, nearly two years after Wesley, in the seventy-sixth year of his age. In his later years, he became depressed and pursued by insane fancies. He fell into the gloom of hypochondria, and believed that he was made of a brittle substance and might be shivered to pieces, or else that he was swelling up into a dangerous bulk and would burst.

Not long before he died, he was visited by a friend who told him of the death of Lady Huntingdon. "Ah!" he said. "is she passed away? Then another pillar is gone to glory, Mr. Whitefield is gone, Mr. Wesley and his brother are gone, and I shall go soon." The friend replied cheerfully: "Yes, Sir, it is not probable you will long survive them; and although some little differences of opinion existed between you here, I have no doubt you will unite in perfect harmony in heaven." "Ay, ay!" said the old man with a placid smile, "that we shall, to be sure; for the Lord washed our hearts here, and there He will wash our brains."

CHAPTER XX

THE FRIENDS OF WESLEY

WESLEY was too busy for the leisurely friendship that likes to fold its legs and have its talk out. He did not positively condemn leisure, and he was extremely well fitted to take a delightful part in familiar or intellectual conversation. But the duties of every day, with him, were definitely arranged, the order of his life forbade any laxity in the use of time.

Then again, Wesley had no home. He was never long in one place. It may be questioned whether, in fifty years, he occupied any house continuously for more than three months. No man was less parochial, or more completely separated from the idea of residence. Most men who knew him well must have associated him always with thoughts of arrival and departure. While the morning congregation was yet under the full influence of his words, Wesley had preached to an afternoon congregation twenty miles away, and he was probably timed to go forward another stage before night and to preach to a third meeting. Such activity could have nothing to do with those quiet, rambling ways in which friends unfold themselves to each other.

It was therefore inevitable that Wesley, though he had a multitude of associates, helpers, admirers and correspondents, should be a man with few intimate friends. Perhaps he was not anxious to have them. In the early days of the Holy Club he had shown a certain exclusiveness, bordering upon civil incivility, which made him seem like a man for whom intimate conversations had no appeal. Yet we know, that no man could have been more cheerful, amusing and loquacious.

We are not surprised to find that most of the men who can be described as the friends of Wesley were clergymen. But we have to remember a very early friend, Ebenezer Blackwell, concerning whom, unfortunately, little can be discovered.

Blackwell joined the Fetter Lane society in his youth; he followed Wesley to the Foundry, and became one of the first Methodists. He was a man of substance, a partner in Martin's Bank, and the owner of a large house at Lewisham. Wesley consulted him on matters of business, and apparently on the choice of a wife, and seems to have spent more time in his house than in that of any other man. Blackwell provided Wesley with sums of money for his poor and helped him in many of his enterprises. Tyerman says that he was called "the rough diamond" on account of his blunt honesty. From another source, we learn that he was bluff, deliberate, and sometimes harsh and domineering in manner. When he died in 1782, Charles Wesley wrote a commemorative poem, in which he extolled his liberality, his piety and justice. He seems to have endured a long illness: in 1764, Wesley wrote to him, with a warning against the renunciation of horse exercise and the too frequent use of a new chariot.

One of the first of Wesley's clergymen friends was Grimshaw of Haworth. Grimshaw was born in 1708 at Brindle in Lancashire and was educated at the grammar schools of Hesketh and Blackburn. At the age of eighteen he entered Christ's College, Cambridge. For more than two years, in spite of a serious boyhood, he gave himself up to the frivolous amusements of the University. However, a disposition for youthful gaiety did not prevent him from taking Orders, which he did in 1731, and quickly became serious again. But he was not yet settled. After a curacy at Rochdale, he moved to Todmorden, where he dropped his pious acquaintances and amused himself with rural sports. He was jolly and popular, careless, and ready for a game or a match or a day with the dogs. In 1734 he began to think seriously again, catechised the children, and exhorted the merry fellows of Todmorden to mend their ways.

Presently he found that his own ways needed mending. For more than three years he was in a state of acute spiritual distress. His conversion was brought about in two stages. First of all, flashes of light from a pewter dish directed his

eyes to a copy of Owen's *Justification by Faith*. He then had
a vision, in which the wall of a dark passage was all that
interposed between him and the fires of hell, while he
listened to God the Father and God the Son discussing his
fate. He was also affected by the Puritan dialectic of the
preceding century. In 1742 he was appointed to Haworth
in the West Riding of Yorkshire, and became a strong
evangelist.

Grimshaw was a man nearly as eccentric as Berridge, but
of a more rugged, and more imposing character. His
utterance was plain and forcible, but not, like that of
Berridge, disfigured by extravagance. However singular he
was in dress and behaviour, he had a cool judgment and was
capable of a firm, steady and regular administration. He
was a man of gigantic build, no fairweather preacher, but
able to face the wind and rain and the cold storms of the
moors. As he gave away clothes, money and food freely,
he had often only one shabby coat and one pair of shoes.
His bluff, hearty manner and the fervour of his spirit gave
a peculiar success to his ministry among the people of
Yorkshire, Lancashire, Cheshire and North Derby—the
wild, rude people of the hills or factories. In his own parish
of Haworth, he quickly raised the number of the communicants from twelve to twelve hundred. Even that was
hardly as remarkable as the fact that he was able to put a
stop to the Haworth races. In the earlier days of his work,
he travelled in the Yorkshire circuit of Benjamin Ingham,
and was occasionally a guest at Ledstone Hall, where he
probably met the "exalted females" of the Hastings family.
He had an argument with Lord Huntingdon, and told
him that his Lordship's trouble was less in his head than in
his heart. Huntingdon was offended and would not see
him again.

Although he was called to account by the Archbishop of
York, Grimshaw was not maliciously persecuted by the
Church, nor was he restrained from carrying out his work
as an itinerating clergyman. The Archbishop, more discerning and more tolerant than some of his fellows, praised
him for what he had done, and impressed upon him the

necessity of prudence. Grimshaw was present, as we have seen, at the Barrowford or Roughlee riot in 1748, and in the following year he published an answer to the *Sermon against the Methodists* by Mr. George White, the leader of the Colne mob.

The methods of Grimshaw were often of a militant kind, and far from gentle. He was a pious autocrat. If he found people idling or sauntering on a Sunday, he would reprove them in the sternest manner. Those who were inattentive in church were rebuked before the whole congregation. While the psalms were being sung, Grimshaw would slip outside, and if he saw any loiterers he would forcibly drive them into the church.

On one occasion, Whitefield preached at Haworth and congratulated the people on having so greatly improved under the ministry of their pastor. This was more than Grimshaw could endure: he rose to his feet and protested loudly, "Sir, Sir! I beg you to say nothing of the kind; do not flatter them; I fear the greater part of them are going to hell with their eyes open."

He literally ruled his parishioners, none of whom dared to do a job of work on a Sunday, no matter how needful, without his consent. He is said to have gone about disguised at night, in order to find out how the people were behaving when they were left to themselves.

But although he may have been fantastically strict, Grimshaw was the kindest and the most humble of men. When the parsonage was full of guests, he would give up his own bed and sleep in the hay-loft, and he might be seen in the morning helping to clean the shoes of his visitors. He had an Alderney cow which would follow him to the church, and he was obliged to sell her, because he could not find it in his heart to drive her away. His last words were, "Here goes an unprofitable servant!"

He died of a fever, which he caught while visiting a sick parishioner, on the 7th of April 1763.

Actually, Grimshaw may be said to have been a link between the Methodists and the unofficial evangelism of the Church of England. Soon after his meeting with Wesley in 1747 he was enrolled in the Methodist societies, and was appointed the "assistant" of the Haworth circuit. He lived on equally good terms with Calvinists and Arminians, though he himself strongly inclined to Calvinism. "I shall be a Methodist," he said, "as long as the Methodists are Churchmen."

In each of the hamlets of his parish he preached three times a month, so that he might be heard by those who were too infirm to come to the church; and in addition to this, he preached in the neighbouring parishes, sometimes as many as thirty sermons a week. For more than fifteen years, he preached not fewer than a dozen sermons each week, and travelled some scores of miles.

He was a tough evangelist of the stirring, manly sort, thinking it shameful to keep silence while so many had never heard, or never felt, the word of God. As he strode or rode over the hills of the West Riding or down the Lancashire valleys he would shout cheerily his loud songs of praise. He was never gloomy or faltering or dejected. There was a resolution, a squareness and energy in his character which made him feared by some and loved by others, but never despised. He is one of the monuments of Methodism.

Wesley first met Grimshaw, on the 1st of May 1747, at Haworth. Grimshaw, in the words of his enemies, had been "preaching damnation beyond all sense and all reason," and the clergy of the diocese were agitating to get him suspended. But Grimshaw had now determined, no matter what occurred, to continue his work as a travelling evangelist, whether inside the Church or outside. Wesley and Grimshaw were soon friends, and Haworth became an important centre of Methodism.

In 1749, Grimshaw assisted John and Charles Wesley at Kingswood. Charles, like his brother, was drawn towards the Yorkshire preacher, whom he afterwards described as "his right hand, his brother and bosom friend." He had met Grimshaw in October 1746, and made the following note in his *Journal*: "I called on Mr. Grimshaw, a faithful Minister of Christ, and found him and his wife ill of a fever.

She had been a great opposer, but lately convinced. His soul was full of triumphant love. . . . We prayed, believing that the Lord would raise him up again for the service of His Church."

Wesley often visited Haworth in the years that followed. The multitudes that came to hear him overflowed the church, and Grimshaw built platforms against the walls for the benefit of those who could not get inside. After the preaching, the Sacraments were administered in the church to one congregation after another, and the number of communicants ran into thousands: it is recorded that, in 1753, thirty-five bottles of wine were used at a single celebration. Nor did the fine results of Grimshaw's ministry cease with his death. In his later visits to Haworth, Wesley usually found a full church and a godly audience. Only once, in July 1770, there was a lapse, and the "poor parishioners were no more affected than stones." But two years later, the old fervour had blazed out again, and Wesley wrote: "Not half the congregation at Haworth could get into the church in the morning, nor a third part in the afternoon. So I stood on a kind of pulpit near the side of the church. Such a congregation was never seen there before; and I believe all heard distinctly."

The loss of Grimshaw was deeply felt by Wesley. Grimshaw was the older of the two by five years, and Wesley had such a high opinion of him that he was appointed, after Charles Wesley, as the virtual head of the Methodist movement if Wesley died before him. There could be no more striking testimony to the gifts and the goodness of William Grimshaw.

Vincent Perronet, the vicar of Shoreham in Kent, was an earlier friend than Grimshaw, whom he resembled in nothing but piety. Perronet, who was ten years older than Wesley, was the son of a naturalised Swiss, who had come to England in 1680. His mother, Philothea Arthur, was the grand-daughter of an officer of the Star Chamber court. He was a scholar of Queen's College, Oxford, and graduated in 1718: in the same year he became the curate of

Sundridge in Kent. He obtained the living of Shoreham in 1728.

Perronet was a gentle, dreamy man whose mind swam buoyantly though steadily upon a placid sea of mysticism. He believed in tokens of a special providence. At the same time, he was never undecided in counsel, and he had a patriarchal appearance of wisdom. Wesley was introduced to him in 1744 by Henry Piers, the vicar of Bexley and one of the first Methodist clergymen. The friendship which was then formed lasted for nearly forty years.

Two of the sons of Vincent Perronet, Charles and Edward, became zealous Methodists, and for some years travelled with John and Charles Wesley. Edward seems to have been a frail youth; he composed one of the best known English hymns: "All hail the power of Jesu's name." Charles was a burly fellow, a little headstrong and turbulent, whose useful bulk was more than once interposed between Charles Wesley and the blows or the sticks and stones of the mob. There were other sons, who did not turn out so well. There was also a daughter, who showed Charles Wesley the cliffs and the hills and the bathing-machines at Margate. "Dudy Perronet," he wrote, "was more rejoiced at the sight of me than I can tell you. . . . She is risen like Venus from the sea, so healthy and handsome you would scarcely know her again." This, presumably, was the lady who so vigorously assisted her father in founding a Methodist society at Shoreham: she was called Damaris. There was another daughter named Elizabeth, who, in 1748, was married by Charles Wesley to William Briggs, one of the Methodist preachers.

The position which Perronet occupied in the life of Wesley and in the history of the Wesleyan revival is unique. He was called the Archbishop or the Umpire of Methodism. He was not a bold, thundering preacher like Grimshaw, he did not go out into the highways or beat up the devil in a circuit of his own. A man rather of contemplation and of mild prophetic raptures, he stayed in his parish, trying to lead men to faith by gentle ways and the example of patience and humility. But although he was a quiet man, he had that serene authority which is a thousand times more convincing than loud assertion. He had a placid belief in divine guidance. Both John and Charles Wesley came to him for advice in their private affairs, as well as in matters of doctrine, policy and administration. He assisted Charles in his courtship by means of a kind letter addressed to Mrs. Gwynne. But he does not seem to have been happily inspired when he advised John to marry, even if he did not know that John had thoughts of Mrs. Vazeille.

A Methodist society was founded at Shoreham, meetings for the villagers were held every Friday in Perronet's kitchen, and everything was done to save the souls and improve the manners of the people. Mr. Kingswood, old Mrs. Lightfoot and her maid, and poor dame Cacket, did their best to help in fighting the heathendom of the place.

The people of Shoreham were tough and rough, and the work of reform was exceedingly slow and difficult. In September 1746, Charles Wesley preached at Shoreham: "As soon as I began," he said, "the wild beasts began roaring, stamping, blaspheming, ringing the bells, and turning the church into a bear-garden." It was not until 1766 that John Wesley could write: "The word of God does at length bear fruit here also, and Mr. Perronet is comforted over all his trouble."

Perronet more than once took up the cudgels in defence of Wesley. He wrote and published a series of smart replies to the dirty pamphlets of Bishop Lavington, and he took the side of Wesley in the Calvinist controversy of 1771.

But the Umpire of Methodism was too gentle and too saintly a man, and also too wise a man, to be seriously concerned with the gestures and proclamations of Pope Joan Huntingdon and her zealous boys. And Pope Joan, for her part, was too genuinely interested in men of piety to quarrel with Perronet: she visited him, with real solicitude, when he was recovering from an illness.

John Wesley found, in the vicarage at Shoreham, a resting-place after his own heart. There was the good, placid man, so luminously pious, with his talk of prophetic fulfilment and his copious erudition; and there was masterful Damaris with her brave society of helpers, and Charles or Edward anxious to labour in wider fields; and there was Charity Perronet, most excellent of wives and housekeepers, careful to provide for the plain comfort of her guest. At Shoreham, Wesley had leisure and quiet for reading and writing; and although he never allowed himself more than a few days of respite from strenuous work, the days at the vicarage must have been happy and recuperative in the highest degree.

There are many entries in Wesley's *Journal* which tell of his concern or affection for his old friend. In January 1778 he noted: "Mr. Perronet, though in his eighty-fifth year, is still able to go through the whole Sunday service. How merciful is God to the poor people of Shoreham! And many of them are not insensible of it." At the end of the same year, he wrote: "I found Mr. Perronet once more brought back from the gates of death; undoubtedly for the sake of his little flock, who avail themselves of his being spared too, and continually *increase*, not only in numbers, but in the knowledge and love of God." And at the end of 1781: "I went to Shoreham, to see the venerable old man. He is in his eighty-ninth year, and had nearly lost his sight; but he has not lost his understanding, nor even his memory, and is full of faith and love."

The death of Perronet, at the age of ninety-one, took place on the 9th of May 1785. Two days before, he had listened with delight to his grand-daughter reading the last chapters of his favourite Prophet, Isaiah. "God bless thee, my dear child," he had said, smiling: "yea, and He *will* bless thee!"—"Oh that I may follow him in holiness," cried Wesley, himself in his eighty-second year, "and that my last end may be like his!"

Fletcher of Madeley was a later friend than either Grimshaw or Perronet. Next to John Wesley himself, he was perhaps the most intellectual and the most fervently religious man in the early history of Methodism. After the death of Grimshaw, Wesley designated Fletcher as the man best fitted to succeed him in the leadership of the great revival.

Jean Guillaume de la Fléchère was born at Nyon in Switzerland in 1729. His father, descended from a noble house of Savoy, was a colonel of militia. Young Jean Guillaume, in spite of a tender conscience, a studious disposition, a good intellect, and the fear of God, wanted to go into the army. After he had passed through the University of Geneva, he went to Lisbon, raised a company of Swiss, and engaged to serve the King of Portugal in Brazil.

But one morning, the maid who waited on him at breakfast dropped the kettle on his legs, and so scalded him that he was kept in bed for many days. The ship sailed to Brazil without him; never had a kettle been dropped so providentially.

He then heard that his uncle, a colonel in the Dutch service, had got a commission for him in Flanders. Joyfully he set out for Flanders, but before he could get there, the war came to an end; and his uncle died soon afterwards. Jean Guillaume, whose father was able to give him a reasonable allowance, therefore decided to come to England. He was introduced to a Mr. Burchell, who kept a boarding-school at South Mimms, and afterwards moved to Hatfield. With Mr. Burchell "he diligently studied both the English language and all the branches of polite literature." In 1752 he was appointed tutor to the sons of Thomas Hill at Tern Hall in Shropshire. The Hill family lived part of the year at Tern Hall and part of the year, during the sessions of parliament, in London. It was in London, and presumably soon after 1752, that he first met John Wesley.

Fletcher, having taken the English form of his name, decided that he would not return to his own country. He came under the influence of the Methodists, and grew increasingly serious. He was tormented by a sense of sin. He had a strange thought: "If I go to hell, I will praise God there." His condition, like that of all those in the stages prior to conversion, became more and more desperate. Satan beset him. If he opened his Bible, he found a mournful pleasure, but no comfort, in seeing how closely he matched the Biblical pictures of wickedness. His actual conversion, which resembled that of other intellectual men, was not the result of a sudden experience. He passed gradually and quietly from a state of misery and fear to a state of happy certitude. Yet, for some time, he doubted whether he was fit to become a minister. Believing firmly in the methods of study and mortification, he sat up for two whole nights every week, praying and reading, and lived on a few vegetables, with milk, bread and water. This austerity had the effect of weakening permanently a body that was never robust.

By 1755, Wesley had become the friend and the correspondent of Fletcher, and he encouraged the young man to persist in piety, though not in ascetic severities, and to take Orders.

In 1757, Fletcher was ordained both deacon and priest by the Bishop of Bangor at the Chapel Royal, St. James's. On the same day, immediately after his ordination, he came to the West Street chapel to offer his services to Wesley. His first sermon was preached at Atcham in Shropshire on the 19th of June, 1757.

For some time, still living at Tern Hall, Fletcher helped the vicar of Madeley, and became fond of the Madeley people. In 1760, he was appointed to the living, which was procured for him by his patron, Hill.

Wesley described Madeley as "an exceeding pleasant village, encompassed with trees and hills." It is now in the blackest and bleakest of industrial regions, not far from the desolate ugliness of Ironbridge. Even in 1760, the place was busy with ironworks and coalmines and full of a rough, grimy people, not unlike those of Kingswood.

Fletcher did not confine his labours to his own parish, but for many years he preached at places ten or sixteen miles away, returning the same night. He was the most exemplary of pastors, attending the sick at all hours, and openly reproving wicked or drunken assemblies without the least regard for personal danger. Like Perronet at Shoreham, his persistence in good works, his love and steady example wore down the beastliness and brutality of his parishioners, and the church at Madeley, scantily attended when he came there, was at last filled to overflowing. In 1764, Wesley affectionately refers to Fletcher as "a Methodist of the old stamp." Fletcher was then thirty-five years old.

Lady Huntingdon, who never failed to discern men of eminent piety, was introduced to Fletcher by Wesley in March 1758. She expressed herself as "both pleased and refreshed by the interview." The young clergyman had resolved "to fly the houses of the great," but now he made an exception. He was not infrequently seen with Lady Selina's travelling staff of chaplains, Venn, Madan and Romaine. He went to assist Berridge, on the suggestion of the Countess, in the winter following the Everton revival.

Fletcher's attitude towards the Queen of the Methodists was at first that of a simple young man, impressed by the beaming condescension of a lady of rank, a lady to whom the Christian faith was so infinitely obliged. "I am greatly indebted to your Ladyship," he said in his ingenuous manner, "for what light I have into the nature of the foundation of Christianity; and although I have great reason to be ashamed of the little use I have made of it, I hope it will work its way . . . through the thick darkness of my self-righteous, unbelieving heart." He told Charles Wesley that, when he listened to the Countess, he felt himself "like Paul at the feet of Gamaliel."

He wrote many letters to Lady Huntingdon at the time of, or soon after, his appointment to the living of Madeley. To her he confided gloomily the state of his two thousand parishioners: "The bulk of the inhabitants are stupid heathens, who seem past all curiosity, as well as all sense of godliness. I am ready to run after them into their pits and forges, and I only wait for Providence to show me the way." In another letter he confessed: "I had a secret expectation to be the instrument of a work in this part of our Church; and I did not despair of being soon a little *Berridge*; and thus warmed with sparks of my own kindling I looked out to see the rocks broke in pieces and the waters flowing out; but . . . I am now forced to look within, and see the need I have of being broken and of relenting myself." And he nearly always signed himself, so true was his reverence and simplicity, "your Ladyship's unworthy Servant."

After the Bath chapel was opened in 1765, Fletcher was one of the men who did duty there. Nay, more: he ministered in the drawing-rooms of Lady Huntingdon to "the elegant and pious persons" who came there so graciously to hear plain men preach the word of God. But the most important result of his friendship with Lady Huntingdon was his appointment to the presidency of the new college at Trevecca in 1768.

In taking charge of this college, Fletcher was not to give up his living. He was to be in residence as often as possible, and to exercise general powers of superintendence. Young men were to be trained, free of charge, for any of the Protestant denominations, and they were to receive one suit of clothes each year. There was nothing in the scheme which could have led any one to foresee the violent attack which the Countess was presently to launch against the Arminian front of John Wesley. Fletcher accepted the post with gratitude and with exultation. To the students, he appeared less man than angel. And it must have been a noble pleasure to the president to come from his dull Shropshire colliers to these earnest, responsive young men.

For a time, all was well at Trevecca. Wesley came there on the 23rd of August 1769, to celebrate the first anniversary of the college, and the birthday of the Countess of Huntingdon. Howell Harris, now in a quiet patriarchial decline, was still presiding over his "family" in the house on the hillside. Wesley exhorted the "family," and then went down the hill to the college, where he was the guest of her Ladyship. He gives an extremely interesting account of the anniversary on the following day:

"I administered the Lord's Supper to the Family. At ten, the public service began. Mr. Fletcher preached an extremely lively sermon in the court, the chapel being far too small. After him, Mr. William Williams preached in Welsh, till between one and two o'clock. At two we dined; meanwhile a large number of people had baskets of bread and meat carried to them in the court. At three I took my turn there, then Mr. Fletcher; and about five in the afternoon the congregation was dismissed. Between seven and eight the love-feast began, at which I believe many were comforted. In the evening, several of us retired into the neighbouring wood, which is exceedingly pleasantly laid out in walks, one of which leads to a little mount, raised in the midst of a meadow, that commands a delightful prospect: this is Howell Harris's work, who has likewise greatly enlarged and beautified his house. So that with the gardens, orchards, walks and pieces of water that surround it, it is a kind of little paradise."

That must have been the last occasion on which John Wesley, Fletcher and Lady Huntingdon dwelt together in unity. In 1770, Wesley issued his anti-Calvinist Minutes. The Huntingdon party rose in a fine predestinarian rage, with cries of Popery! horror! and abomination! Those at Trevecca were called on to denounce the Minutes, under pain of being expelled. The headmaster, Benson, and the president, Fletcher, resigned their posts.

In the controversy that followed, Fletcher published his famous *Checks to Antinomianism*, in defence of Wesley and the wider Methodist movement. These *Checks* were distinguished not only by a complete mastery of English, by strength and clarity of argument, but also by gentle and courteous restraint: they are patterns of polite repartee. The fourth *Check*, under the heading of *Logica Genevensis* and in the form of a series of letters addressed to the Hills, was published in 1772. *Logica Genevensis* was continued in two further parts in 1774, in which year Fletcher produced nearly six hundred pages of graceful and gently ironical polemic.

Wesley lamented the fact that his friend Fletcher was thenceforth tied down to the limited ministry of a country parish. "He was full as much called to sound an alarm through all the nation as Mr. Whitefield himself: Nay, abundantly more so, seeing he was far better qualified for that important work. He had . . . a richer flow of fancy, a stronger understanding, a far greater treasure of learning, both in languages, philosophy, philology and divinity." But Fletcher believed himself set apart for a humbler work; nor is it likely that he had the bodily strength for the life of an itinerant preacher.

In 1776, indeed, he was clearly in a consumption. First, he retired to Stoke Newington for health and rest, and then he moved to the house of a religious friend, Mr. Ireland, at Bristol. In 1777, he attended Wesley's Bristol Conference. As he entered the room, a pale, ghostly figure, leaning on the arm of his friend, the entire assembly rose to their feet and Wesley advanced to meet him. Fletcher began to speak, but Wesley, fearing that the sick man would strain himself, knelt by his side and began to pray. Again moved by a spontaneous and beautifully appropriate emotion, the company of preachers dropped on their knees and joined in the prayer.

Fletcher, though steadily declining, lived for another eight years. At the end of 1778, he set out for Switzerland, accompanied by Mr. Ireland and some other friends. He was no sooner in France than he appeared better, and when he reached Nyon and was among his own people it seemed as though he might be completely restored. He made a tour through part of Italy, and visited Rome. He saw the Pope in an open landau, waving his hands as though he was swimming, and poor Fletcher "longed to bear a public testimony against Antichrist." Yet he allowed the Pope to be "a man of sense and humanity." He returned to England in the spring of 1781, and in the same year he married a pious Methodist lady, Miss Bosanquet. He had known Miss Bosanquet for twenty-five years, and had felt that, if he ever married, she would be the proper wife for him.

For some time after his marriage and return to Madeley, Fletcher seemed greatly improved in health. But the improvement was illusory. He was nursed with sublime care and devotion by his wife through the last years of his illness, and died on the 14th of August 1785, at the age of fifty-six.

A few days before his death, the dying man (for so he was) had taken the service in the church at Madeley.

Blackwell, Perronet, Grimshaw and Fletcher were certainly the men who, after his brother Charles, were dearest to the heart of Wesley. He had other friends, but none who could be placed on a level with these. Yet we should mention briefly two men for whom he had a more than ordinary regard in the later years of his life. Both of these men were natives of Brecon in South Wales, and both of them were born in the same year—1747. Their names are Thomas Coke and Walter Churchey.

Of Coke we shall speak more fully hereafter: he took the degree of D.C.L. in 1775, and became the leader of Episcopalian Methodism in the United States.

Churchey was a lawyer, and as he never made any money, we must assume that he was a rather singular man, with no sense of professional advantages. He wrote a prodigious quarto of religious verse, which, in the sharp words of his biographer, "is not generally accepted as poetry." He married Miss Mary Bevan of Clyro, died at Hay in 1805, and was buried in the Priory Churchyard of Brecon. Wesley had a warm liking for this Welsh lawyer, to whom he wrote many affectionate letters, and whom he consulted about the *Arminian Magazine.*

In all the friends of Wesley, the outstanding and indisputable quality was a sense of religion. Religion of the rugged, crusading kind was the leading character of Grimshaw; in Vincent Perronet we have the softer and more speculative religious mind; in Fletcher, a pure, burning, transcendent piety. And it was certainly Fletcher whose mind and spirit most closely resembled those of Wesley and approached most nearly to Wesley's own idea of Christian perfection.

CHAPTER XXI

HIS WORK PROSPERS

FROM 1760 to 1770 the advance of Methodism was never seriously checked. There were local fluctuations, as in Cornwall, but the general tendency was one of steady ascent. Mere physical violence was almost restricted to Ireland, where people were ready to kick Wesley's hat or to run after his preachers with halberts.

It was not often, now, that Wesley had any need to compare his listeners to dead stones or dry bones. The ordinary people of England were not affected by Lavington's *Enthusiasm* or Warburton's angry book on Grace, or Foote's *Minor* (1760) or the dull and dirty abuse of poems and pamphlets. The new industrials were beginning to look on Wesley as their own particular leader in spiritual affairs, and as the working Englishman has always been, and still is, fundamentally religious, Wesley already took his place among the treasured properties of the nation.

The Methodist societies had now assumed the character of the old German *Collegia Pietatis*, for they aimed at the general promotion of holiness without separation from the Church. At least, that was the aim of the leader, and for the time being the idea of separation was not much in evidence. But no one could say that Wesley insisted upon conformity to Church procedure. In 1761, he not only tolerated, but encouraged, the first woman Methodist preacher, Sarah Crosby. Sarah was but the first of a host of others, including Miss Bosanquet (Mrs. Fletcher), Mary Barnett and Hannah Harrison.

In 1761 there was a truce, if not a compromise, between Wesley and the Calvinistic preachers. Venn came to see him when he was on the northern circuit during the summer; at the end of their conversations Wesley was able to say, "I believe there is no bone of contention remaining." In the following year, Lady Selina herself attended the Leeds Conference.

Trouble seemed more likely to come from within the ranks of the Methodists, but not of a serious kind. "In the year 1762," said Wesley, "there was a great increase in the work of God in London"; but he was obliged to add, "five or six honest enthusiasts foretold the world was to end on the 28th of February (1763)." By the term "honest enthusiasts" he included Thomas Maxfield, one of his first preachers, and George Bell, an ex-corporal of the Life Guards.

Maxfield had become noisy, fanatical and rebellious. He had been mildly reproved, but had turned upon the Wesleys with insane bitterness and accused them of preaching a false doctrine. Bell announced that he was completely sanctified and had the exclusive right to represent God in the metropolis. He gathered round him a band of crazy followers who believed themselves as perfect as angels, with power to cure the blind and raise the dead. Towards the end of 1762, the corporal announced the end of the world.

It is not improbable that Hogarth had such men as Bell and Maxfield in his mind when he produced his etching of *Credulity, Superstition and Fanaticism* (1762). But all the direct references in this ugly satire are references to the Calvinist party: the "New and Correct Globe of Hell by Romaine," the lines from Whitefield's hymn on the clerk's desk, and the copy of Whitefield's *Journal* in the basket.

Bell, in particular, must have exposed Methodism to contempt, and it is odd that Wesley tolerated and admonished him for so long, and waited until he removed himself from the Society of his own accord. Bell and Maxfield withdrew from the Foundry early in 1763, taking with them some thirty or forty enthusiastic followers.

On the 27th of February, Corporal Bell and his disciples walked to a little hill near St. Luke's Hospital to have a last look at the wicked world. But here Mr. Bell was rudely arrested by two constables, with a warrant from a magistrate in Long Acre, and he was taken away to jail. Whitefield observed wisely that it was a pity Bell was taken up, and that it would have been better to have left him alone.

Dr. Johnson, on the 30th of July 1763, paid his first tribute to the Methodists. He admitted their success. "Sir," he observed, "it is owing to their expressing themselves in a plain and familiar manner, which is the only way to do good to the common people, and which clergymen of genius and learning ought to do from a principle of duty, when it is suited to the congregation."

He was right, but only partly right. Methodism grew, not merely because it spoke in a plain familiar manner, but also because it reached the vast masses of the people to whom "clergymen of genius and learning" had nothing whatever to say.

The leadership of the revival, in every respect, was more and more settled upon Wesley. His brother Charles may be said to have retired. Whitefield, though he was in England for eight years between the summers of 1755 and 1763, was becoming less active and was hindered by asthma. Grimshaw and Berridge could never have been leaders, though both were sources of volcanic energy; and Grimshaw died in 1763. But Wesley had set up an almost perfect organisation, and he had a volunteer force which was continually adding to its ranks. Indeed, the seemingly spontaneous growth of Methodism and its appearance of natural vitality may obscure our true view of the leadership, the genius and the inspiration of Wesley.

And yet Wesley, if you can possibly conceive of such a thing, was like a general who was always in the firing-line. On nearly every day of every year he was riding and preaching, preaching and riding. That is why many people find his *Journal* a rather monotonous record; the adventures, they think, are too few; there is a continued repetition of expression and experience.

"We designed to take horse at four, but the rain poured down so, that one could scarce look out. About six, however, we set out and rode through heavy rain to St. Claire. . . . Soon after my mare dropped a shoe, which occasioned so much loss of time that we could not ride the sands, but were obliged to go round through a miserable road to Llanellos. . . . I began expounding, a second time, after an interval of above twenty years, the First Epistle of St. John. . . . At nine I preached in the same place to a far more serious audience. Between eleven and twelve I preached at Westcombe, and in the evening at Frome. . . . I preached, about one, at Whitchurch, and then rode to Basingstoke. Even here there is at length some prospect of doing good. . . . I returned to London, and found our house in ruins, great part of it being taken down in order to a thorough repair; but as much remained as I wanted; six feet square suffices me by day or by night."

So it goes on, page by page, month by month, year by year. Here and there you have an account of some notable conversion, of some strange happening—a ghost, an earthquake, the fall of a cliff, a body mysteriously burnt; but in general the record shows a noble simplicity and similarity. He goes on, not doggedly or grimly, but with steady fervour, steady concentration of purpose. He is not kindling in the minds of a few ignorant people a flickering and fugitive hope; he is bringing back to England a consciousness of belief in the Christian revelation.

It would be wrong to suppose that the preaching of Wesley was universally successful. The movement continued to be chiefly effective in the industrial regions of England. In Ireland, there was a general increase in the numbers of the societies, there were larger meetings and a greater readiness to listen quietly; in Scotland, "they knew everything, and so learnt nothing"; in South Wales, the societies were thinly scattered, but the people of Gower were "the most plain, loving people in Wales."

The number of the English circuits had risen in 1765 to twenty-six. There were four circuits in Scotland; Wales had only two; and there were eight in Ireland.

Several rules or modifications were introduced by the Conference of 1765. A fund was established for the relief or support of aged preachers and their families. Chapels were to be supplied with sash windows, opening downward.

There were to be no "tub pulpits" and no backs to the seats. Men and women were to sit apart. The foolish custom of breaking bread to each other at love-feasts was to be abandoned. Singing was to be greatly encouraged, and taught to the societies and congregations. There was to be intercession on Fridays, and fasting was advocated Preachers were neither to take snuff nor to drink drams: they were to reprove those who snuffed in sermon time, and they were not to admit the excuse that drams cured colic and helped the digestion. The people were to abstain from useless compliments, silly ejaculations and words without meaning. They might call each other brother and sister if they pleased. Late preaching, except at harvest time, was forbidden; every one should be at home by nine o'clock. Finally, there was a new humanitarian ordinance: no preacher was to ride hard, and every preacher, having arrived at a hostel, was to see with his own eyes that his horse was properly rubbed, fed and bedded.

At this time (1765) Methodism in America was but loosely organised, if organised at all. Whitefield, who spent so much of his time in America, had no capacity for administration. He was content to stir people to a lively realisation of faith, and then to leave them to themselves. Beyond a doubt he had accomplished in America a work of tremendous importance, for he had gallantly revived religion among a people who were naturally preoccupied with questions of exploitation and settlement, and people in whom religious tendencies were not greatly encouraged. He had done what was most difficult and most necessary; he had given the people a new mind and a new spirit. But spirits are not commonly perceptible or effective unless they have bodies, and no religion can live long without the codes, the guidance and the outward solidity of a church. True, the spirit may be overcome by the body; the church may miserably collapse under the dead load of its own tradition; yet there can never be a lasting faith without substance or without its appropriate doctrine, legend, rules, rituals and architecture.

Ireland, mother of missions, sent to America the men, and the woman, who were to organise Methodism.

In 1766, the organisation of Wesleyan Methodism in New York was begun by Philip Embury, one of Wesley's Irish converts, and by Captain Webb, an officer in the British army. These men were afterwards assisted by another Irishman, Robert Strawbridge, and by one of the most remarkable of Methodist women, Mrs. Barbara Heck. It was not until 1769 that Wesley himself dispatched two volunteer preachers—Pilmoor and Boardman—to New York. A large sail-loft was rented in 1767 by Embury, Webb and other Irish Methodists, and in that year the New York society had a membership of over two thousand. It should be remembered that Pitt had denounced the Stamp Act in 1766, and that Americans were already talking in no ambiguous way of their constitutional claims.

At the end of 1767, or early in 1768, Wesley was appointed one of the domestic chaplains to the Countess of Buchan: the other two were Henry Venn and John Berridge. This appointment was not a matter of any consequence, nor had it any results (as far as we know) beyond the preaching and publishing of one sermon; it is only interesting on account of the fact that Wesley chose to accept it.

From this period onward, the history of the Wesleyan revival is one of a steady advance, not equally maintained in all places, and almost exclusively confined to the middle and labouring classes. The rules, character and purpose of Methodism were clearly established. Adherence to the Church of England, if not loudly insisted upon, was implicit in the entire doctrinal scheme. In 1766, Wesley had written, "I see clearer and clearer, none will keep to us, unless they keep to the Church." Yet the advance was not to proceed without shocks or collisions, and the events which led to the most serious of these collisions began to take shape in 1768.

On the 12th of March 1768, six students were expelled from St. Edmund Hall, Oxford. It was alleged, that they had held or frequented conventicles, and had preached and prayed *extempore*, particularly in the house of a stay-maker, a woman who pretended to be religious; moreover, some of them were low fellows, one had been a weaver and kept a tap-house, one had been a barber and one a draper; all of them were illiterate, incapable of performing what was required by the University, and they were maintained *at the charge of persons suspected of enthusiasm*. In addition, they were attached to a sect known as Methodists, and believed in salvation by faith alone; and some of them had very rudely argued with their tutor and had purposely sought occasion to vex him. The Principal of the Hall defended their doctrines as being consistent with the Thirty-nine Articles of the Church, and spoke in the highest terms of their piety and good conduct; but the sentence of the University was against them, and they were duly driven out of Oxford.

It is extremely difficult at the present time to form a just opinion of this procedure. There is little doubt that the six students were maintained at Oxford by Lady Huntingdon. With the exception of Erasmus Middleton, they seem to have been obscure, uncouth lads, more likely to have "attracted the ridicule of the gay townsmen" than to have "excited the jealousy of the Church." Their language and manners may well have been flagrantly indiscreet. Charles Godwyn says they called themselves "ambassadors of King Jesus" and behaved with ignorance and assurance, in a way more likely to do harm than good. The account in the *St. James's Chronicle* is reticent, with a slight though perceptible bias against the Vice-Chancellor. To Lady Huntingdon, the persecuted lads were "faithful and devoted souls, and active in diffusing the light and love of which they were the happy recipients." Dr. Johnson bluffly and roughly denounced them. "Sir," he said with anger, "that expulsion was extremely just and proper. What have they to do at a University, who are not willing to be taught, but will presume to teach? . . . Sir, they were examined, and found to be mighty ignorant fellows." Boswell observed indulgently that they were *good beings*. "Good beings!" cried the Doctor testily. "I believe they might be good beings, but they were not fit to be in the University of Oxford. A cow is a very good animal in the field, but we turn her out of a garden."

None of the students had been associated with Wesley, and he did not feel that the expulsion involved any principle which he was called on to defend. But the affair was taken up hotly by the Calvinist party as a challenge to their position. If Lady Huntingdon's young men were to be kicked out of Oxford, she would have a little university of her own; and so the college of Trevecca was founded.

And that was not all. The immediate result of the expulsion was to bring to the surface, in a seething medley of wild speeches and fierce pamphlets, the whole question of Calvinism within or without the Church of England. In this regrettable discussion, very congenial to young men with hot theological fancies, two new pamphleteers became conspicuous: Richard Hill, the eldest son of Sir Rowland Hill, and Augustus Montague Toplady. Both these men became the bitterest opponents of John Wesley, and the most enthusiastic defenders of uncompromising predestination.

Richard Hill (afterwards Sir Richard) was born in 1732. He graduated M.A. in 1754, and afterwards travelled on the continent with the Earl of Elgin. Having returned from his travels, he became a follower of Whitefield and the Calvinist Methodists.

After the St. Edmund Hall affair, Hill flounced truculently into the argument with a tract of eighty-five pages called *Pietas Oxoniensis*. He was answered by Dr. Nowell of St. Mary's Hall, who maintained that the Calvinist doctrines of Lady Huntingdon's young men were contrary to the teaching of the Church of England. But Hill was a mild rebuker compared to the impetuous, foaming Toplady.

Augustus Montague Toplady was the son of Major Richard Toplady, and was born in 1740. He was educated at Worcester (Oxford) and at Trinity College, Dublin. He had been converted by one of John Wesley's preachers in a barn at Codymain, and had then accepted the Wesleyan point of view. In a little time he had changed his opinions and become a fiery predestination man. He was ordained in 1762, and became the curate of Blagdon in Somerset.

In 1764 he was the curate of Fairleigh, Hungerford; and in 1766, by means of a dubious transaction, he acquired the living of Harpford with Venn-Ottery in Devon, and in 1768 that of Broad Hembury. He was the particular friend of Berridge and Romaine. One of the compositions of Toplady is known to millions, for he wrote one of the most popular of English hymns: "Rock of Ages."

Toplady came to the assistance of Richard Hill, who was counter-attacked by Dr. Nowell, in 1769. He wrote *The Church of England vindicated from the Charge of Arminianism.* In the same year he committed himself to a *guerre à l'outrance* with a pamphlet of a hundred and thirty-four pages, called *The Doctrine of Absolute Predestination Stated and Asserted, Translated, in great measure, from the Latin of Jerom Zanchius.*

Zanchius-Toplady, with the copious energy and sublime assurance of youth, not only damned, elected and predestinated mankind in general, but also brayed most hideously against the Arminian clergymen, and thus against the entire body of Wesley's followers.

Wesley hated nothing more than controversy, which he regarded not only as a waste of time, but as a thing which soured and corrupted the better part of a man's nature. He hated arguments about religion. He had given sound advice to a young lady when he told her to "beware of the reasoning devil!" And in 1768 he had written to Mr. Plenderleith: "I did attack predestination eight-and-twenty years ago; and I do not believe now any predestination which implies irrespective reprobation. But I do not believe it is necessarily subversive of all religion. I think hot disputes are much more so; therefore I never willingly dispute with anyone about it."

Yet there were some things which Wesley could not endure in silence, and Mr. Toplady's writings were among them. It must not be forgotten that Wesley believed the idea of absolute predestination to be an error. He was never disposed to answer personal attacks, but he felt himself obliged to oppose the "horrible decree" of Calvin's mechanistic theology. But we may question whether his method of answering Toplady was in keeping with sound controversial tradition. He made an abridgement of the Zanchius translation and published it as a penny pamphlet under the initials of Toplady. At the foot of this questionable abridgement he printed the following note:

"The sum of all is this: One in twenty (suppose) of mankind are elected; nineteen in twenty are reprobated. The elect shall be saved, do what they will; the reprobate shall be damned, do what they can. Reader, believe this, or be damned. Witness my hand.

"A—— T——."

"This," observes Tyerman, "was the whole of Wesley's offending." But surely the offence is not a slight one, nor can it be viewed with anything but surprise and regret. It cannot be said that a pamphlet offered to the public was intended for private or limited circulation, nor can it be admitted that it was really "an honest abridgement."

A man with more dignity and more wisdom than Toplady might have exploited this blunder to his own advantage. Instead of making a sane use of the opportunity, Zanchius-Toplady lost his head in a crazy outburst of rage. Toplady was not without learning, nor did he lack force and brilliance as a writer, but he had no restraint. "Tenderness," he said, "has no good effect on Mr. Wesley and his pretended family of love. . . . The envy, malice and fury of Wesley's party are inconceivable." He therefore printed, early in 1770, a *Letter to the Revd. Mr. John Wesley.*

Toplady's *Letter* begins with a justifiable complaint and an equally justifiable assertion. "Why did you not abridge me faithfully and fairly? Why must you lard your ridiculous compendium with additions and interpolations of your own, especially as you took the liberty of prefixing my name to it?" And he observes in reference to the note at the end. "In almost any other case, a similar forgery would transmit the criminal to Virginia or Maryland, if not to Tyburn." So far, Toplady had the upper hand, but he fell, almost at once, to a level of scurrilous and muddy abuse. After observing that "controversy, properly conducted, is a friend to truth, and no enemy to benevolence," he proceeded to conduct his own controversy, and to exhibit his own benevolence, in such terms as these:

"Your piddling extract from the pamphlet . . . your illiberal and malevolent spleen . . . you are a Dissenter of the worst kind . . . your followers are working all manner of iniquity with greediness . . . your own hare-brained (sic) perfectionists . . . I do not expect to be treated by Mr. John Wesley with the candour of a gentleman or the meekness of a Christian. . . ."

It is necessary to remind ourselves that Toplady was not a mere abusive pamphleteer. Much of his polemical and expository work is of a high order. He could write charming essays on birds, meteors, the sagacity of brutes, and the solar system. In practice, he was charitable. His faults were conceit, thinly veiled by a pretence of indebtedness to God, and a lack of balance. At the beginning of this controversy, he was twenty-nine years old, and he died eight years later.

The importance of these pamphlets, trivial enough in themselves, is that they brought the Calvinist controversy to a point of explosion, and thus helped to define and divide sharply the two schools of theology within the Methodist revival. Up to this point, the gentle intervention of Howell Harris and the powerful pleading of Whitefield might have effected a compromise. But now Harris was too old and too exhausted to make an effort, and Whitefield, sinking in health, was away in America.

At this stage, Wesley felt it necessary to explain the position of his own societies. He had already made concessions to Whitefield on the subject of election, and this had tended to bring about some confusion in the ranks of his followers, and particularly among those who did not believe in the importance of good works. The skirmish over Zanchius, and the generally aggressive appearance of the Calvinist front, led Wesley to issue a manifesto. This manifesto was contained in the Minutes of the Conference of 1770. It is a declaration of doctrine. The historical importance of this declaration makes it necessary for us to review its critical theses:

"We have leaned too much towards Calvinism. Wherein?

"With regard to *man's faithfulness*. Our Lord Himself taught us to use this expression. . . .

"With regard to *working for life*. This also our Lord has expressly commanded us. . . .

"We have received it as a maxim, that 'a man is to do nothing in order to justification.' Nothing can be more false. Whoever desires to find favour with God should 'cease from evil and learn to do well.'

"Review the whole affair: Who of us is *now* accepted of God? He that now believes in Christ with a loving and obedient heart.

"As to *merit* itself, of which we have been so dreadfully afraid; we are rewarded 'according to our works,' yea, 'because of our works.' How does this differ from *for the sake of our works*? And how differs this from *secundum merita operum*? as our works *deserve*? Can you split this hair? I doubt I cannot.

"The grand objection to one of the preceding propositions is drawn from matter of fact. God does in fact justify those who, by their own confession, neither feared God nor wrought righteousness. Is this an exception to the general rule? It is a doubt, God makes any exception at all. But how are we sure that the person in question never did fear God and work righteousness? His own saying so is no proof; for we know how all that are convinced of sin undervalue themselves in every respect.

"Does not talking of a justified or sanctified *state* tend to mislead men? almost naturally leading them to trust in what was done in one moment? *Whereas we are every hour and every moment pleasing or displeasing to God, according to our works; according to the whole of our inward tempers and our outward behaviour*."

We have already seen the effect of these Minutes upon Lady Huntingdon's party. On the one side the Calvinist, on the other the Arminian, began to waste their energies over the old, hopeless problem of destiny and freewill, of grace and election, the incomprehensible nature of a God whose power and foresight are both unlimited, the opposition of choice and necessity, and the question of our dependence upon law, accident or compromise. Into such follies are we led in our frantic pursuit of the unsearchable.

CHAPTER XXII

THE GRAND ADVANCE

WHILE the excited young men of Trevecca, and all My Lady's Preachers, were so eagerly defending their doctrine of doom, John Wesley, having now left his own defence to Fletcher and Sellon, was placidly going about his work. In the autumn of 1770 he was in Cornwall. He took a walk on the hill of Carn Brae, and looked, with a pious contempt not unlike that of Dr. Johnson, at the granite monuments which were then called the altars of Druids. They might, he said, be coeval with Pompey's Theatre, or even with the Pyramids; and did that make them any the better? It was of no consequence to the living, whether they had stood there for three hundred or three thousand years. He came down again and preached to attentive multitudes, living souls indeed, and ready to hear the word.

Wesley had won Cornwall. Even the boorish people of Newlyn, who used to gape so stupidly or shout so provokingly, were now quiet listeners. There were no more bullies in St. Ives, no more cries of Canorum! at Falmouth. "All our enemies," said Wesley, "are at peace with us."

When he returned to London in November, he heard the sad news of the death of Whitefield. He was desired by the executors to preach the funeral sermon at the chapel in the Tottenham Court Road. It had, in fact, been agreed between the two men that whoever survived was to preach at the funeral of the other. Whitefield had hoped that he might be buried in his London chapel, with the Wesleys beside him; he did not think that he would leave his bones in America, to be handled by casual sightseers.

The funeral sermon was preached by Wesley to an immense concourse of people, both in the Tottenham Court Road and at the Moorfields Tabernacle; it had been composed in the quiet retreat of Blackwell's house at Lewisham. "It was an awful season," wrote Wesley; "all were still as night; most appeared to be deeply affected."

Generous enemies might have sought on this occasion for an honourable truce, and nothing could have been more to the mind of the great evangelist whose memory they were celebrating. We know the sentiments of Wesley in regard to his dead friend. A lady asked him if he thought he would meet Mr. Whitefield in heaven. After a pause he replied, "No, Madam." "Ah!" said the enquirer; "I was afraid you would say that." Wesley continued, "George Whitefield, Madam, will be so near to the throne of Grace, that a sinner such as I am will never get a glimpse of him."

But the Calvinist party had settled to a grim, vigilant opposition, and the publication of Wesley's funeral oration was made the occasion, not for a truce, but for a new attack. Wesley had said nothing of election and the final perseverance of the saints. His doctrine was "defective, abortive and precarious." And so the dismal controversy was carried on, and Wesley had cried in vain, "Take away from us all anger and wrath and bitterness, all clamour and evil speaking!"

In 1771, Benson was dismissed from Trevecca because he defended the Wesleyan Minutes, and Fletcher followed him. Lady Selina, in conference with her cousin, the Honourable and Reverend Walter Shirley, decided upon an open attack upon the Arminian lines. There was a preliminary bombardment in the *Gospel Magazine*, which, under its mild title, printed the most vigorous colloquial abuse. In June, a circular letter was issued from the Calvinist headquarters. This letter proposed a meeting of predestinarian supporters at Bristol at the time of Wesley's annual Conference: it was addressed to "Christian friends, real Protestants, both clergy and laity," and to all who disapproved of Wesley's doctrines, even among the Dissenters. The predestinarians were to hold a joint meeting, and were then to proceed in a body to the Conference and to *insist* upon "a formal recantation" of the offensive Minutes. Those Minutes were described as injurious to the very fundamentals of Christianity, and as a heresy of the most dreadful kind. If Wesley refused to listen, the agitators would draw up and sign a combined protest. Lodgings would be provided for the attacking force. An answer was requested, to be sent either to Lady Huntingdon or to any one of her agents, whose names and addresses were appended in a postscript.

With due allowance for those who took the strange view that Wesley was really the enemy of true religion and was promulgating a dangerous doctrine, it is not easy to find an excuse for this astonishing circular. Such a move can be reconciled with a privileged eccentricity, but hardly with the cool, reasoning mind of Shirley, or with the attitude of anyone who had even a moderate amount of common sense. That Lady Huntingdon and her men should "insist" upon a recantation on the part of the Wesleyan Conference was a proposition which bordered upon the limits of absurdity. They were certainly entitled to protest in any way that seemed proper, but not to assume the tone of a synod of bishops.

It is to be observed that neither Toplady nor the Hills, men usually without discrimination or reticence, took part in this mad proposal. The plans for a mass attack failed miserably. We do not know what excuses were made by the captains upon whom Lady Huntingdon was probably relying; nor do we know who did, and who did not, answer the circular. But when the Calvinist forces moved to their lodgings in Bristol they were found to consist only of nine persons. Shirley was there, and two other ministers; John Lloyd of Bath, Ireland of Bristol, Cornelius Winter, and two raw, excited boys from Trevecca College.

This was a most disheartening response to a call for a general insurrection of the pious. No doubt Lady Selina had seen herself advancing to the Conference with an overwhelming multitude of the elect. She would have led them, an awful accusing figure, like a fiery pillar moving in a cloud of righteousness. What could she do with a mere handful of six men, and two boys who ought not to have left their class-room? The idea of facing John Wesley in his own convocation with such a feeble retinue was too much, even for the seething enthusiasm of poor Lady Selina.

Shirley now realised that he was in a position which was no longer tenable. The Conference was to open on the 8th of August. On the evening of the 7th Wesley received two letters, one from Lady Huntingdon and one from Walter Shirley. Both letters were apologetic. Her Ladyship assured Wesley that she and her friends had intended no personal disrespect, and pleaded "a degree of zeal against the principles established in the Minutes." Shirley regretted that he had spoken of such a thing as a formal recantation; he did not really mean anything of the sort; he wanted to send Wesley "a respectful message imparting their design"; and he kept himself in countenance by stating that the doctrines of the Minutes were "evidently subversive of the fundamentals of Christianity."

Although Wesley did not answer these letters, he agreed to receive the Calvinist deputation (for such it had now become) at the first session of the Conference.

Shirley, after some discussion, presented to the Conference a statement on the doctrine of justification by works, to which he requested that all would set their hands. After a few alterations had been made in the text of this document, it was signed by John Wesley and fifty-three of his preachers. Charles Wesley was not present. Shirley was then asked to state openly that he had mistaken the real meaning of the Minutes. With a little hesitation, he agreed. In the brief note in his *Journal* which relates to this momentous Conference, Wesley, speaking of the discussion with the Calvinist deputies, wrote: "We conversed freely for about two hours; and I believe they were satisfied that we were not so 'dreadful heretics' as they imagined, but were tolerably sound in the faith."

There was little to be gained by this compromise. Wesley, with his preachers united solidly behind him, might courteously and firmly have refused to examine any criticism of his Minutes, which could have been regarded as a reasonable and final announcement of his doctrinal belief. The Minutes were not ambiguously worded, and no one with any sense could possibly have regarded them as favouring the idea of justification by works alone. By signing Shirley's paper, the Conference had admitted an appearance of ambiguity in the Minutes. There was no need for such an admission, and it did but prepare the way for further troubles.

Wesley had sent to the printer a copy of Fletcher's *Vindication of the Minutes*, and Shirley now asked for the immediate withdrawal of the manuscript. Wesley refused. By this refusal he reaffirmed his readiness to uphold the Minutes as they stood, and made the signing of Shirley's paper a gesture of no significance. Shirley himself, quite correctly, took this point of view, and accused Wesley of bad faith and treacherous behaviour. Richard Hill, and his young brother, Rowland, who had left Cambridge not long before, joined Toplady in a crude violence of attack.

No purpose would be served by quoting the poisonous articles which now appeared in the *Gospel Magazine* or the tracts and pamphlets which were too freely produced by both parties. If Wesley had acted with a view to conciliation, as he probably had, it is to be feared that he had not chosen the proper means or the proper moment. At the same time, it is necessary to read the letter which he sent to Lady Huntingdon, presumably written at Hay on the 14th of August:

"My dear Lady,
"The principles established in the Minutes I apprehend to be no way contrary to that great truth, Justification by Faith, or that consistent plan of doctrine which was once delivered to the saints. I believe whoever calmly considers Mr. Fletcher's *Letters* will be convinced of this. I fear, therefore, that 'zeal against these principles' is no less than zeal against the truth, and against the *honour* of Our Lord. . . . These *Letters*, which could not be suppressed without betraying the honour of Our Lord, largely prove that the Minutes lay no other foundation than that which is laid in Scripture, and which I have been laying, and teaching others to lay, for between thirty and forty years. Indeed, it would be amazing that God should at this day prosper my labours as much if not more than ever, by convincing as well as converting sinners, if I was 'establishing another foundation, repug-

nant to the whole plan of man's salvation under the
covenant of grace, as well as the clear meaning of our
Established Church, and all other Protestant churches.'
This is a charge indeed! But I plead Not Guilty: and till
it is proved upon me, I must subscribe myself, my
dear Lady,
> "Your Ladyship's affectionate but much
> injured Servant
> "John Wesley."

My Lady's Preachers, those noisy predestinarian lads of
whom Wesley could never speak without a shade of ex-
asperation, fluttered out from Trevecca and fervently
exhorted people in every part of the country. Wesley ran
across these young men in all sorts of places. He found
them at Dover: "They had gleaned up most of these whom
we had discarded. They call them My Lady's Society, and
have my free leave to do them all the good they can." *The
Gentleman's Magazine* for the 23rd of September 1772
reported: "A prodigious concourse of people assembled on
Tower Hill, where a temporary stage had been built with
back seats, on which appeared eight divines, seven of whom
had been educated at the sole charge of the Countess of
Huntingdon, who was present." On the 14th of August
1772, after preaching at Hay on the previous day, Wesley
paid a visit to his old friend Howell Harris at Trevecca.
Harris took him into his confidence. He said: "I have
borne with these pert, ignorant young men, vulgarly called
students, till I cannot in conscience bear any longer. They
preach bare-faced Reprobation, and so broad Antinomianism,
that I have been constrained to oppose them to the face,
even in the public congregation." Wesley observed: "It
is no wonder they should preach thus. What better can be
expected from raw lads of little understanding, little learning,
and no experience?"

Wesley could hardly have approved of Lady Huntingdon's Calvinistic incubator, which was hatching out so
many twittering chicks. But Wesley himself, except on the
points of absolute predestination or Roman theology, was

never dogmatic. He did not even refuse to admit a Calvinist to his own Society. "The distinguishing marks of a Methodist," he said, "are not his opinions of any sort." He was ready enough to leave particular views to the individual conscience, as long as they were not incompatible with harmonious relations, and a life which exhibited in all its ways true goodness and piety. Think, and let think. But he could not allow misrepresentation. He owed it to himself, to his preachers and people, that the faith of a Methodist should not be challenged. Neither could he tolerate schismatic preaching within his ranks. "I have no more right to object to a man for holding a different opinion from mine than I have to differ with a man because he wears a wig and I wear my own hair; but if he takes his wig off and shakes the powder in my eyes, I shall consider it my duty to get quit of him as soon as possible."

In general, Methodism was advancing all along the line. America, preparing for the struggle of her United States against the rule of Britain, was producing large Methodist communities. Pilmoor and Boardman had been sent to America by the Conference of 1769; and they were followed in 1771 by Francis Asbury and Richard Wright. Thomas Rankin was sent over in 1773. The first Methodist Conference in America was held in 1774.

It is extremely interesting to find that Wesley himself had considered the desirability of a second voyage across the Atlantic. In 1770, he wrote to Lady Maxwell: "I have some thoughts of going to America, but the way is not yet plain. I wait until Providence shall speak more clearly, on one side or the other." And in 1771, he wrote to an anonymous correspondent: "My call to America is not yet clear. I have no business there as long as they can do without me. At present I am a debtor to the people of England and Ireland, and especially to them that believe."

The part played by Methodism in the American fight for independence has never been adequately studied, but it certainly cannot be regarded as a very important factor. Wesley's own opinions, and the corresponding tone of his words and writings, appear to have changed considerably between 1770 and 1775. At first he had considered that America was treated unwisely if not unrighteously. But he could never agree with methods of violence. The affair of the Boston tea-ships in 1773, and the obvious tendency to armed resistance, must have filled him with alarm. Like Johnson, he was a stout monarchy man. He had very orthodox views about the Constitution. If he did not resemble the orthodox patriot in every respect, it was only because he could not applaud the use of a military force in the suppression of grievances.

In the summer of 1775 he wrote, from Armagh, a letter to the Prime Minister, Lord North. He stated that he was "a High Churchman," bred in the highest notions of passive obedience to authority; yet he could not help thinking that the Americans had asked for nothing more than their legal rights. And waiving all question of right and wrong, he asked whether the use of force could be reconciled with common sense. "These men [the Americans] think one and all, be it right or wrong, that they are contending *pro aris et focis*, for their wives, children and liberty. What an advantage have they over many that fight only for pay! none of whom care a straw for the cause wherein they are engaged, most of whom strongly disapprove of it." He then pointed, with remarkable astuteness, to the military difficulties of conducting a war at such a distance from a base. He advised North that the temper of the British people was dangerous, if not ready for rebellion. On all counts it would be a grave mistake to launch an expeditionary force of any magnitude on a mission of such a questionable nature.

It is a little difficult to reconcile the admirable tone of the letter to North with that of Wesley's famous political tract, *A Calm Address to our American Colonies*.

The *Calm Address* was published in the summer of 1775. In spite of its title, it proved to be a pennyworth of high explosive. Wesley had read the *Taxation no Tyranny* of Johnson, and his own tract was nothing more than a palpable abridgement of Johnson's, with no acknowledgement to the original.

This procedure was certainly indiscreet. At the same time,

it is entirely reasonable to suppose that Wesley and Johnson had discussed the matter. Johnson had a profound respect and a warm liking for Wesley, and he was not the man to endure in silence a flagrant act of piracy. In February 1776, Johnson wrote a letter to Wesley in which he said frankly: "I have thanks to return for the addition of your important suffrage to my argument on the American question. To have gained such a mind as yours may justly confirm me in my own opinion." This is not the language of a man who has to complain of a literary theft; it is the cordial compliment of a friend. But nothing can save Wesley from the charge of indiscretion. If he was convinced by *Taxation no Tyranny*, he was right in letting people see that he had changed his views; he was wrong in allowing himself to be accused of a bungling, gratuitous plagiarism.

No sooner had the *Calm Address* been circulated than a score of venomous pamphleteers were busy answering it in anything but a calm manner. Caleb Evans, a dissenting minister at Bristol, was one of the first to print his reply. He charged Wesley, not with plagiarism (perhaps Johnson's tract was unknown to him) but with inconsistency.

Wesley at once reprinted the *Address* with a preface. In this preface he says: "I was of a different judgment on this head, till I read a Tract entitled *Taxation no Tyranny*. But as soon as I received more Light myself, I judged it my Duty to impart it to others. I therefore extracted the chief arguments from that Treatise, and added an application to those whom it most concerns." He then proceeds to examine, and to demolish, the arguments of Mr. Evans.

Toplady could not let the occasion pass. He printed a tract of twenty-four pages called *An Old Fox Tarr'd and Feather'd*. This is the most crazy and the most indecent of his attacks on Wesley. It begins thus: "Whereunto shall I liken Mr. John Wesley? I will liken him unto a low and puny tadpole in divinity, which proudly seeks to disembowel a high and mighty whale in politicks." After much dull buffoonery of the same kind, he printed in parallel columns passages from Johnson's *Taxation* and Wesley's abridgement, showing (what anyone could see for himself) an almost exact identity in thought and expression: indeed, the actual wording of Johnson is only slightly varied.

In 1776, Wesley published a *Seasonable Address*, in which he deplored the hideous war in America, pleaded for a more conciliatory temper and for a chastened spirit of humanity and penitence. But after the Declaration of Independence, he issued, in 1777, *A Calm Address to the Inhabitants of England*, in which he took the side of an outraged nation against her rebellious subjects. It was a die-hard call to loyalty. We are familiar with such calls, but this one had the unusual merit of being sincere. North himself could not have desired a more sturdy protest, a more vehement defence. The shortest way to peace was a victory for the British arms in America. The liberty mob was already on the run. And it is not a little astonishing to find these words in a *Calm Address*: "Whatever they do, they will not fight. I believe they cannot, for the hand of God is upon them. But they can rob and plunder and destroy, and turn a well-peopled and fruitful land into a wilderness. They can burn houses, and drive men, women and children into the wild woods, in the depth of winter . . . these brawlers for liberty. . . . No man there can say that his goods are his own. They are absolutely at the disposal of the mob, or the Congress." Perhaps the most charitable thing that can be said for Wesley's American tracts is that the author managed, with perfect honesty, to get on the wrong side every time.

But there was another matter in America, besides the question of independence, which claimed the attention of Wesley. He was appalled by the horrors of negro slavery, and still more appalled, as well he might be, by the general toleration of those horrors.

Thoughts upon Slavery was published in 1774. At that time negroes were not merely treated with far less consideration than dogs or cattle, but often with an excess of diabolical brutality which is almost beyond credence. Lynching and burning, ghastly as they are, and at variance with any standard of civilisation, are mild methods compared with the slow and systematic tortures inflicted by slave-owners in the eighteenth century. Negroes were hung in cages, and left to be consumed by birds and insects. They were whipped raw, and rubbed with salt and pepper. Hot sealing-wax was dropped on their skin. They were pinned to the ground and slowly roasted by the application of burning sticks. The ordinary conditions of their labour were known to be such, that many drowned themselves before they could be led to the plantations.

Wesley's tract on slavery is a noble, forcible and vivid appeal. It has the manly directness of assertion, the sharp, hammering logic and the clear, nervous phrasing of his best essays. It is pleasant to find it cordially approved by the *Monthly Review* for September 1774.

In 1773, Wesley was seventy years old. Although he frequently reflected, with gratitude and amazement, upon the excellence of his health, he was no longer able to endure long days of travel on horseback. The distances which he travelled were not less, but from 1773 he made use of a carriage of his own.

Though he was not a powerful man, Wesley had an extraordinarily good physique. He was very seldom ill, and in all probability he was never dangerously ill. His biographers have been misled by the anxious concern with which he describes his symptoms, forgetting that both anxiety and concern were the results of impatience and of a limited personal experience of sickness. To be kept in the house, unable to carry out his full programme of work, was the most distressing of calamities to this active man.

On the 28th of June 1774 he wrote in his *Journal*:

"This being my birthday, the first day of my seventy-second year, I was considering how is this, that I find just the same strength as I did thirty years ago? that my sight is considerably better now, and my nerves firmer than they were then? that I have none of the infirmities of old age, and have lost several that I had in my youth? The grand cause is, the good pleasure of God, who doeth whatsoever pleaseth Him. The chief means are, (1)

My constantly rising at four for about fifty years. (2) My generally preaching at five in the morning, one of the most healthy exercises in the world. (3) My never travelling less, by sea and land, than four thousand five hundred miles in a year."

Perhaps the most serious of his illnesses was that which fell upon him in the summer of 1775, while he was in Ireland. The acute stage of this illness, which looks remarkably like influenza, lasted for three days. He was in a high fever, his throat was dry, his understanding was confused, his memory failed, and for two or three days he had no clear impression of what was going on. Fortunately, he was in the house of a friendly gentleman near Lisburn. A week later, he was on the road again. On the 10th of July, he resumed his regular preaching. On the 26th of the same month he wrote: "I found one relic of my sickness; my hand shook so that I could hardly write my name; but after I had been *well electrified* by driving four or five hours over very rugged broken pavement, my complaint was quite removed, and my hand was as steady as when I was ten years old." Nothing seems to justify Tyerman's assertion that the illness had "nearly proved fatal."

By the end of 1775, it was considered advisable to build a new Methodist headquarters in London. The famous Foundry was only held on a lease, and there seems to have been a doubt as to its renewal. Apart from this, a more commodious and a more dignified building was clearly desirable. The authorities readily granted a new site in the City Road. In August 1776, Wesley appealed for subscriptions, and raised more than a thousand pounds at three meetings. In November, the architect's plans were accepted. The first stone was laid by Wesley in the following April, and on the 1st of November 1778 the new chapel was opened. Another large chapel was opened by Wesley at Manchester in 1781.

One of the men most closely associated with the early preaching in the City Road Chapel was Dr. Thomas Coke. Coke was a man by no means lacking ambition or a sense of personal importance. But however pompous, however fond of authority he may have been, no man could have been more sincere in his profession of religion or more zealously evangelical. He was the son of Bartholomew Coke or Cooke, an apothecary of Brecon, who attended the family of Marmaduke Gwynne at Garth. His grandfather was the rector of Llanfrynach. Thomas was educated at Jesus College, Oxford. He took his B.A. in 1768, and in 1771 he was a bailiff and alderman of the borough of Brecon and a Justice of the Peace. He was examined for priest's orders at Abergwilli, and was ordained in 1772. His first curacy was at Road in Somerset, and he was thence transferred to South Petherton in the same county. He was led towards evangelism by Maxfield, who had become a clergyman in the Established Church. Coke was harshly persecuted on account of his Methodist views, although he was a stiff Churchman. He took the degree of D.C.L. in 1775. Wesley first met him in 1776 at Kingston, near Taunton. "I had much conversation with him, and a union then began which, I trust, shall never end." In the following year, Coke was driven out of his parish and formally joined the Methodists. He attended Wesley's Conference at Bristol in August, and soon became one of the most capable and most valued of preachers and administrators.

Dr. Coke was precisely the assistant that Wesley needed. He was a sturdy, rather truculent little man, driving ahead with never a thought of compromise or prevarication, and perhaps not less useful because he desired to rise to a position of command. He was a scholar, a clergyman, and a man of some breeding. If he had gone into a fighting service, he would have been a brave, ambitious officer, with a rigid though exalted conception of duty, and an honest belief in the justice of his own promotion.

And Wesley, in spite of the grand advance of Methodism, was never in greater need of good officers. His political writings on the subject of America had given his enemies an opening of which they were not slow to avail themselves.

In addition to this, a final attack was being launched against the whole system and practice of Methodism. This attack reached a phase of incredible violence between 1777 and 1779. Satirical poems, with indecent engravings, were produced by the dozen. Maxfield published a sorry libel. Rowland Hill exceeded Toplady (who died in 1778) in frothy vituperation.

According to gentle Rowland, Wesley was "the lying prophet of the Foundry," he was "a dealer in stolen wares . . . unprincipled as a rook and silly as a jackdaw . . . a liar of the most gigantic magnitude, a disappointed Orlando Furioso, a miscreant apostate," and so on. All this was loudly applauded by the *Gospel Magazine*: "Hob in the well again, or Pope *John* once more in the suds! Seldom has literary punishment been administered with greater keenness or spirit . . . When you take Old Nick by the nose, it must be with a pair of red-hot tongs."

Wesley refuted the libel of Maxfield because it reflected upon his relations with Whitefield's followers in 1741: the rest he ignored. But he could not let the lively and literary fellows of the *Gospel Magazine* have it all their own way, and in 1778 he started the *Arminian Magazine*, which became one of the most famous of religious periodicals, and was continued as the *Wesleyan Methodist Magazine*.

Under the date of the 15th of February 1777, there is a very significant entry in Wesley's *Journal*: "At the third message I took up my cross, and went to see Dr. Dodd in the Compter."

The sad history of Dr. Dodd is well known, chiefly on account of Johnson's defence. He had been a gay and brilliant young man, who took Orders and became one of the most fashionable clergymen in London. He was at one time the lecturer at St. Olave's, Hart Street, and the Lady Moyer lecturer at St. Paul's. For more than twenty years he was a favourite, not only with people of rank and elegance, but with men of learning. He was a foppish man, and was called "the macaroni parson." Dodd became one of the royal chaplains and a prebend of Brecon, but, with all his brilliance, he was a weak, frivolous creature, ruined by a taste for luxury, gaiety and ostentation. In 1774, he tried to bribe Lady Apsley, the wife of the Chancellor, in order to get the living of St. George's, Hanover Square. He was then struck off the roll of the king's chaplains, and was driven out of the country by contempt and ridicule. After living in France and Switzerland for some time, he returned to England. In February 1777, he forged the name of Lord Chesterfield, his former pupil, to a bond for £4200. He was tried at the Old Bailey, found guilty, and sentenced to death.

It should be remembered that Dodd had been one of the most resolute opponents of John Wesley. He had accused the Methodists of plain Dissent, and of being "the source of innumerable evils." "To hear such men disclaiming separation," he said, "has something in it so double and offensive as to raise the indignation of every serious and reasonable Christian." He did not attack Wesley in scurrilous terms, but he taxed him with contradiction and with "fighting against everybody."

Now, just before his removal to Newgate, Dodd sent three earnest appeals to Wesley. That he should have sent three times is a proof that Wesley hesitated. And as he went to the Compter, Wesley felt that he had "taken up a cross." He believed that he could do little good to a man who had so debased his vocation, and he could only anticipate an interview of the most painful kind. It was his conviction that Dodd merely wanted him to use his interest, and to intercede with men who might be able to save him from the awful penalty of his crime. But when he saw Dodd, he was surprised: the wretched man was "deeply affected, yet thoroughly resigned to the will of God." Three days later, he visited him again.

On the 24th of May, both Charles and John Wesley visited poor Dodd in Newgate: his appeal had failed, in spite of Johnson's rotund eloquence, and the day of the execution was already fixed. Wesley was at once impressed by the unusual quiet of the prison. Every one seemed anxious not to disturb Dodd, and to show respect for his sorrow and penitence. It is doubtful if Wesley, in all his experience of prison work, had ever been more deeply moved. On the 25th of June, two days before the execution, Wesley saw Dodd for the last time. "He was in exactly such a temper as I wished. He never, at any time expressed the least murmuring or resentment . . . but entirely and calmly gave himself up to the will of God. Such a prisoner, I scarce ever saw before, much less a condemned malefactor."

So the man who had vigorously opposed Wesley and all his works turned to him in the hour of misery, in order that misery might be turned to resignation and fear to repentance. If Wesley hesitated, if he went without a hope of doing good, he quickly perceived his error. There were few scenes in Wesley's life more affecting than his prison interview with the man who had spoken of the Wesleyan preachers as "the source of innumerable evils."

CHAPTER XXIII

METHODISM TRIUMPHANT

THERE is not much in the record of Wesley's last years to remind us that we are following the record of a very old man. A man who, at eighty-three, scrambles down the rocks of the Land's End, and who, at eighty-six, briskly jumps into his carriage at four o'clock in the morning, makes us forget that he has lived beyond the ordinary limits of an active life.

Those who saw Wesley in old age were delighted by his cheerfulness, the grace of his manner, his abounding vitality. Nor could they have seen one who was more charming, more happy in appearance. He was fresh and clear in colour, with a bright, piercing, yet always benevolent glance. He wore his long hair, as he had always worn it, parted in the middle, and falling on each side to the rolling curls on the shoulders; but now it was hair of a snowy whiteness. His neat figure, small, agile and firm, gave an impression of health and vigour not usually conveyed by the figures of ancient men.

No one represented in a more striking way the elevation of the human character, no one had more gravity or a sweeter decorum, yet Wesley had a rare flow of spirits and could talk in a way that pleased equally the critical mind of Dr. Johnson and the homely taste of a working man. He could be austere, but never bitter; firm, but never angry or truculent. Even those who were most prejudiced against him felt, when they were actually in his presence, an immediate sensation of reverence and wonder. He is thus described by one who knew him well in his later years: "So fine an old man I never saw. . . . Wherever he went, he diffused a portion of his own felicity. Easy and affable in his demeanour, he accommodated himself to every sort of company. . . . While the grave and serious were charmed with his wisdom, his sportive sallies of innocent mirth delighted even the young and thoughtless; and both saw in his uninterrupted cheerfulness the excellency of true religion."

The last ten years of Wesley's life were certainly years of triumph. He had worn down the grosser kinds of opposition, and he was popular in the best sense of the word. His likeness, whether engraved or in coloured pottery, was exhibited in thousands of English and American homes; and a living likeness was impressed on the hearts of the multitudes who had listened to his preaching.

It is true that he could still say in 1789, less than two years before his death, "I have not been so tried for many years: every week, and almost every day, I am bespattered in the public papers." He could well have ignored the muddy escapades of journalism. Even the Calvinistic opponents had sought a sullen truce, and were occupied with their own precarious affairs.

Of the triumph of Methodism there could be no doubt at all. In 1780 there were eighty-four circuits, with a total membership of 52,334: in 1790 the number of the circuits had risen to two hundred and forty, and of the members to 134,549. The most astonishing advance was in America, where the number of the circuits had risen in these ten years from twenty to one hundred and fourteen, and the membership from 8504 to 57,631. No other Protestant organisation could produce statistics in any way comparable to these.

The wider view of victory is made yet more striking by details of the advance. On the 31st of October 1780, Wesley preached at Oxford. He had never before had such a large University congregation. He was astonished to observe that even "the young gentlemen" behaved properly. Every one listened to him with attention and reverence. The idea of a merely personal success was never present in the mind of Wesley, but he must have felt, when he saw a well-behaved congregation in Oxford, that God had indeed chosen him to be an instrument of extraordinary power.

The Church, at last, was beginning to take the same view. The London churches which had angrily shut their doors in the face of Wesley now opened them to receive him.

"The tide is now turned," he said, "so that I have more invitations to preach in churches than I can accept of."

It was the same everywhere, and yet Wesley, so far from thinking of retirement or a purely administrative control, was never more active. At seventy-nine, he said, he felt the infirmities of age no more than he did at twenty-nine. A computation of distance will show that he travelled over as much ground in his eightieth year as he had in his fortieth, preaching as many sermons in as many places. The *Journal* entries for two consecutive days in 1781 may be quoted as evidence:

"Sunday, July 1.—I preached, as usual, at Misterton, at Overthorpe, and at Epworth.

"Mon. 2.—I preached at Scotton about eight; at Brigg at noon; and in the evening in the old church-yard at Grimsby."

We have seen Wesley in a prison scene with Dr. Dodd: in December 1780, he received two messages from another prisoner—Lord George Gordon.

There appears to be no adequate reason for describing Lord George as a lunatic. It is true that he became a Jew, but he did so upon religious, and not upon social, principles. To call a man a lunatic because he changes his religion, or his clothes, is hardly fair. Gordon may have been ill advised to accept the presidency of the Protestant Association in 1779, but he could not have foreseen that an association with such a respectable name was to be the cause of such appalling riots. He himself had no authority over the savage mobs which burnt Newgate, the King's Bench prison and the New Bridewell. Nor can it be doubted that the cry of No Popery! was a mere excuse for violence on the part of those who disliked the government. And what is more, every one knows that prisons are periodically destroyed by the populace in every civilised country. Twenty thousand troops were called out against the rioters, three hundred of whom were killed in the fighting; twenty-five were executed, and Lord George Gordon was clapped in the Tower.

After the second appeal from this fantastic but humane

nobleman, Wesley obtained a permit from Lord Stormont, and went to see Gordon. The prisoner was only twenty-nine years old. There is something exceedingly strange and affecting in the interview between the old Methodist clergyman and this peculiar, unfortunate youth.

Their conversation turned "upon Popery and religion," and Gordon showed that he was well acquainted with the Bible. The room was full of books; it was less like the room of a prisoner in a fortress than the study of some quiet recluse. Lord George impressed Wesley by his placid tone, and the entire absence of complaint. When, about a fortnight later, Wesley heard that Gordon had been indicted with high treason, he cried out that such an indictment was "a shocking insult upon truth and common sense." He must have been glad when Gordon was acquitted.

Wesley had talked to the young man in the Tower upon "Popery and religion." In his mind, the two things were incompatible, they were as opposite as light and darkness. At the beginning of 1780 he had himself published a letter in support of the Protestant Association. The letter was not a good one, and perhaps it contained only one defensible proposition—that Roman Catholicism could not safely be tolerated by any save a Catholic government.

It is by such an argument that we are reminded of the unflinching Protestantism of Wesley, whose maxim of "think and let think" was not to be too widely interpreted in religious matters. He found himself in the ambiguous position of one who declared that a Methodist could profess any form of the Christian belief, but that no Methodist was to consider himself as anything but a subscribing member of the Church of England.

To him, the Church of England represented the supreme Church of the world. He disobeyed her laws only that he might promote her vital welfare. He conceived of the Methodist revival as a thing always within the ecclesiastical plan, with the United Societies always a part of the Establishment. Yet from the very beginning of the revival the question of separation had risen again and again, and it was to be the one vexation of his closing years. He could not see, or could not allow, that separation in every practical way had already taken place. He could never have agreed that Methodists were bound to the Church only by a thread of sentiment. He could never have been persuaded that he was fighting, and fighting almost alone, for a mere formality.

At the Conference of 1788, the question was formally discussed, and the sum of that discussion was (1) That in the course of fifty years the Methodists had not willingly varied from the Church in one article, either of doctrine or discipline; (2) That they were not conscious of any difference in doctrine; (3) That they had, through necessity and not by choice, gradually varied in some points of discipline, by preaching in the fields, by extemporary prayers, by the use of lay preachers, by forming societies and by holding a Conference; but they could not have refrained from these things, except at "the peril of their souls."

But two actions of Wesley in 1784 showed how great was the actual distance between Methodism and the Church. First came the Deed of Declaration, and then the ordination of the American preachers.

The Deed of Declaration was more than a matter of policy, it was a statement of unity and independence, a legal charter. It made the Conference a permanent institution, bound the societies together, and secured the ownership and administration of all Methodist properties. The Deed was signed by a special convocation of a hundred preachers, and was enrolled in the Court of Chancery.

This Deed gave rise to some argument, but nothing compared with that which was produced by Wesley's decision in regard to America.

We have noted the astonishing growth of American Methodism. That growth had been particularly rapid during the War of Independence; partly, no doubt, because the Church was supposed to have associated herself with the policy of the British government; and partly because the clergy of America were leaving the country, and their churches were falling in ruins. Francis Asbury, a man of extremely fine character and splendid courage, had preached with a success almost equal to that of John Wesley himself. He is the most romantic figure in Methodism, a pioneer in rough, unsettled regions, riding through the dark woods and over the high, stern mountains of the new world.

After the War, the American Methodists were deprived of all benefits of clergy. They had begged for some kind of indulgence which would allow their own preachers to administer the Sacraments. Asbury had prevailed with them to leave the matter to Wesley, and Wesley had told them not to think for a moment of irregular practices. But obviously the situation could not be allowed to continue. Wesley therefore asked the Bishop of London to ordain a preacher who could visit the United States; and the Bishop refused.

For many years Wesley had believed in the sovereignty of the presbyter, and he now resolved to confer ordination upon such men as he judged fit for his purpose. He chose his most able assistant, Dr. Coke, and determined to send him to America with extraordinary powers. Coke, after a little hesitation, agreed to go, if Wesley, "by the imposition of his hands" should give him the right to ordain others.

But why should Coke have demanded the "imposition of hands?"—he was a clergyman, he was ordained already. If Wesley had the right to ordain, so had Coke. The answer is that Coke was an ambitious man; he had his eye on the dignity and the privilege of a full-blown, lordly *episcopos*. He wanted a sort of double ordination, the unmistakable guarantee of "extraordinary powers."

On the 20th of September 1784, Wesley called to his rooms at Bristol, Dr. Coke, and two lay preachers, Richard Whatcoat and Thomas Vasey. The two preachers were "set apart" as presbyters, and Coke was ordained "to the office of Superintendent of the Societies in America." After he had reached America, Dr. Coke was to ordain Asbury as Associate Superintendent.

No formalist can justify Wesley in taking this course, but the formalist is not always right. It is true that Wesley had not used the term "ordination." Yet the effect, the designed effect of his action was precisely the same as that of regular ordination by a bishop. Charles Wesley was logically right in viewing this action with horror, and in speaking of schism and dissent. Lady Huntingdon's preachers, driven under the shelter of the Toleration Act, had begun to "ordain" men in 1783; but the case was not parallel, for they had definitely placed themselves outside the Establishment.

Soon after his arrival in the United States, Coke officially described the American Societies as the Methodist Episcopal Church. Less than five years later, Coke and Asbury presented an address to Washington in which they deliberately styled themselves *bishops*. No one was more indignant at the assumption of this title than Wesley, and to say that he intended to make Coke a bishop is the most arrant nonsense.

But Wesley did not hesitate to ordain other men. In 1785 he laid his hands episcopally upon three preachers from Scotland; in 1786 he ordained two more for Scotland, one for Antigua, and one for Newfoundland. In 1787, five others were thus ordained, and in 1788 nine more were "set apart," including Mather, who was made a superintendent. Finally, in 1789, Wesley ordained Henry Moore and Thomas Rankin. That makes a total of twenty-six ordinations. Of these ordinations Winchester very correctly observes: "It is best to admit frankly that Wesley's conduct, however described, was inconsistent with any strict churchmanship, and to be defended only by those who consider forms of church constitution and government to be matters of expediency, and not of universal obligation. To those who so believe, it will be sufficient to say that Wesley was fully justified in breaking with usage and discipline when convinced that only so could the religious welfare of great numbers of his fellow men be conserved. That is the opinion of the vast majority of Methodists on both sides of the Atlantic; that will probably be the verdict of the impartial historian of the future."

Until he reached the eighty-first year of his life, Wesley had never taken a real holiday. In the summer of 1783 he paid a visit to Holland. According to Moore, he went "partly for relaxation, and partly to form an acquaintance with the truly pious in foreign nations."

Holland pleased him mightily. The trim parks and avenues, the bright waterways, the noble houses, the cleanliness and propriety of the towns were all to his liking. He observed a hundred things with curiosity and delight. He noted the window-glasses, placed so as to reflect the moving pictures of the streets; he looked with approval at the tall battalion of the Swiss Guards, whose whiskers were as black as their boots; he admired the beauty, the gravity and the plain clothes of the women and children; even the gallows, he saw, was pleasantly situated in a cluster of trees by the canal—so that the dying man, whatever his next prospect, could have one last fair green view of the earth. He was charmed, too, by the people. "How entirely were we mistaken in the Hollanders, supposing them to be of a cold, phlegmatic, unfriendly temper! I have not met with a more warmly affectionate people in all Europe; no, not in Ireland!" He declared that he found himself "as much at home in Utrecht and Amsterdam as in Bristol and London."

He preached in several places in Holland, both in churches and in private houses. The people he met, and there were many English among them, were pious, charming and hospitable. At the Hague, he was entertained by Madame de Vassenaar, who received Wesley and his friends "with that easy openness and affability which is almost peculiar to Christians and persons of quality." In the house of Madame de Vassenaar he expounded a text from Corinthians to several ladies of rank, and "two most agreeable gentlemen," one of whom was a colonel in the Prince's Guards. So great was his pleasure in all that he saw and heard, that he must have wished he had been there before, and he resolved to visit Holland at least every other year. Certainly no other country in Europe could have pleased him better; it is doubtful if any could have pleased him so well.

In August 1786, Wesley paid a second visit to Holland. Again he records a series of cheerful impressions, with one harsh reflection upon the University of Utrecht, which he considered far worse than either Oxford or Cambridge. In general, he gives pictures of grave elegance or homely charm. Holland is "one of the pleasantest summer countries in Europe." He was always a happy man, but he found a new happiness in these two delightful excursions.

Yet it would seem that Wesley had no need of rest. The activity of his last years is truly astonishing. He still preached, nearly every morning, at five o'clock. In 1787, finding the chaise too slow on bad roads, he rode a horse over the Irish hills. In the same year, he was delayed in his journey to Birmingham by the collapse of two coaches: he arrived late, after a very tedious and exhausting journey, but, finding his congregation waiting for him, he stepped out of the carriage at the door of the meeting-house and at once began to preach. Later, he sailed with Coke (who had returned from America) from Yarmouth to the Channel Islands.

But Wesley felt one of the sorrows of an old man: he had outlived the dearest of his friends. Ebenezer Blackwell had died in 1782. Fletcher and Perronet had both died in 1785; and in 1788 he lost his brother Charles. None of the younger men could make up for these losses, for none could share with him the memories of trial and triumph of half a century of splendid perseverance and zealous effort.

In 1789, at the age of eighty-six, Wesley visited Ireland for the last time. He was there from the 29th of March to the 12th of July. On the day before his embarkation he had travelled seventy-eight miles. He preached and prayed, made up quarrels and talked with old friends, in every part of the Irish circuit. There were very few interruptions; even the poor sinners of Sligo were not entirely without hope. The soldiers, to whom Wesley had nearly always been welcome, offered him rooms in their barracks. He was struck, in nearly every place, by the seriousness and attention of the people. Only at Lisburn, "some things called gentlemen" walked to and fro and talked loudly during the greater part of the sermon: "If these had been poor men, probably they would have had common sense!" On the 3rd of July he presided over the Dublin Conference.

In the same year (1789) Wesley paid his final visit to Cornwall. He had a special fondness for the Cornish people; the people who had once so furiously opposed him, but who were now gaping at him "out of stark love and kindness."

When he stood for the last time in the green amphitheatre of Gwennap he saw before him a multitude of more than twenty-five thousand people. His voice, he knew, could not reach them all. Wherever he went, at Redruth, at Penzance and St. Ives, he found large and attentive congregations. "So," he said, "there is a fair prospect in Cornwall, from Launceston to the Land's End."

It was only now that he began to feel the physical effects of age. He was accustomed to review the state of his health, in later life, each year on his birthday, the 28th of June. When he was in Ireland in 1789 he made the following entry:

"This day I enter on my eighty-sixth year. *I now find that I grow old.* My sight is decayed, so that I cannot read a small print, unless in a strong light; my strength is decayed, so that I walk much slower that I did some years since; my memory of names, whether of persons or places, is decayed, till I stop a little to recollect them. What I should be afraid of is, if I took thought for the morrow, that my body should weigh down my mind, and create either stubbornness, by the decrease of my understanding, or peevishness, by the increase of bodily infirmities: but Thou shalt answer for me, O Lord my God."

On New Year's Day, 1790, he wrote:

"I am now an old man, decayed from head to foot. My eyes are dim; my right hand shakes much; my mouth is hot and dry every morning. I have a lingering fever almost every day. . . . However, blessed be God, I do not slack my labour. *I can preach and write still.*"

Certainly there was no slackening of labour, even then. Two months after he had written this, he was on the road. On the 1st of March he was at Brentford; in the evening he preached at Newbury; on the following day he was at Bath. From the 4th to the 14th he was at Bristol. On the 15th he went to Stroud, and the next day he was at Painswick and Gloucester. On the 17th, after calling at Tewkesbury, he went on to Worcester. He was at Stourport on the 18th, at Quinton on the 19th, and on the evening of the same day he arrived in Birmingham.

In the summer of this year (1790) Wesley was in Yorkshire, as brisk and as busy as he had been fifty years before. At Beverley he was met by a company of friends from Hull, some in carriages and some on horses. They all dined together at the inn, a cheerful company, delighting to honour their leader and to see him smiling and talking at the head of the table. But when the talk was most lively, and the good people had forgotten all in the joy of this extemporised festival, Wesley took out his watch, jumped up, said good-bye, ran out to his carriage, and was on the road to Hull before the others had time to slip the harness over their nags. So all the company, with their horses and carriages, pursued Wesley along the road, and were just in time to give him a welcome to the town.

At the end of July 1790, Wesley presided over the Bristol Conference. To those who saw him, he appeared feeble in body; he could not read the hymn-book; but his voice was clear and strong, his manner was brisk and cheerful, and his spirits were as lively as ever.

In September he wrote to his friend Brackenbury:

"My body seems nearly to have done its work, and to be almost worn out. Last month my strength was nearly gone, and I could have sat almost still from morning to night. But, blessed be God, I crept about a little, and made shift to preach once a day. On Monday I ventured a little farther; and after I had preached three times (once in the open air), I found my strength so restored that I could have preached again without inconvenience."

About three weeks after writing this, he preached in the open air for the last time: at Winchelsea, on the 7th of October.

As Wesley stood in the green square of Winchelsea, under an ash-tree in the churchyard, he saw before him "most of the inhabitants of the town." It was not a large congregation, but a quiet one, with many reverent people, and many who were "almost persuaded." The wood of the ash-tree was afterwards lopped and chopped by shameless Methodistical souvenir-makers, for snuff-boxes, paper-knives and other trinkets; until a lay preacher, caught staggering off with a whole branch, was threatened with transportation.

In the same month (October 1790) he preached at Colchester, Norwich, Yarmouth, King's Lynn, Diss, and Bury St. Edmunds.

His Colchester sermon was heard by a remarkable youth, Henry Crabb Robinson. As the youth looked at Wesley, standing in a wide pulpit, and supported by a minister on each side of him, he felt "a respect bordering on enthusiasm." "His discourse," Robinson tells us, "was short— the text I could not hear. After the last prayer, he rose up and addressed the audience on liberality of sentiment, and spoke much against refusing to join with any congregation on account of difference of opinion."

On the 22nd of October, Wesley returned to London, and the last entry in his *Journal* was made two days later. It seems probable that he continued to make short journeys, during the remainder of the year, into Bedfordshire, Hertfordshire and Kent.

CHAPTER XXIV

SOLI DEO GLORIA

AT the beginning of 1791, Wesley found that his strength was failing rapidly. But his courage and cheerfulness never failed, nor did he think for one moment of giving up his work. " I am still enabled to scrawl a little," he wrote to a friend, "and to creep, though I cannot run." He made his usual arrangements for his journey to the north, which he intended to begin early in March; he sent his carriage to Bristol in advance, and took places in the Bath coach.

On the 17th of February he preached at Lambeth. On the 22nd he spent a busy day, preaching in the City Road Chapel, dining with a friend at Islington, attending to his ordinary routine affairs, and meeting his leaders. On the following day he got up at four in the morning and set off for Leatherhead, where he preached in a private house. That was his last sermon; and the next day he wrote what is believed to be his last letter. The letter was written to that gallant youth, William Wilberforce, already beginning his great fight for the abolition of slavery. Wesley had always been a zealous advocate for abolition, and we have seen that he composed one of the most powerful of his tracts on this very subject; he wrote to Wilberforce with all his cordial enthusiasm, and with a striking vehemence:

"My dear Sir,
"Unless the Divine Power has raised you up to be as Athanasius, *contra mundum*, I see not how you can go through your glorious enterprise in opposing that execrable villainy which is the scandal of religion, of England, and of human nature. Unless God has raised you up for this very thing, you will be worn out by the opposition of men and devils; but *if God be for you, who can be against you?* Are all of them together stronger than God? Oh, *be not weary in well doing.* Go on, in the

346

name of God and in the power of His might, till even American slavery, the vilest that ever saw the sun, shall vanish away before it.

"Reading this morning a tract wrote by a poor African, I was particularly struck by that circumstance that a man who has a black skin, being wronged or outraged by a white man, can have no redress; it being a *law* in our colonies that the *oath* of a black against a white goes for nothing. What villainy is this!

"That He who has guided you from your youth up may continue to strengthen you in this and in all things is the prayer of,

"Dear Sir,

"Your affectionate Servant,

"John Wesley."

On the day after that on which he wrote this letter, Wesley came back from Balham to his rooms in the City Road.

The steady ebbing of his life, which his friends now perceived clearly enough, was not accompanied by pain or by any distress. He was feverish, torpid; but all his expressions were those of a happy, composed man, willing to resign his body, and looking with a bright, untroubled hope towards the vision of God.

He recognised the friends who came to his bedside, smiled at them affectionately, and whispered thanks or praise or the comfortable words of faith. At times he was gently delirious, thinking that he was addressing one of his congregations, or a meeting of preachers. On Sunday morning, the 27th of February, he seemed better; he got up, sat in his chair, and drank a cup of tea. Then, with a clear voice, he repeated a verse from one of his brother's hymns:

"Till glad I lay this body down,
Thy servant, Lord, attend;
And O! my life of mercy crown
With a triumphant end."

Soon after, speaking in a particularly earnest manner, he said, "Our friend Lazarus sleepeth." He tried to talk to the friends who were near him, but he was soon exhausted, and had to lie down. By the evening he was very feverish and drowsy, and for the greater part of the following day he was asleep.

Death came to Wesley with no fears, no ugliness. His calm soul was ready, nor was there any doubt or shadow or vain reproach in the mind of this holy man. The men and women who reverently stood or knelt in his room saw the supreme reward of one who lived in the light of truth. "Sir," said one of them, "we are come to rejoice with you." With such reverence, and such a conviction of triumph, men have watched the last earthly moments of saints or philosophers, disciples have listened eagerly to the last words of those almost in sight of the opening heavens.

On the morning of the day before his death, Wesley rallied a little. He sang two verses of a hymn, and then called for pen and ink. But he was too feeble to write. Some one said, "I will write for you, Sir; tell us what you desire to say." "Nothing," he replied, "but that God is with us." In the forenoon he said, "I will get up." While they were making ready his clothes and his chair, he sang, with a vigour which surprised them, a verse from one of his favourite hymns, by Dr. Watts:

> "I'll praise my Maker while I've breath,
> And when my voice is lost in death,
> Praise shall employ my nobler powers:
> My days of praise shall ne'er be past
> While life and thought and being last,
> Or immortality endures."

After this, he was no longer able to speak much. In the afternoon he said clearly, "The best of all is—God is with us." And again, raising his hand, "*The best of all is—God is with us!*"

One of the last to come to the bedside was Sarah Wesley, the widow of his brother Charles. "He giveth his servants rest," said the old man, affectionately pressing her hand; and as she moistened his lips with a little water, he was heard to say, "We thank Thee, O Lord, for these and all

Thy mercies: bless the Church and King; and grant us truth and peace, through Jesus Christ our Lord, for ever and ever." During the night, he tried to repeat the verse of the hymn: "I'll praise—I'll praise——"

Wesley died at about ten o'clock on the morning of the 2nd of March 1791. A few moments before his death, he had opened his eyes, and, seeing his friends near him, had placidly said "Farewell."

No purely formal analysis can bring to a reader's mind the true picture of John Wesley. His bright serenity, his godliness and courage are easily perceived. The glowing faith, which gave such peculiar charm to his face in old age, can be described in simple terms as the sign of Christian love and Christian practice. But no simple terms can reveal the deeper things of the spirit, or disclose the source of that abounding piety which makes a man at once so truly human and so truly divine. Wesley, above all, was a man of God, striving to reach nothing short of perfection, yet always humble, and always perceiving clearly the distance between desire and attainment.

His own attainment in bringing men to religion, in preaching and travelling, in setting up a disciplined organisation of believers, guided by his ordinance and cheered by his example, may be compared with that of St. Paul. Birrell has described him as "the greatest force of the eighteenth century." That he was the greatest power for good within the region of Protestant activities, is not a matter for doubt. But we are not to think of the Wesleyan influence as a thing confined within sectarian boundaries. The good of Methodism flowed far beyond the limits of its own official cognisance. Wesley set before the English people a new conception of the sovereign merit of goodness, a new standard of honesty and industry, a new way of accepting cheerfully the duties of life.

Our desire to know something of the closer and more familiar aspects of this remarkable and lovable man can hardly be satisfied by a mere conspectus of attributes. We should like a more vital representation. It would please us to know more exactly how he moved and spoke, and what he thought about the smaller, persistent things of human experience. We should like some of those vivid trifles which, like appropriate notes in a picture, show us how we can meet illustrious men in the common field of humanity. Every man, too, has faults, failures and limitations; the actions of every man, however deliberate they seem, are changed or tempered by weakness, by vagaries of health, by the innumerable accidents of life.

Unfortunately, there is no contemporary portrait of Wesley by a great writer, or even by a very competent writer. The men who knew him and wrote about him in his later life—Coke, Moore, Whitehead, Hampson and Clarke—were not men with literary skill, and they were chiefly concerned with a purely objective account of Methodism. There is no Methodist Boswell; no shrewd yet loving observer; no scribbling, journalistic friend. The busy life of Wesley, and the nature of his occupation, kept him apart from the pleasant meetings of intellectual society and from the companionship of men of letters. He had no leisure; no time even for those wholesome amenities which would have been so congenial to him. Johnson said of him that "he could talk well on any subject," and we know the Doctor's almost querulous complaint, "that he was always obliged to go at a certain hour." If Wesley had not been always obliged to go at a certain hour, if he could have lingered in Bolt Court or strolled with Johnson down the Strand, we might have had a memorable account of his appearance and conversation. As it is, he touches the literary life of his age with only a brief, peripheral contact. Walpole gives a terse note of his appearance, Johnson observes that he can talk well, young Walter Scott is just in time to hear him preach, and that is all. The plain, honest men who had known him, and who took such pains to set down the mere facts of his life, were not writers. Wesley himself remains his best biographer, and the *Journal*, with all its *lacunae*, is the best record of his life. Wesley, when he wrote for his friends or the Press, knew what to omit; but he was incapable of the least falsehood. His *Journal* is not only a document of immense value to the social historian; it is unique as an autobiography, for it certainly contains, if not the whole truth, at least nothing but the truth.

There are, of course, many sources—indeed, almost innumerable sources—from which we can add details to our general view of Wesley. It is only by making use of these sources that we are able to supplement Wesley's account of himself, and to check the statements of his earlier critics and biographers.

Every one who has written about Wesley has displayed clearly enough the form of his religious character. Of that character, in which the antique spirit of Christianity was revived, nothing more need be said.

Perhaps the secondary characteristics of sense, coolness and humanity have also been sufficiently described; and they are obvious in all the decisive movements of his life. Too little attention has been given, we may think, to his learning, to his lively interest in scientific knowledge, to his alertness in recognising the immense possibilities of research. But there is another matter, more problematical and more liable to the distortions of prejudice: it has been asserted that Wesley was absurdly credulous.

The charge of credulity has two implications. Either it is applied to a man who is readily deceived by simple imposture, or to one who does not require proof of all that he believes. Both of these applications were involved in the charge against Wesley.

At the present day, with materialism forcibly ejected from our current views of science and philosophy, we are inclined to regard the credulous man with tolerance, or even with profound respect. Credulity almost appears to be a condition of intellectual advance. Being deceived in a particular instance does not prove that a man is wrong in a general supposition; and it would hardly be incorrect to say that men of science are now the most credulous of all. Indeed, the capacity to assume without proof, to rely more and more upon hypothesis, distinguishes every process of the higher scientific thought. Scepticism, not credulity, has become disreputable, and the sign of inferior intelligence.

But in Wesley's day, to call a man credulous was tantamount to calling him a fool. People were eagerly peering through improved microscopes and telescopes, and handling with delight what seemed to them to be instruments of incredible delicacy and precision. Final discoveries appeared to be imminent; men were on the point of explaining, in quite a simple way, the ultimate secrets of the universe. Mystery was being abolished. Newton, our greatest man of science, had opened a new view of the material universe, and the men who followed him had gone on zealously from one proof to another. Everything was being reduced to a neat system of incontrovertible facts. Archæology was already beginning the dullest, the blindest and least profitable of all investigations. A few daring men were guessing at the true meaning of fossils, without renouncing the idea of diluvial catastrophe. Unless a thing could be seen, felt, weighed or measured, there was no reason for believing that it existed; and since the movement of matter seemed to explain every believable thing, it was unnecessary to retain the hypothesis of God, except as the possible cause of original momentum. Anyone who could still believe in divine guidance, in diabolical agency, in apparitions of the dead, in second sight or prophecy, in the inexplicable nature of phenomena, was to be looked on with pity or contempt. And Wesley believed every one of these things.

If Wesley had lived to-day, he might have been a spiritualist. He certainly had faith in communion with the dead. In a letter to Lady Maxwell, written in 1769, he is quite explicit on this point:

"I have heard my mother say, 'I have frequently been as fully assured that my father's spirit was with me, as if I had seen him with my eyes.' . . . I have myself many times found on a sudden so lively an apprehension of a deceased friend, that I have sometimes turned about to look; at the same time I have felt an uncommon affection for them. . . . In dreams, I have had exceedingly lively conversations with them; and I doubt not but they were then very near."

In the same year (1769) he read Glanvill's *Sadducismus Triumphatus*: "All his talk of Aerial and Astral Spirits, I take to be stark nonsense. Indeed, supposing the facts true, I wonder a man of sense should attempt to account for them at all. *For who can explain the things of the invisible world but the inhabitants of it?*"

He believed in prowling devils, and in the good angels who, like the Olympian gods of Homer, sped from heaven to save men from tragedy or death. When the horses bolted with his carriage and ran with it to the edge of a precipice, only stopped in the nick of time by a brave rider, Wesley observed: "I am persuaded both evil and good angels had a large share in this transaction; how large we do not know now; but we shall know hereafter."

He gives a long account (May 1768) of Elizabeth Hobson of Sunderland, who appears to have been a first-rate medium: Elizabeth saw luminous apparitions of those who were about to die, she was frequently visited by the ghost of her uncle, she heard inexpressibly sweet music, saw the apparitions of those drowned at sea, and was at one time regularly visited by the spirit of a wicked grandfather.

In 1788 he was convinced that Margaret Barlow of Darlington "had frequent intercourse with a spirit that appeared to her in the form of an angel." Margaret Barlow announced the destruction of the wicked, and on the appointed day the effect of her prophecy was considerably heightened by a thunderstorm. The wicked not only survived, but they persecuted Margaret so vigorously that she fled to America: but what has that to do with the angel?

Again, in the matter of divine interposition, Wesley has been exposed to ridicule. Often, while he preached, he observed that a cloud would pass between him and the sun, keeping him in a cool shadow until the sermon was over. Or the wind, blowing hard a moment before, would suddenly die away. Or the rain, instead of falling on him, would pass to right and left and leave him dry. In these things he saw the hand of God. Why is it necessary to suppose that he was mistaken?

Credulity, in the ignoble or derogatory sense, was not one

of Wesley's failings. Indeed, if we look for failings of the ordinary kind in the character of Wesley, we are not likely to find them. It is easier to see his limitations.

Perhaps he was too ascetic, too severely opposed to recreation, to play and amusement. Perhaps he was unjustly impatient with those who built mansions and planted avenues and turned their gardens into elegant representations of Stygian banks or Elysian groves. His remark on the British Museum is worth remembering: "One large room is filled from top to bottom with things brought from Otaheite; two or three more with things dug out of the ruins of Herculaneum! Seven huge apartments are filled with curious books; five with manuscripts; two with fossils of all sorts; and the rest with various animals. But what account will a man give to the Judge of quick and dead for a life spent in collecting all these?" He was frankly shocked by nude statues, and by pictures of a too luscious kind—which is no doubt equivalent to saying that he had no appreciation of art. He could only see a definite value in what was clearly good for the spiritual welfare or the bodily soundness of his fellows; which is a palpable limitation.

Wesley has also been charged with a lack of humour. Yet, by whatever standard humour is to be judged, it is not easy to refuse it to a man who could write such an anecdote as this: "I talked with a warm man, who was always very zealous for the Church when he was very drunk, and just able to stammer out the Irish proverb, 'No gown, no crown!' He was quickly convinced that, whatever we were, he was himself a child of the Devil. We left him full of good resolutions, which held several days." Or take another short story: "One came to me, as she said, with a message from the Lord, to tell me, 'I was laying up treasures on earth, taking my ease, and minding only my eating and drinking.' I told her, 'God knew me better; and if He had sent her, He would have sent with her a more proper message.'"

Yet another accusation, and one by no means without weight, is that Wesley was entirely wrong in his views on education, and that he imposed upon the school at Kingswood, and advocated elsewhere, rules that were intolerably harsh and showed a complete failure to understand the needs and nature of the growing mind. Wesley's condemnation of *Emile* is a sufficient proof of his own views; but we have to remember that he was only accepting the current ideas of his age. The eighteenth century believed in the subjection of women and children; we have seen how Mrs. Susannah Wesley insisted on "conquering the wills" of her own children, and teaching the poor little creatures "to cry softly." Wesley had inherited the views of his mother, with the addition of an exceptionally severe attitude in regard to games and play. "Methodist parents!" he cried, "who would send your girls headlong to hell, send them to a fashionable boarding-school!" In 1783, in view of the endless troubles at Kingswood, the Conference decided, "that either the school should cease, or the rules of it be particularly observed; particularly, that the children should never play, and that a master should be always present with them."

This attitude towards play helps us to understand his general attitude towards our natural desire for leisure and recreation, for pure amusement and all the trivial and pretty things which help us to brighten or decorate the cheerless rooms of life. To him, nothing was of value, nothing was to be tolerated, unless it could be said to promote the knowledge of communion with God; all the rest was mere vanity, emptiness and vexation. Even reading, unless it tended to help the soul, or to keep the body in health, was to be carefully controlled. It was for this reason that he wrote or edited such a number of profitable works for his societies.

There is certainly a tendency to under-estimate the importance of Wesley as a writer. His style is plain, direct and vigorous. He strikes to the heart of the matter with keen, steady reasoning; never wasting his words, but always choosing them with the good taste of a trained exponent. His shorter writings, his tracts and appeals, are perfect examples of clear argument and of neat English prose. In polemical writing he is said to have taken as his pattern the First Epistle of St. John; in more discursive essays he was admittedly inspired by Swift. We are too ready to suppose, without looking at them, that sermons must be dull reading and inferior literature; the published sermons of Wesley are anything but dull or inferior; they are concise, deeply religious, and phrased with an admirable sense of balance. He wrote and preached for simple people; but he never blundered into clownish colloquialism, like Berridge, or assumed the lofty tone of a superior.

He was a slow writer, and the great number of books and letters which he wrote in the course of a busy life is the more astonishing. His letters are composed with care, and have the keen, emphatic quality which is found in all his written work: they are excellent letters, full of good, concise thinking, and often with touches of delicacy or affection that show the warmth of his heart.

In the great majority of his books, pamphlets and letters he had in view the promulgation of the Methodist doctrines. We have already displayed those doctrines in the course of the present work; they are few and simple. Perhaps it will not be inappropriate to summarise the basic ideas of the Wesleyan theology, as they were taught by Wesley himself.

The vital teaching of Wesleyan Methodism is the necessity for religious experience. Wesley speaks of this as the *experimental knowledge of God.* A merely passive belief, or the formal subscription to dogma, is not religion. Without experimental knowledge no rational creature can be happy. A man who knows religion is at all times intensely conscious of communion with God, he is aware of the divine fellowship and has entered upon harmonious relations with the universal Presence. Religion is thus a matter of spiritual perception, distinctly emotional in quality, and not to be confused with experience of any other kind.

Regeneration may be described as the phase which marks the fully conscious reception of this experience. Without regeneration there is no salvation for anyone who has been brought to a knowledge of the Christian doctrines: but those who lived before Christ, and those who by reason of immaturity, mental defect or unavoidable ignorance cannot receive the Word, are not to be regarded as irrevocably lost. The Christian is therefore responsible, in a large measure, for his own salvation; he is to seek God; he is to pray for grace; on no account is he to lapse into a state of Moravian stillness. All means by which salvation may be secured are to be fully employed. "God deliver me," said Wesley, "and all that seek Him in sincerity, from what the world calls Christian prudence!"

And since religion is a matter of the direct relations between the soul and God, there is no human authority in religion. "I must insist," Wesley said, "on the right of private judgment. I dare call no man Rabbi. I cannot yield either implicit faith or obedience to any man or number of men under heaven."

Wesley regarded the religious consciousness as advancing from a lower to a higher condition; he believed in a law of ascending evolution, with a corresponding ascending scale of moral values and responsibilities. It is possible, while in the body, to reach a state of Christian perfection; but not of sinless perfection, for that would make of no account the sacrifice of Christ. "By perfection," said Wesley, "I mean perfect love, or the loving of God with all our heart, so as to rejoice evermore, to pray without ceasing, and in everything to give thanks. I am convinced every believer may attain this; yet I do not say he is in a state of damnation or under the curse of God till he does attain. No, he is in a state of grace, and in favour with God, as long as he believes."

The idea of absolute predestination is rejected, even if this rejection involves a difficulty in the question of divine omniscience. Man is born free. Some may be elect: "I do not deny this," said Wesley, "though I cannot prove it so." But, "I cannot believe, that all those who are not elected to glory must perish everlastingly, or that there is one soul on earth who has not ever had a possibility of escaping eternal damnation."

John Wesley believed in the existence and purpose of hell, nor did he shrink from occasionally revealing "the terrors of the Lord." Yet God would not require of any man that of which he was incapable. The one sin which must infallibly lead a soul to destruction is the denial or the mockery of Christ.

Ultimately, the Wesleyan theology rests upon what Wesley considered to be the correct interpretation of the Bible. In his view, the Bible was a full, plain, unmistakable revelation of God's nature and purposes. It was "the only and sufficient rule both of Christian faith and practice." Wesley had nothing to add to the Scriptures; he was going back, as he believed, to the faith of the Primitive Church. His appeal is to the inward experience of man, to his absolute conviction of religious truth. With regard to subtleties of dogma, a Methodist could think as he pleased, with certain reservations in the case of those dogmas for which, in the opinion of Wesley, there was no scriptural foundation. Broadly speaking, he considered that the Church of England was the supreme guardian of the faith, though possibly in error in some matters of ritual and discipline.

Revival is not revolution, and Wesley is not to be thought of as a revolutionary, or even as a man whose views tended towards political socialism. It is true that Methodism had a political influence, but that influence was definitely conservative. Wesley upheld the divine right of kings and he taught implicit obedience to the laws of the country. If he protested vehemently against the appalling evils of drink, slavery, electoral corruption and the growth of extravagance, he never for a moment believed that a radical change in the Constitution would improve matters. True religion and proper thinking were to be the cures for every social disorder. When George II died, Wesley wrote in his *Journal*, "When will England have a better prince?" There could not be a more convincing proof of blind loyalty. In his *Free Thoughts on Public Affairs*, written in 1768, he claimed that the advantage he had over both parties was that he was angry with neither; but he spoke of Wilkes as "a person of a complete, uniform character, encumbered with no religion, with no regard to virtue or morality." He talked about "French gold" with all the ingenuous horror of a patriotic journalist. He defended vigorously the family and the person of George III, and composed his *Thoughts upon Liberty* as an answer to the *Letters* of Junius.

He had done much to prepare England for the shock of the French Revolution. It is not too much to say that he was a chief agent in the stabilisation of the national temper at a critical period.

We cannot give John Wesley a place among the great intellectual reformers of the Church; we cannot set him by the side of Wycliff or Luther, Calvin or Melancthon. But if we place what is purely spiritual above what is purely intellectual, if the elevation of philosophy is yet below the elevation of saintliness, then we can surely place him in the highest company of all. "I do indeed live by preaching," he said. He was a great light, rising in a time of darkness and confusion, and showing men that a vital religion was the one thing which could give them happiness and security and peace.